African Philosophy and Enactivist Cognition

Bloomsbury Studies in World Philosophies

Series Editor
Monika Kirloskar-Steinbach

Comparative, cross-cultural and intercultural philosophy are burgeoning fields of research. Bloomsbury Studies in World Philosophies complements and strengthens the latest work being carried out at a research level with a series that provides a home for thinking through ways in which professional philosophy can be diversified. Ideal for philosophy postgraduates and faculty who seek creative and innovative material on non-Euroamerican sources for reference and research, this series responds to the challenges of our postcolonial world, laying the groundwork for a new philosophy canon that departs from the current Eurocentric sources.

Titles in the Series:
Andean Aesthetics and Anticolonial Resistance, by Omar Rivera
Chinese Philosophy of History, by Dawid Rogacz
Chinese and Indian Ways of Thinking in Early Modern European Philosophy, by Selusi Ambrogio
Indian and Intercultural Philosophy, by Douglas Berger
Toward a New Image of Paramārtha, by Ching Keng
African Philosophy and Enactivist Cognition, by Bruce B. Janz

African Philosophy and Enactivist Cognition

The Space of Thought

Bruce B. Janz

BLOOMSBURY ACADEMIC
LONDON • NEW YORK • OXFORD • NEW DELHI • SYDNEY

BLOOMSBURY ACADEMIC
Bloomsbury Publishing Plc
50 Bedford Square, London, WC1B 3DP, UK
1385 Broadway, New York, NY 10018, USA
29 Earlsfort Terrace, Dublin 2, Ireland

BLOOMSBURY, BLOOMSBURY ACADEMIC and the Diana logo are trademarks of Bloomsbury Publishing Plc

First published in Great Britain 2023
This paperback edition published 2024

Copyright © Bruce B. Janz, 2023

Bruce B. Janz has asserted his right under the Copyright, Designs and Patents Act, 1988, to be identified as Author of this work.

For legal purposes the Acknowledgments on p. vii constitute an extension of this copyright page.

Series design by Louise Dugdale
Cover image © Olga Kurbatova/Getty Images

All rights reserved. No part of this publication may be reproduced or transmitted in any form or by any means, electronic or mechanical, including photocopying, recording, or any information storage or retrieval system, without prior permission in writing from the publishers.

Bloomsbury Publishing Plc does not have any control over, or responsibility for, any third-party websites referred to or in this book. All internet addresses given in this book were correct at the time of going to press. The author and publisher regret any inconvenience caused if addresses have changed or sites have ceased to exist, but can accept no responsibility for any such changes.

A catalogue record for this book is available from the British Library.

A catalog record for this book is available from the Library of Congress.

ISBN: HB: 978-1-3502-9218-5
PB: 978-1-3502-9222-2
ePDF: 978-1-3502-9219-2
eBook: 978-1-3502-9220-8

Series: Bloomsbury Studies in World Philosophies

Typeset by Newgen KnowledgeWorks Pvt. Ltd., Chennai, India

To find out more about our authors and books visit www.bloomsbury.com and sign up for our newsletters.

Contents

Foreword   vi
   Souleymane Bachir Diagne
Acknowledgments   vii

Introduction: Spaces of Thought in African Philosophy   1
1   The Ceremony Found and a New Human Problematic: Sylvia Wynter after Humanism   23
2   Vitalism and Bantu Philosophy: Placide Tempels and Jamaa   45
3   Sasa, Zamani, and Myths of the Future: John Mbiti, Memory, and Time   69
4   Oginga Odinga as Sage Philosopher: H. Odera Oruka and Historicity   93
5   Ubuntu as Enactivism: Mogobe Ramose and Be-ing   115
6   A Literary Tradition of Thought: Sophie Olúwọlé, Euphrase Kezilahabi, and a Literature of Philosophy   135
7   How Do We Speak of Our Place? Achille Mbembe's World   161
8   "The Poet Becomes a Prophet": Suzanne Roussi Césaire's Négritude   195
Conclusion: Future Events?   215

References   231
Further Reading   241
Index   253

Foreword

Souleymane Bachir Diagne

In the young history of African philosophy as a field that is now more and more present internationally in academia, the question about "African philosophy" has moved from one of existence to one of definition. After works such as Placide Tempels's *Bantu Philosophy* (1959), published just after the Second World War, were considered a revolution simply because they presented the continent as a place for philosophy, the issue has become, since the 1970s, that of a definition of a field that obviously exists as a continuously expanding library. The proof of the pudding is in the eating, as the saying goes.

The issue is the following: can there be a definition by intension, in other words a notion of "African philosophy" under which all texts belonging to the field are subsumed, or should we simply accept that given the openness and the diversity of the field we can only work with a definition by extension? After all, is there any region of the world that has a definition by intension of "its" philosophy? Or consider it important to have one?

Beninese philosopher Paulin Hountondji famously proposed the following definition by extension: "By African philosophy I mean a set of texts, specifically the set of texts written by Africans and described as philosophical by their authors themselves" (1996a: 33). By being thus minimalist this (non)definition obviously puts to rest the intractable question of the "identity" of African philosophy by focusing on its reality and its becoming: what I would call its "existence in movement."

Bruce Janz's book is important as a bold response to the challenge of proposing a definition by intension of African philosophy that also captures its existence in movement. It makes the case that such a definition is provided by the concept of enactivism, a concept in cognitive science expressing the position that cognition is not the representation of reality but arises through the interaction, which is an embodied process, of the organisms that we are with the reality of our environment. No doubt that the claim, brilliantly illustrated here by the demonstration that major texts in African philosophy lend themselves to an innovative enactivist reading, will put *African Philosophy and Enactivist Cognition: The Space of Thought* at the center of important debates in the field of African Philosophy.

Acknowledgments

Thanks to all those who have read excerpts of this book, or commented on parts of it, or otherwise contributed to its production. This includes Mason Cash, Jonathan Chimakonam, Souleymane Bachir Diagne, Edwin Etieyibo, Michael Onyebuchi Eze, Grant Farred, Shaun Gallagher, Alex Gil, Anke Graness, George Hull, Andrea Hurst, Jeanne-Marie Jackson-Awotwi, Chike Jeffers, Ward Jones, Monika Kirloskar-Steinbach, Kai Kresse, Dwight Lewis, Bernard Matolino, Achille Mbembe, Thad Metz, Motsamai Molefe, Uchenna Okeja, Abraham Olivier, Shelley Park, Leonhard Praeg, Gail Presbey, Angela Roothaan, Michael Strawser, Pedro Tabensky, Samantha Vice, Charles Villet, as well as others who I have talked with about the book over the past few years. I would also like to thank anonymous reviewers for their suggestions. My apologies if I have forgotten to include anyone here. No one listed here is responsible for any of the views expressed in this book.

Thanks as well to the University of Central Florida, which provided a research leave in 2017–18, when the early structure of this book was being drafted.

Introduction: Spaces of Thought in African Philosophy

The Place of Philosophy in Africa

In what follows, I aim to develop two complementary and intertwined lines of inquiry. The first focuses on the question of what constitutes a space of thought in philosophy, and the changes or ruptures that make spaces of thought possible. The second focuses on the development of African philosophy as it is practiced in Africa and elsewhere. The first line of inquiry is meant to be a generalizable but not replicable approach to opening up philosophical thought to new concepts and by extension new voices from all places. It uses African philosophy as a prime example of how that might happen. The second line makes a case that academic African philosophy has developed over the past number of decades in a manner that tends to limit rather than expand the space of thought available to it. This does not mean that it has restricted those who can or do participate (although that might also happen, in principle or in practice) but that in its form and in the way it defines its objects of inquiry and interrogates its own texts, it has tended to give answers meant to consolidate African philosophy as a set of related and mutually reinforcing positions rather than a space in which radically different kinds of thought might coexist.

Already, readers are likely thinking of counterexamples to this second line of inquiry. Surely African philosophy is as diverse as any other tradition of thought! People disagree about all sorts of questions! We can find rough equivalents of analytic philosophy, continental philosophy, pragmatism, and a host of other approaches! We can find philosophers who start their inquiry with current culture, others who start with ancient Egyptian thought, and others still who look to tradition! This cannot possibly be correct.

And of course, all of this is true. Diversity does exist at those levels. But my interest is different—it is with the story we tell about the development of African philosophy, a story that defines the nature of much of African philosophy. If one takes an African philosophy course, there is a common narrative told about the development of academic African philosophy since about 1945. It often starts with Placide Tempels and the publication of *Bantu Philosophy*, although it might stretch a bit further back than that to include Négritude. With more work being done on earlier philosophical figures such as Zara Yaqob and Wilhelm Amo Afer, the narrative is pushed back, although the self-conscious narrative about the African-ness of African philosophy remains a relatively recent one. It proceeds through a number of figures who pose pivotal questions or formulate central concepts for the contemporary narrative about African philosophy. There are early reactions against Tempels, coming to a head with Paulin Hountondji's discussion of "ethnophilosophy." There are key concepts that are developed—Mbiti's approach to time, Odera Oruka's sage philosophy, various versions of Ubuntu, African concepts of personhood, and so forth. These might be framed chronologically or thematically. Various philosophers excavate history and culture to demonstrate that philosophy existed in Africa since the beginning of recorded history, and others make the case that this ancient philosophy was in fact the progenitor of philosophy elsewhere, especially in Europe. Each of these is a step in the story of how African philosophy is both truly philosophical and truly African. Each event is a moment in the tale of African philosophy's development.

There might be hesitation about the first line of inquiry as well, concerning what constitutes a space of thought. Has philosophy not always been preceded by the careful application of reason through dialogue mitigating any one person's blind spots and prejudices to arrive at concepts that fairly represent reality? What need is there to engage a metaphilosophical inquiry that has been largely settled? Or, alternately, have we not had a host of attempts to describe, advocate, or create ruptures of thought? Is this not what we have for every philosopher who announces a new turn, a new program that will wake philosophy itself from its dogmatic slumber? Philosophy not only continually returns to its sources or foundations, whatever individual philosophers consider those to be, but it is also addicted to new beginnings, at least in the modern West. It is perhaps a kind of envy of science and its seeming progress and paradigm shifts that lead to new explanations and new ways of connecting phenomena together, but the rupture and the new start seem to be a common feature of European philosophy since at least Descartes.

Obviously, I do not think that the metaphilosophical questions are settled at all nor that there is nothing more to be said about the ruptures of thought that can create something new. My argument here will be that there are discontinuities in philosophical inquiry, which come about not only because of concepts generated within philosophy itself but also because of a host of factors that define the space of philosophical inquiry. The point is not that there are material conditions for the production of philosophy but that the inquiry itself—what counts as a concept, what questions are available and how they are framed, how the encounter between currents of thought happens in dialogue or other ways—resists linear development (or rather can only be described linearly after the fact and only by leaving out elements of the narrative that were formative conditions for those engaged in the space of thought at the time). Further than that though, there is a sense that philosophical "progress" is the result of a kind of subjectivist enterprise of discovery and representation of the true nature of human experience and the structure of reality. In this picture of how philosophy operates, then, discontinuities in philosophy come about when we realize that there is something fundamentally flawed about how we represent human experience or the world and we correct it.

It is this picture of progress that I am questioning, along with the picture of individual reflective minds as the drivers of change. The conditions that rupture or redirect the path of philosophy are its events, and I am interested here in both the rational or conceptual interventions that change philosophical narratives and also the affective and intuitive moments that might prefigure a new direction or give hints that all is not well in the received story. One reason for focusing on African philosophy in this story is that it is, I think, a space in which the development of thought has been a deliberate project over the past number of decades. It is a kind of natural experiment, in that it is a space of thought that has not been integrated into the "mainstream" of philosophy (and I recognize that even using a term like that diminishes African philosophy and assumes something about where the most important narratives and developments have been within philosophy). It has reflected on its own nature fully cognizant of what was happening in the rest of the world of philosophy, but without the rest of the world caring much about its development until recently. This has been understood as marginalization and discrimination against Africa in philosophy, and it has certainly been that, but it has also been an isolation in which currents of thought have developed with different vectors of influence. Some of those vectors, of course, are the reality and residue of colonialism and other brutalizing encounters with the West, including systems such as apartheid, and the continuing influence of neoliberal economic and political agendas meant to "reform" Africa. Others, though, are indigenous and neo-indigenous forms of thought, ways of thinking responsive to lived experience in contemporary Africa.

The answer of a great deal of African philosophy has been to create a philosophical space similar to but different from Western space. It has been a new foundation for a different ethics, a different theory of personhood, a different set of political theories, and so forth. This "similar but different" sensibility inevitably does not stand as Western philosophy's shadow but Western philosophy stands as its shadow. The result of this similar but different space has been a relative narrowing of the potentiality of philosophical discourse in Africa. As long as the implicit imperative has been to find an "African" approach to something—knowledge, action, logic, governance, whatever—the result is to create a space in which homogeneity of thought rather than heterogeneity is a central value.

I am interested in the making of events, that is, the decisions that individuals make in order to move forward in an epistemically uncertain world as well as the moments that individuals might not even recognize until after the fact but that nevertheless represent the foundation for a new space of thought. We have sometimes thought about a philosophy as a set of rules for understanding and living, based on a representation of reality as it is. It is this view that I want to bracket off for the moment. The move of the thinker thinking in a place using the concepts and tools available in that place is not always simply applying an abstraction to the particulars of the world and deriving an account of things and a plan of action for the future. Sometimes the arrow goes the other way, and in fact there is a complex relationship between action and thought. It is not even a circle; it is more of a set of shifting but repeatable and rhythmic currents that can be known but not predicted with any degree of certainty. The world is not ordered and made rational by philosophy; rather, the potentialities of the world are drawn out when the tools of philosophy intersect with the contingencies of the world.

In this book, I want to call into question the story about philosophy's inherent ability to change itself using only its own tools and the genius of its practitioners. African philosophy has been on a mission to change philosophy (as have of course other philosophical traditions and interests) by carving a space for itself and others who have not historically fit into the model of philosophy. Since philosophy was assumed to have neither debts nor duties to any place, the platializing "African" part of African philosophy must be irrelevant and a distraction. Since philosophers were not assumed to have any identity other than as the rational inquirer (using a specific definition of rationality that did not include contingent concerns of race, gender, history), many of the thematic areas were at best to be regarded as "applied" philosophy, something that followed the real philosophical work worked out in metaphysics, epistemology, value theory, and logic. Whether or not this was made explicit as a set of parameters for inquiry, it certainly defined the narrative in European philosophy and elsewhere in the world that held European philosophy as a model or ideal of philosophical activity.

In my earlier book, *Philosophy in an African Place* (2009), I argued that the natural conclusion of these parameters was for African philosophers to try to carve out a space on the philosophical map by finding methods, themes, or concepts that were truly African and truly philosophical. While this was an understandable response, it resulted in a search for some foundational concept or concepts that would guarantee these conditions. The ones I addressed in that book were tradition, reason, wisdom, culture, language, and practicality. I argued that none of these contenders for such a concept could accomplish this goal but that the problem was not with the concept but with the goal itself. It was what I termed at the time "spatial philosophy," that is, finding the space on the map that African philosophy was entitled to, defining who was a citizen of this intellectual country, defending the borders, and establishing the conditions for life within that space. I suggested that this question of spatial philosophy did not lead to creating the conditions for new thought, and that a different approach that I termed "platial philosophy" was more likely to be successful. These two were typified by fundamentally different questions: in the case of spatial philosophy, it was "Is there an African philosophy?" (a question that I argued was not itself an African question but a challenge from the outside), and in the case of platial philosophy, it was "What does it mean to do philosophy in this (African) place?" (a question that led to something more like a phenomenology of intellectual experience and that also allowed a complex and sophisticated approach to the conceptual unities and disjunctions within Africa).

In this book, I want to rehabilitate the notion of the spatial but not by revisiting the question that grounded spatial philosophy in the earlier book. That question still seems to me to be an external challenge and is no more likely to engender creative thought now than it did then. Attending to platial philosophy, though, can afford spaces of thought, and that is what I want to work out in this book. African philosophy is an ideal space in which to see this for the same reason it was an ideal space to think through platial philosophy—it is in a self-conscious process of determining its own identity. It continues to react to developments in world philosophy while recognizing the problematic effect that world philosophy has had on its own development. Thinking about the concepts that emerge in place can lead to opportunities for new philosophical development, which is something that a significant number of African philosophers have tried to develop in recent years.

This is the outcome of thinking in place—in the case of African philosophy, we can see not only how concepts emerge that are adequate to their places but also how spaces might be created for new thought. African philosophy uses its past and present but is always in a process of becoming-philosophy. The question "Is there an African philosophy?" is therefore illegitimate for another reason—it is not only a non-African question, meant as a challenge and a demand for definition against the backdrop of already-existing philosophy elsewhere in the world, but it also frames African philosophy as something that does or does not exist, rather than something that is becoming-philosophy. All philosophies worth the name are becoming-philosophy, and if they are not, they are at best history of ideas. They are records of the passage of thought under conditions that are no longer extant, they are not enacting thought in the space of current conditions. History of ideas might, of course, become part of the conditions of current thought, but then we find ourselves back at the question of becoming-philosophy.

What I am calling "thinking in place" is this process of awareness of the vectors of place, while at the same time the recognition that all awareness is inevitably partial and, in most cases, comes too late. Thinking in place involves the creation of concepts that are adequate to their places. Every concept is a multiple—if we think of something like freedom, for instance, or race, or gender, or anything else that might be of philosophical interest, we are met with a cloud of concepts under the term we use, and that cloud refers both to contextual differences in the usage of concepts as well as to differences in the ways concepts have emerged, given specific histories. It also means that these concepts are themselves within a space afforded by a question, and they do not precede the questions we ask.

Thinking in place is what I see as this process of rupture in philosophy, not simply paradigmatic change of explanatory structure but a disequilibrium of thought that produces a new problematic. This is not a new *grand récit* but a new space of thought.

The goal of this book is to do just such an interrogation of the nature of philosophical activity itself. It will, at the same time, establish a space of thought by offering a fundamentally different approach to African philosophy from the most common mainstream academic one. I will call my approach an "enactivist" African philosophy, a term that comes out of contemporary phenomenological cognitive sciences. The idea, though, is not to impose another external approach on Africa to substitute for the external questions I have argued are already there. Enactivism is already present in African philosophy and has been for a long time. The goal will be to draw out a way of doing philosophy that is already present in many major works but remains implicit. It is a potentiality that has not been taken up, mainly because the assumptions about what constituted "real" African philosophy were set, and so the potentiality remained unrecognized.

Enactivism

How is enactivist cognitive science relevant to African philosophy, or to philosophy in general? Enactivism, as a project within the cognitive sciences, is focused on giving an account of cognition. It is, as Daniel Hutto puts it, a "broad church" approach (2017: 377), which means that it is not a single theory of cognition but a diverse family of approaches that deploy similar concepts to provide an alternative to standard accounts of brain-based cognition.

The use of enactivism here is not an attempt to give an account of cognition within an African context, as if that might be different from a generalized theory of cognition elsewhere. It is an attempt to move away from thinking of philosophy as necessarily beginning from classical categories of metaphysics, epistemology, value theory, and so forth and think instead about the constitution of thought itself. This move is not, of course, anything new in a Western context—it was the project of thinkers as diverse as Hegel, Marx, Wittgenstein, Heidegger, Rorty, Deleuze, and many others. This is not to say that all of these engaged in what we might think of as research in cognition but rather that all saw the mode of thought as relevant to the practice of thought and its results.

We will see in upcoming chapters some elements of what an enactivist African philosophy looks like. The bulk of the book works through a series of cases that show that this enactivism has, in various ways, been present in pivotal literature within contemporary African philosophy. For now, though, we can see at least a few concepts that will be important in this project. These can be described as we think about the production of philosophical knowledge within the African philosophy tradition.

We start with *intentionality*. Classically, we tend to think about the products of African philosophy as both rooted in African culture and the result of the attention that individual philosophers have given to that culture. Content is represented, and it is assembled through the collective efforts of individuals as they attend to various aspects of African culture. There is therefore the potential of evolution in the kinds of areas that receive focus—there was a time when almost no attention was paid to questions of the environment, for instance, or to the place of women in African philosophy, and that has changed. In an enactivist version of African philosophy, intentionality works not as the contingent representations of individuals but as the dynamic space of meaning made available within the places of African life. We act based on what we know and experience in those places, and they likewise act on us. Place, in this case, has *focal length*—we might use a long focal length and call it "Africa" or zoom in much closer on "Kenya," "Nairobi," "sage philosophers," and so forth. Everyone lives in a range of these places simultaneously, and while in some cases they might be subsets of each other, in others they are plateaus, different levels of complex interaction that encounter each other transversally. Place is a *nonrepresentational, non-reductionist site for concept emergence*, that is, it is the wellspring of philosophy (Janz 2022). Concepts are adequate to their places (or not, in which case they come under scrutiny and revision, but their inadequacy is often felt before it is theoretically recognized).

One way to think about this is in terms of our *first-*, *second-*, and *third-person self-understanding in philosophy*. If philosophy is representational when it comes to self-understanding, it is almost invariably first-person. In other words, it is an attempt to describe a state of affairs that is based on a first-person subjective experience of the world. It is *my* experience and *my* knowledge, and I am a (perhaps partial) window on reality through that experience. I have analyzed elsewhere the debts of philosophy to linguistics and literature in its sense of orientation toward its subjects of analysis (Janz 2018b). What is noteworthy is that it is conceivable to foreground the second-person and the third-person, but these are rarely taken seriously as modes of philosophical production of self-knowledge or for that matter of any other kind of philosophical knowledge. A third-person self-understanding prioritizes the reports of others (e.g., a community) over one's own self-understanding, and a second-person self-understanding (e.g., Martin Buber's dialogical philosophy) suggests that we come to who we are in dialogue with another.

If we decenter first-person constructions of the self, we can see that African philosophy's preference for communal modes of social organization can account for forms of the construction of the self that look like enactivism's extended social cognition. Individuals matter, of course, but they are not the necessary starting point for accounting for selves. There is reciprocity in our philosophical cognition; there is group cognition; there is social scaffolding; there is motivated theorizing; there is after-the-fact justification and theorization of actions that have already taken place. Philosophical production, in other words, simultaneously works out a theoretical point and accomplishes something within a place. We can see all of these interactive modes as forms of *dialogue*, as long as we do not think about dialogue as just the comparison and assessment of claims (Janz 2015). Productive dialogue starts with listening and questioning rather than speaking (Janz 2018a).

Philosophy is not, in other words, simply a set of mental representations and their artifacts, such as propositions, claims, systems, and theories. An enactivist version of intentionality in African philosophy means that the driving force is the *question*. Propositions, claims, and the like still exist, of course, but they are treated as transitional moments to the next question, not the payoff and stopping point of philosophical inquiry. The question, properly asked, produces a *problematic* triggered by an *event* (or virtuality) in thought that engenders a new working-out of concepts. This working-out produces new places—it is a mistake to think of any place, particularly African place, as static. These new places become part of the focal length of place, that is, they become new ways of understanding place. The long focal length of a place such as "Africa" allows (and may cover over or obscure) a great deal of *autopoiesis*, that is, a great deal of organization of complexity, but that creativity still exists (we will see this worked out by Sylvia Wynter in Chapter 1 and Suzanne Roussi Césaire in Chapter 8). *Philosophy-in-place*, which is my term for this whole creative process, is a philosophy of dynamical and emergent systems rather than first principles or models.

The place in which philosophy happens is its *literature*, which makes available a range of mutually intelligible but contingent and potentially incommensurable ways of reading (Chapter 6 will address this). This is a *nonlinear space of thought*, that is, it is a space in which we do not simply make deductions from first principles to arrive at reliable conclusions. As Africa is read by philosophers, it is read in a range of ways. Sometimes those ways hew to familiar patterns—they work out a longstanding question. Sometimes they ask new questions, thus creating a new problematic. That new problematic is a discontinuity, a rethinking of terms, no different from the ways in which a literature can admit widely different modes of reading. But this literature is not just an archive or an oeuvre. It has a history, not a coercive one but one that is usable in the project of becoming-African (for more, see Chapter 5). It is also a conflicted battleground, a space in which writing itself is fraught. Philosophy does not come easily, because the literature on which it is based and to which it contributes stands in a history of slavery, colonialism, and apartheid (see Chapter 7 for more on this). Despite the challenges of grounding philosophy in a literature, though, there is the benefit that it takes us away from thinking of philosophy as a *mode of thought*, that is, as a unifying theoretical representation of African culture that serves as a standard to adjudicate new work in philosophy. While it still makes sense to ask whether someone "gets it right" when representing cultural or intellectual practices in African society, the more interesting philosophical question is what that text makes available as a new way of becoming-African.

Philosophers do not simply theorize and abstract on cultural content, and they do not simply sit in their offices as individuals and construct systems of thought. Philosophy is *shared cognition*—it is thinking together and it is thinking that is not simply located within individual minds. In other words, it makes sense to talk about the philosophy of a place in a way that is not simply reducible to the individual opinions of people who inhabit the place. This is not some version of idealism; instead, it is a shared set of practices and implicitly agreed-upon questions and problematics. It emerges from traditional concerns but also from present ones. Places *scaffold* philosophical thought, which means that any philosophical investigation externalizes its line of thinking into practices, materials, curricula, institutional structures, and so forth. Philosophy is *incentivized* in a range of ways, including the promise of jobs, tenure, advancement, publication, and social recognition. It scaffolds *scholarly cognition* around itself, ways of supporting particular lines of inquiry. These can expand and extend into national and international structures such as philosophical societies. They can define the priorities of granting agencies, publishing series, disciplinary standards, and national research ranking priorities, among many other things. These are not simply downstream aspects of the professionalization of philosophy (and thus, at best, incidental to philosophical creativity), they are integral parts of philosophy's way of engaging its world. These are a feature of any philosophy anywhere, but they become particularly obvious in a pursuit like African philosophy, which has grappled with its relationship to its own history and that of others, and its own social and political structures. We will see some of this worked out in Chapter 8.

In other words, African philosophy (and indeed any philosophy) does not exist only as a set of claims about some feature of the world. It is not pragmatic in the sense that there exist a set of goals or objectives and philosophy enables them to be achieved and is judged by its success in achieving them. Philosophy is generative—it asks questions based in place that act as events to create new problematics, new spaces of thought. Its cognitive space is both that of disciplined logical argumentation and of engagement at other levels of meaning, involving *affect* and *empathy*. There are *normative* implications as well—philosophy in Africa neither simply represents African culture nor randomly follows any and every possible line of thought. It recognizes its debts and duties to its places, and its choices of spaces of thought reflect value to culture. Philosophers have the reputation of being attracted to the abstract and seemingly impractical lines of thought, but one great virtue of philosophy is this idea of asking new questions that produce new problematics, which might only end up gaining widespread application long after the initial investigation of a space of thought. One might, for instance, see something like Ubuntu as an African metaphysic and ethic deeply rooted in the past, but its investigation now by a range of thinkers gives it vitality in the current space of thought, and critiques it, that is, explores its scope and limits and interrogates the new and often unexpected places that come to exist in the presence of a living philosophy like this.

There is, then, what might be called "mindshaping," following Tadeusz Zawidzki (2018). The social cognition of philosophy is not about our individual minds working separately to represent this shifting and changing cultural place, as I have described it. Instead, we rely more on "embodied capacities to shape each other's minds, e.g., imitation, pedagogy, and norm enforcement" (736). The "embodiment" (or perhaps, following Chakravarthi Ram-Prasad (2018: 13–16), the "bodiliness") part of this is important. We rarely think of philosophy as bodily, but that does not mean that it is not. Zawidzki points out that some of the most sophisticated mindshaping happens by "matching the behavior of fictional models like protagonists of myths or morally ideal agents" (2018: 742). In other words, shared cognitive practices can involve narrative elements and exemplars. These include social narratives, including normative stories within culture, depictions of forms of oppression and opportunity, inclusion and exclusion, in short place construction of all sorts. This is the space in which philosophy operates. We do, of course, convince people using reasoning and argumentation, but we do that in the context of these shared projects of meaning-building, place-building, norm-creating, and norm-defending. We are bodily in these spaces, and even in an age of electronic communication, it still matters which place we are bodily part of, and what the various networks are that we are engaged with.

This bodiliness, along with the ways in which culture, technology, institutions, practices, and so forth are the ground of thinking, contributes to what I am calling the *enactive* approach in African philosophy. The conviction is that thought does not precede either individual or group action. Thinking is a form of acting, and acting is a form of thinking. The philosophers' conceit that we must first arrange our mental and conceptual space, and then that causes us to act in culture and undergirds everything else, is at best a partial and misleading picture. We do, of course, think before we act, but if we want to understand how philosophy actually is a constitutive aspect of being human, we have to recognize that our mental activity proceeds within a space made available by culture and responds to questions that exist in a reciprocal relationship with that space. We ask about what our places prepare us to ask about. Enactivist African philosophy, then, starts from the idea that the function of thought is to live in this complex world and not simply to construct abstract structures that refer to some aspects of this world. Abstraction is not ruled out, by any means, but it always remains tied to the questions enabled and authorized by place. The creative and constructive goal of philosophy is to push the boundaries of these questions, to ask questions that enable us to live in the world, but also to create a new world out of the material of the place.

A philosophical space of thought is something we can see in hindsight but cannot predict in advance. It is not simply the linear investigation into ontology or the methodical analysis of knowledge or ethics. Terms like that are high-level concepts, a little like "African Philosophy" itself, which encompasses much and is sometimes useful, but which also serves to cover over the dynamism within the space. African philosophy has tried various versions of *vitalism* at times, usually as alternatives to more linear or modern senses of "Western" time (and, of course, "Western" is another long focal length concept that can cover over much), and in fact without its metaphysical or theological commitments, vitalism can look much like the autopoietic emergence I describe here (see Chapters 2 and 3 on this). This emergence leads us toward a revised version of humanism, what we might call "ahumanism"—the recognition of the embeddedness of human action and consciousness within a set of transversal intersecting networks, some of which we are aware of and harness and some of which we are not, but which nevertheless shape the kind of space we operate in (see Chapter 1 for more on this).

As an analogy, consider our biological and evolutionary development. We might imagine that we are something like computers, with a kind of source code in our genes that defines who we are at a fine-grained level. What has become apparent in recent years, though, is that this story of the implementation of code as a control mechanism to define the creation and function of our bodies is at best partial. There are other transversally intersecting networks, often ignored in the past but which both affect the how this "code" is made manifest and also stand in symbiotic or reciprocal relationships with that code. We exist in the context of a bacterial and viral world, suffused throughout our bodies and, as importantly, embedded within our genetic code. Some of the code strings we have in our DNA are from bacteria. We exist as organisms within the networks of other organisms, again affected by complex emergent networks that create virtualities at their intersections. What we are, at the interstices of these networks, are not beings that dominate, nor minds that bestow meaning on a world that has none. We are ahuman—not nonhuman or antihuman or post-human but humans that find themselves as emergent properties of our constitutive and intersecting networks. We are, in fact, becoming-human, a task that is renewed with each decision we make and with each engagement with the world.

And this is why enactivism offers something important to the contemporary practice of African philosophy—it does not ask the question, "What does it mean to be African?" but rather, "Given the place of life and the space of thought, as well as the existing activated concepts in this place, what might emerge as African here?" Put positively, an enactivist approach to African philosophy reorients "the human as a problem to be interrogated and as a process that can be mobilized for interventions, rather than weighting it as an object of knowledge" (Narkunas 2018: 3–4). The human, in other words, becomes less an object of inquiry and more a site of creativity. That means that traditional questions within African philosophy about things like the nature of personhood become less interesting, not because it is not possible to identify salient differences between concepts that come out of an African place and those developed elsewhere but because even if we manage to find an African version of personhood, that tells us little about the potentialities made available for new thought adequate to African places. Granting that there is such a thing as African personhood (and that is itself still debatable), focusing only on that does not tell us about the contingent space in which such a person might operate and does not raise the likelihood that greater agency, value, or determination will accrue to the person.

This implies, at the least, a tentative relationship to humanism. Enactivism takes seriously the embeddedness of all human knowledge, decision, and action within a space of technology, nature, economies, and a host of other forces. Humanism, of course, like any concept, is a multiple, that is, it has many elements in its provenance, not all commensurable with each other. It is pressed into service in many ways. We will see this ahumanism in the chapter on Sylvia Wynter and humanism (Chapter 1). In the space of the ahuman, there are dividuals (Ott 2018; Deleuze 1992). These are not individuals, subjects acting out of their own representational mechanisms, exerting their wills on the world to shape it. Dividuals act and respond in networks, are subject to controls but are also nodes of becoming. We can, after the fact, narrate these as individuals, actors that represented their reality and exerted their wills in order to bring about change, but those narratives are always after the fact. Their stories always oversimplify.

We see this dynamic in the context of discussions of race. The majority of them are representational in one way or another, in the sense that the goal of discourse on race is to represent race, or racialized experience, or racialized subjects, or the ways that race functions within systems of colonialism or domination. Race is biological, or race is not biological but social, or it is neither but it is produced by some other phenomenon—politics, religion, language, and so on. And there is nothing wrong with the project of representing race, but if that is the only way to talk about it, the result is always to assume race as either a property of a subject or a group, or foundational to a subject or group, or formative of subjects and groups. In all these cases the impulse is toward theories of being, descriptions of race's modes of existence within human experience. Representations of race lead to questions of comparison between representations—which is better, which is more accurate to reality or experience?

The phenomenology of these experiences can, though, be assembled into something else, into versions of race that focus on the modes of becoming, not only of racial subjects but of race itself. It is the viscosity of race in its space. "The spatiality of race is not one of grids or self/other dialectics, but one of *viscosity*, bodies gradually becoming sticky and clustering into aggregates. Battling against racism is then not a question of denying race, but of cultivating its energies against the stickiness of racial segregation" (Saldanha 2006: 10; original emphasis). Race emerges like slime molds do, sometimes as individuals and sometimes as myriad separate cells: "The trick is to explain how, *even then*, we are faced with the slime molds of racism, sexism, capitalism, and what have you" (18; original emphasis). The manifestation of this complex emergence cannot be ontologized in a singular fashion but must be understood as existing in multiple or singular form depending on the vectors of the environment.

The point here is not to say that a slime mold, or for that matter race, is nothing at all. The point is that their manifestation changes at a fundamental level, and the conditions of those changes are complex. If we are still engaged in representationalism, we might name the complexity and call it a day. It is a slime mold, and under that signifier there is hidden a range of changes, all easily ignored in favor of the stable entity we can think of as an individual. But it is an individual only under some conditions, and so the ontology chooses one manifestation as determinative of its form. A slime mold is a thing, unless and until it is not. A flock of birds is many things, even if it acts as one and is encountered as a singular thing, such as with a murmuration of starlings. A person in Africa is an individual, until he or she is not—a member of a social group. Prioritizing one ontological state over others obscures how any of these things become what they are, and are not-yet.

Enactivism as philosophy makes it possible to both achieve Paulin Hountondji's goal of having an African philosophy not reducible to anonymously held static worldviews, and at the same time have a philosophy that takes seriously the complexity of the African experience. It leverages elements of the existing African philosophical tradition, which anticipate and run parallel to enactivism as an explanation within cognitive science. It allows a rethinking of philosophy itself, and a deeper interrogation of the human within a space of thought. We move from here to consider some elements of this approach to philosophy more closely, to lay the conceptual groundwork to see how this can be worked out from the texts within the literature of African philosophy itself.

The Structure of the Book

The core of the book is in the investigations of a set of specific texts. This core is framed by two chapters that are meant to serve as restatements of a narrative, a redirection toward something other than the story about the development of African philosophy we have grown used to. The front end of that frame, in Chapter 1, is a consideration of Sylvia Wynter's work on humanism. In her two essays "The Ceremony Must Be Found" and "The Ceremony Found," she suggests how we might consider emergent thought within a space, thought that comes to terms with its past but is not bound by it. The back end of the frame, Chapter 8, is a reconsideration of Négritude, mainly through the work of Suzanne Roussi Césaire. Her work is often not included in the story we tell about Négritude, but she tells a different kind of story about the function and power of Négritude than is often seen when the work is considered in more reductionist terms.

These two texts are by women of the African diaspora, not from the continent. I use them as a frame because I want to consider the turn of events, the might-have-been and might-still-be, the becoming-philosophy, the joyful potentiality. I want to unseat a comfortable narrative that puts African philosophy in a specific place within world thought and suggest that there is much more potential that exists within the texts themselves.

A frame must frame something, and that is the six case studies focused on specific texts in the history of African philosophy. As already mentioned, some of these are classics and some are less well known. I make no claim that these are all the major turning points in African philosophy—far from it. When writing this book, it quickly became apparent that the problem would be how to choose between the texts I could have written about. So, many prominent texts are not included here. What I have included is here because it gives a particular turn on how the narrative of African philosophy is told, and what the relationship between philosophy and meta-philosophy is. I start where the story often starts, with Placide Tempels and *Bantu Philosophy*. The investigation in this chapter moves between two things—the concept of *elan vitale*, the life force that is so crucial to his thought, and the fact that there was a robust community that emerged out of *Bantu Philosophy* and Tempels's work, the Jamaa community, which is largely ignored by philosophers and yet raises interesting questions about how we should take his work. The argument will be for an enactivist approach to philosophy, one that takes seriously the idea that practice does not simply follow abstract thought but is embedded with it, and that philosophy is a kind of cognition within a place that enables us to cope with our reality.

John Mbiti's work on time is the focus of the next chapter. He is usually seen as trying to describe something about African culture, a unique sense of time. My goal in this chapter will be to suggest a less representational and more autopoietic sense of his project. Almost all the work on Mbiti on time focuses on a small section of his book, and a different picture emerges as we take the whole text seriously. It is possible to understand Mbiti's version of time as one directed at the question of how to live well, as opposed to one directed at describing a metaphysics of time in an African context.

Odera Oruka's book *Oginga Odinga* stands as an unusual entry into his sage philosophy project. On the one hand, Oruka is clear that it is sage philosophy—he spends significant time discussing sage philosophy at the beginning and argues for Odinga to be considered as a sage. At the same time, the book itself reads completely differently from any other sage philosophy interview Oruka ever did. This text seems to fall outside of his sage philosophy method, and yet, it also seems that he saw the book as the first in a series of extended sage philosophy books that he wanted to do. The contrast between the bulk of his work and this volume is remarkable and yet has not been remarked upon. This chapter's focus will be on Oruka's introduction, for the first time, a sense of temporality, historicity, and place into the project. I will consider how that functions in a project that tended, before this point, to emphasize the abstract and invariant in African conceptual life.

Much work has been done on Ubuntu, and it is not my intention to take up the vast literature that works out various aspects of it. There is one work, though, which suggests a unique approach. Mogobe Ramose's *African Philosophy through Ubuntu* (1999) explicitly sees Ubuntu not as an ethical code, a body of cultural knowledge, or a generalized African philosophy, but as a cognitive strategy. He works out a theory of questioning that lies at the heart of Ubuntu. His version is a kind of cognition in place, and shared cognition, which suggests strategies for encountering a chaotic and uncertain future by honoring the past but not being bound by it. An enactivist version of Ubuntu moves us away from trying to explicate its propositional content and toward asking about how it enables the creation of new concepts.

Sophie Olúwọlé's "The Africanness of a Philosophy" (1989) seems on the surface to be a contribution to spatial philosophy. It looks like it is trying to identify what is truly African about philosophy. What she actually does, though, is more interesting. She argues for a literary tradition of thought. In this chapter I investigate what she means by this, and what it implies. I connect her desire for a literature of African philosophy to Euphrase Kezilahabi's thoughts on the philosophical function of literature, as outlined in his doctoral dissertation.

Finally, the last of these six chapters considers Achille Mbembe's essay "African Modes of Self-Writing" (2002) along with its reception and other later writing of his that continues his arguments in that essay. Most critical attention is given to the modes of self-writing he sees as limited or inadequate. I am interested in what he points to, in this essay and his other work, as generative. My argument here is that in this and other works, Mbembe is imagining an exhaustion of place in various ways, along with proposed responses to that exhaustion. I draw a parallel to ways of addressing torture and argue that this too is an attempt to respond to a threat to embodied place. Mbembe's "self-writing" becomes a writing of place within non-place, within a place stolen and defiled and drained of the potential for meaning. He imagines a "world" that is in the end one, and this is the response to what seems to be an impossible writing in a place where justice for the sins and outrages of slavery, colonialism, and apartheid (along with torture) will not find satisfaction.

What I hope to have accomplished by the point that we reach the chapter on Suzanne Césaire and Négritude is a revisioning of what African philosophy might be. I hope to suggest an enactivist, autopoietic, generative version of African philosophy, one that does not depend on representing culture but that is embedded within culture and acts out of culture. It is a version of African philosophy focused on what intellectual apparatus is needed to navigate African space, and how that apparatus can develop to meet new challenges. Some of these challenges, both old and new, include those defined by the mechanisms of colonialism in general, and racism, sexism, and other forms of oppression and marginalization. None of these are static—they change and morph to maintain a hold, they move between material and symbolic registers, they co-opt attempts to challenge them. A robust African becoming-philosophy must be able to meet these challenges, and this is what I describe in these classic texts—the tools and strategies already developed within the tradition to do just that.

I hope to offer a different possibility of thought within African philosophy, one that will orient thinkers toward the future, toward the creation of concepts adequate to African experience. My focus here has been on texts, for a simple reason—they are my major access point to African philosophy. They are what have been put out there. They are not just windows but creative engines of thought, and we need to see the accumulation of texts within African philosophy as having done the work not only of representing culture but also of establishing ways of thinking. To the extent that those ways are not reflected upon, they become modes of thought. The argument here is that they need to be spaces of thought, which can happen only as we think both about the representations of thought and the meta-philosophy that that creates. This is why philosophy is, ultimately, enactivist—the act of engaging in it produces its conditions and lays down a narrative about what belongs in thought and how it must be done. More than that, engagement produces surprises and new directions. The concepts of philosophy are a complex system, and as those concepts engage with each other and with other systems, there are autopoietic events that can lead to new problematics, that is, new areas of inquiry. The goal of this book is not to try to make that happen but to recognize that it has happened and is happening.

Reading the Book

Each chapter can be read as a general introduction to the central theme of the respective text. As such it will be useful to the beginning student in African philosophy. But this is not the only path through the book that one might take. These chapters can also be seen as transversal readings of these classic texts. There is something interesting in each of these texts that might only be apparent at a distance or by taking a non-direct approach to the reading. The texts served specific purposes at the time they were written, and almost all were part of specific conversations. My objective is to find alternate readings, minor notes, and new implications that come from asking different questions about these pieces. This is an exercise in destabilizing the canon.

As a study of events, it is important to note that, in this reading, I am not suggesting that I have any special insight into the intentions of the authors. I am not proposing to enumerate and correct errors of the past. These texts were put into the world, in the context of a conversation, and I am giving a reading that diverges in most cases from the standard one in African philosophy. In some sense, I do not even have to make the case that my new readings are the best ones. I simply need to pry open the tendency within African philosophy of texts to converge on a relatively commonly held view of what African philosophy actually is. These readings start from a different premise than most African philosophy—that the primary goal of philosophy is not to represent but to create. If we can reach the point of seeing that there is not *an* African philosophy but *many* African philosophies that are non-reducible to each other and that are part of the vitality of the space of thought, then the goal of philosophy as a creative enterprise will be met.

These readings can be seen as both introductory and transversal, but they also are arranged with a kind of narrative arc. My purpose here is to advance thinking in place, which is the idea that philosophy that attends to its places has creative potential. The goal, in other words, is to offer a new way of creating concepts within African philosophy. This arc is a kind of narrative, and it could be seen as a phenomenological or hermeneutical reading of this project. In this sense, this book is an extension of *Philosophy in an African Place*, even though this book might also be seen as a significantly different approach to the nature of place.

There is more than one narrative potentiality, though. The Wynter and Césaire chapters are meditations on the limits and possibilities of humanism. Wynter rethinks humanism (it is the point of her "ceremony") as the potential for the emergence of new forms of life rather than the production of a civilization that is limited only to some. Césaire draws the forward-looking aspects from Négritude to imagine a creative and vibrant civilization foreseen in Leo Frobenius's idea of *paideuma*. These are both versions of humanism but not as it is commonly understood in Western thought. It is closer to what J. Paul Narkunas calls the "ahuman condition," the condition of human life in the space of complex and unpredictable systems, in which human life is not thought as sets of immutable attributes but are "concatenations of individuations that immanently come together through their interaction and create several simultaneous possibilities for actualization within the flux of life" (2018: 264).

The chapters between Wynter and Césaire are rereadings that posit a nonrepresentational sense of African philosophy, one that does not start from the idea that the central project is to identify an African form of humanism, different from but equal to Western humanism. The chapters are not, though, antihumanist, trans-humanist, or even post-humanist. The point is to create a different problematic within African intellectual space, one that does not attempt to ground philosophy in a humanist project analogous to that which grounded European philosophy for so long. The ahuman asks the question of how to proceed in a complex space, and how to regard the human as a site of knowledge rather than an object of knowledge. These chapters argue that this question has existed in a range of writings within African philosophy for years, sometimes as minor notes but sometimes as potentialities that could not be recognized due to the prevailing humanist readings given to them.

Another arc is the move in these chapters from time to text. Perhaps more accurately, it is a set of meditations on the implications of time for text and text for time. Wynter thinks through a different trajectory from the past into the future than the current one. She suggests an event, the "ceremony," that takes us on a path toward a future of creation (although not the creation of the future). Autopoiesis is emergence, and we need the skills to deal with the encounter with the emergent future. We then go into three chapters that, in one way or another, deal with time. Tempels's vitalism is a version of what Wynter calls autopoiesis. Mbiti, read in the context of his whole book rather than just a small section, looks less like a metaphysician of time and more like one who is sketching modes of encounter, and the nature of the uncertainty we live in vis-à-vis the future. And Oruka, in his late work, adds an unexpected element to sage philosophy—historicity. He opens the door to moving past sage philosophy as a window into an unchanging cultural past and suggests how the political helps to shape the future.

The chapter on Ramose, in this approach, is the fulcrum between time and text. Ubuntu, as Ramose conceives it, is a space of thought. It depends on a version of time as developed in the previous three chapters and is a kind of textualization, as will be spelled out in the next three. Ramose's Ubuntu is a unique explication of the concept among the large number of scholars of Ubuntu because it emphasizes both a futurity and a theory of action based in Ubuntu and also the interpretive potential, in the form of becoming, that Ubuntu thought has. He is less interested in laying out a list of qualities and characteristics and more interested in describing a mode of thought, one that was overwhelmed by the instruments of colonialism but nevertheless retains its vitality.

The next two chapters deal with elements of text, or rather, rethink how textuality relates to thought. In Chapter 6, Sophie Olúwọlé argues that philosophy requires a literature, and she suggests that any candidates we have seen to this point are inadequate. Euphrase Kezilahabi turns the question around to think about the ways in which philosophy informs literature. Between these two, the creative potential of philosophy becomes apparent. Finally, Achille Mbembe raises the question of self-writing. My exploration here is to understand his examples of mis-writing, both as imposed by external forces (slavery, colonialism, and apartheid) and as adopted in response to these forms of mis-writing (nativism and Afro-radicalism) as examples of the loss of place. I put these in relation to the phenomenology of torture, as the erasure of self-writing of the body in the form of the loss of embodied place. All these amount to ruptured and exhausted places, and they stand as currents of existence that undermine the kind of enactivism I have been arguing for.

This brings us to Suzanne Césaire's reading of Négritude. It is creative, it is the formation of a text, a poetic, surreal text designed to make it possible to, again, dwell in one's native land. It is not the land it was, but it is a potentiality emerging from the pain. It depends on a form of surreal temporality—not linear, not dialectical, not eschatological, but transversal. If the work has been done in the first part of this section, we have a vitalist version of time that moves into an uncertain future and engages in the task of avoiding the forms of capture that have existed. The ahumanism of Wynter's ceremony becomes the surrealism of Césaire's Négritude. And, that which is produced, a new space of thought, is a new text in the literature of African philosophy, one in which self-writing happens in a new way.

There are, no doubt, other narrative arcs through the book, but this should hopefully give a picture of the space of thought I believe exists within work in African philosophy, and which could exist in new ways in the future.

1

The Ceremony Found and a New Human Problematic: Sylvia Wynter after Humanism

Sylvia Wynter has, over a long academic career, sought to rethink what it means to be human. Marshaling a vast and diverse literature, she both makes an argument for and models what it means to realize potentialities implicit within our devices for and habits of meaning-making. Most scholarship on her understandably focuses on the arguments she makes. Their richness and subtlety require careful attention to detail, both to understand what she is arguing and to avoid superficialities and missteps.

I will depend on that subtlety of argumentation in this chapter, but I am just as interested in the way she models what she argues for. I take her primary goal to be not exegetical or interpretive but creative. She shows us what it means to create, to work within a space of thought rather than engage in a mode of thought, and to activate the thought from people and groups previously ignored or deemed irrelevant. Her goal is to create such a space of thought, to establish a new problematic rather than work within the mode of thought of Renaissance humanism. The path from the mode to the space is not easy, because it means breaking the terms of the mode from within, but this is exactly what she does in order to answer the question of what comes after humanism.

Modeling a space of thought is important for the project of this book because this is exactly what I propose to do in the chapters that follow. There is a space of thought available within the literature of African philosophy. It is one that allows creation of new concepts. Just as Wynter shows us what it means to not just imagine a utopian space of thought that overturns and denies what came before but rather recognizes its "genre-specific" nature and helps it to move beyond that, so too has African philosophy formed a genre of thought, one that can use its own existing literature to broaden and realize the richness available in a space of thought. What Wynter sets up for us here are two themes that will figure in the following chapters—the theme of literature and the theme of temporality.

Each is recognized as having been restricted by what I am calling a mode of thought and what she calls genre-specific reality, and rethinking each is the key to another kind of life.

This chapter will give an overview of Sylvia Wynter's account of the human. It will include several of her key concepts that will be useful for the rest of the studies in this book. What she calls humanism has some elements in common with what I call ahumanism.

Wynter is opposed to a subjectless structuralism (Scott and Wynter 2000: 120), but she is clearly not interested in the classical alternative—a Renaissance humanism that defines the subject in a specific racial and cultural way. Much of her work is aimed at imagining a version of humanism that can be recovered and relaunched from that dominant model. She analyzes the reasons why that form of humanism became dominant in the first place.

For most writers, the "human" has too much baggage as a concept to be useful. Apart from its historical specificity in a European narrative, it also suggests a kind of essentialism as well as a kind of anthropocentrism that makes it untenable in a world where neither of these are easily defensible. Wynter's project, then, is ambitious and, it should be said, not entirely clear at first glance. Why recover this concept at all? Has it not simply run its course, and does it not deserve to be consigned to the history of philosophy, as a moment we can point to on the path to our current better and more inclusive ways of thinking?

The answer to this question lies in determining what kind of question she is trying to answer. Is it simply descriptive, a way of accounting for the evident injustice and differential application of the human to different people and groups, both historically and in the present? There is certainly plenty of description, and Wynter's writing requires of the reader a robust familiarity with a wide range of scientific, historical, philosophical, and literary texts. Is this, like at least some of Fanon, therapeutic? Is she, in other words, giving an account that can help to address the existential and psychological trauma experienced by those who have suffered from a particular version of the human, one that has served colonialists and capitalists but not nonwhites and workers? Again, there is an element of this, even though she is not, like Fanon, a trained psychiatrist, and the impetus of her writing does not come from observing patients and their mental afflictions and realizing that it is not that they are mad but that the system in which they exist that is mad.

Is she giving us a diagnosis of the cultural illness we find ourselves in and which overwhelmingly affects nonwhites? It is partly this, yes, inasmuch as a diagnosis is both an explanation and a plan of action to remedy an illness, but if we are to continue this medical metaphor, she is interested in what we might call wellness, and the myriad ways that it might be possible, not just the myriad ways it fails to be realized and is thwarted.

My interest, though, is in another agenda she has. This is the creative agenda, that is, the question of how we might live as human into the future, and how all of us have been held back from that creative existence through a complex system of capture of energies and signifiers that has seemed to benefit some and not others, but that in fact has benefitted no one, once there is a clear understanding of what becoming human entails.

The plan for this chapter is as follows. We will first unpack some central concepts she uses to make her case for what comes after humanism. We begin with her appropriation of Fanon's concept of the sociogenic and move to Maturana and Varela's concept of autopoiesis. With these in hand, we will be able to understand why she searches for and finds a ceremony, rather than a theory, a praxis, or something more familiar to theorists. From there, we can look at how she thinks about "literature" (which appears extensively in "The Ceremony Must Be Found" [1984]) and "genre" (used extensively in "The Ceremony Found" [2015]).

Once these are clear, we can look at her theory of the human again. We will argue that it actually comes closer to the "ahuman," since taking seriously both the conditions of creative thought as well as cognitive and systems theory implies that seeing Renaissance forms of humanism as a form of capture of otherwise fluid system relations means recognizing that there is no further capture possible. Wynter is not arguing that we simply got the definition of the human wrong under Renaissance models, and now we can get it right by foregrounding the currently marginalized. She is arguing for something more radical than that. The ahuman is not the nonhuman, or the antihuman, or the trans-human, but rather the becoming-human, the possibility of being other than what we are (as opposed to the program of Renaissance humanism, which strove to become more of what we already were, more of that seed of human greatness as represented by European heterosexual adult property-owning males).

Sociogenesis

Relating insights from the natural sciences, Wynter's thesis lays the groundwork for what she has defined as a new science of human systems:

> It is these schemas and the coercive nature of their systems of meaning that make it possible for each mode of sociogeny and its artificially imprinted *sense of*

self to be created as one able to override where necessary, the genetic-instinctual sense of self, at the same time as itself comes to be subjectively *experienced as if it were instinctual*; it is thereby not only to reoccupy the formerly hegemonic place, of the genetic self, but also to harness its drives to its now culturally defined sociogenetic own. (Wynter 2001: 47–8; original emphases)

The implication remains that the discourse of race, "by mapping or totemizing negative/positive meanings (as part of a cultural series) on the non-humanly instituted difference (as a natural series)," activates by a process of semantic reprogramming the opioid system in genre-specific terms, thereby illustrating that the "*objectively* structured biochemical system … determines the way in which each organism will perceive, classify, and categorize the world in adaptive terms needed for its own survival and reproductive realization as such an organism" (Eudell 2015: 240–1; original emphasis).

Sylvia Wynter engages with the implications of neuroscience, biology, and evolution in her program of rethinking the human. Her account of the social is not simply about the actions of individuals but about a social rooted in the biochemical, the neural, and the adaptive.

Fanon only mentions "sociogeny" once:

Reacting against the constitutionalizing trend at the end of the nineteenth century, Freud demanded that the individual factor be taken into account in psychoanalysis. He replaced the phylogenetic theory by an ontogenetic approach. We shall see that the alienation of the black man is not an individual question. Alongside phylogeny and ontogeny, there is also sociogeny. In a way, in answer to the wishes of Leconte and Damey, let us say that here it is a question of sociodiagnostics. (2008: xv)

Sociogeny, or sociodiagnostics, is Fanon's clinical tool to diagnose the neurotic structure of colonialism. It stands alongside phylogenesis (the development of species) and ontogenesis (the development of individual embryos). It is worth noting a few things about the framework into which the sociogenic fits. Putting it alongside phylogeny and ontogeny suggests that it is about development. In the case of these two, which are rooted in nineteenth-century science and revived by Vygotsky, they refer to morphological development. Ontogeny typically charts the forms that individual life takes at various stages of development from (in the case of mammals) the fertilization of an egg up to birth and then throughout life. Phylogeny, on the other hand, refers to the methods of classification and systematization within evolutionary development of species throughout their histories.

The purpose of these two ways of structuring biological life has varied over time. Phylogeny has always been an attempt to understand relationships over time in order to understand the lines of descent of species. Scientists such as Ernst Haeckel held forth hope in what was called the "recapitulation theory," which was succinctly phrased as "ontogeny recapitulates phylogeny" or, put less pithily, the development of the individual mirrors the evolutionary development through speciation over time. This theory has no merit in contemporary biology (despite having been taken up in weak versions by Piaget and Freud, among others), but it does point to the idea that finding morphological patterns in life over time might reveal something about its forms of adaptation.

Wynter's use of Fanon's sociogenic puts her in this space of thought. When encountering a concept, it is useful to ask what question the concept was created to answer, and what other concepts are within its ecosystem that allow it to succeed at answering this question. Phylogenesis is a concept of emergence, and it is a concept that works only by looking backward. In other words, the evolutionary scientist looks at existing and extinct species in order to tell how they relate to each other, and to be able to work out the forces that came to bear upon natural selection in order to produce particular outcomes. This does not work into the future—we cannot predict evolution using phylogenesis. Why is that? Not because we have insufficient knowledge about species (that would suggest that all we need to do is expand our knowledge) but rather because there are transversal forces in biological development that make speciation in principle unpredictable. As for ontogenesis, there is also an ordering, mostly in relation to what is "normal" within a particular species. This idea of "normal," though, is a highly selective one. Mutation still happens within individuals, as does selection for specific traits based on a host of factors, as does individuation, and all of these point to variation within the development of any particular individual. A species is not, in other words, a single thing but a range of related things.

So, what question is sociogenesis meant to answer? One question clearly concerns the lack within this account of the phylogenetic and the ontogenetic of any influence of social relationships on development. From a biological point of view, this seems jarring—does the social influence either evolution or individual development? That is not the vantage point of the issue, though. The vantage point is that of the present, and it is an attempt to explain the situation of humanity when we recognize the vastly unequal and racist conditions in which many live. Adding the sociogenic to these others is an attempt to place the social development of humans at a level as basic as the biological development, and also to use the resources of evolutionary theory to think about how the social can succeed or fail, in particular cases.

Wynter's development of the sociogenic principle is likewise an attempt to represent forms of development and relation that can explain, in particular, what it is like to be Black, not just as an existential fact but as a way of thinking about consciousness (2001: 31). She describes it as follows:

> Fanon's explanatory concept of sociogeny put forward as a third person response to his own first person questioning, serves, when linked to the insights of Thomas Nagel's 1974 essay "What it is like to be a bat" (Epigraph 2), to verify Chalmers' postulate with respect to the empirical functioning of psychophysical laws, as these laws function at the level of human experience. Further, that such laws are not only redefinable at this level as sociogenetic or nature-culture laws, but also as ones whose processes of functioning, while inseparable from the physical (that is, neurobiological) processes which implement them, would, at the same time, be non-reducible, as the indispensable condition of what it is like to be human, to these processes alone and, therefore, to the laws of nature by which those processes are governed. Further, if, as Nagel proposes, an organism can have "conscious mental states" only if "there is something it is like to be that organism," something it is like for that organism, for, therefore, its identity as such an organism, then Fanon's exploration of the "lived experience of the black," and thereby, of the processes of functioning of these psychophysical laws within the terms of our present hegemonic modes of identity, (as itself, but one variant of the hybrid nature/culture modes of being unique to us as humans), can at the same time also provide insights into the functioning of these laws as they function at the level of purely organic forms of life. That is, insights into the laws which govern the realm of lived subjective experience, human and non-human, which govern, therefore, the interrelated phenomena of identity, mind and/or consciousness. (32)

There are several things to note about this concept as Wynter describes it. First, sociogeny has a law-like structure, one that links first-person observation to third-person response. The first-person experience cannot, in other words, simply remain as a subjective (and hence easily dismissable) experience. Second, sociogeny is linked to consciousness, which is something that cannot be said about phylogeny or ontogeny. Consciousness is a way of functioning of an organism that links its biology to its social experience. Wynter draws on David Chalmers's famous "hard problem" in cognitive science, which is the question of how consciousness can arise from physical processes in the brain.

Her solution is not to propose a mechanism that explains this but to propose the sociogenic principle. (For a useful overview of consciousness that includes nonrepresentational versions sympathetic to Wynter's approach, see Hutto [2011].) The third thing to note is that if sociogeny functions like its parallel developmental areas, it is not actually a principle (despite Wynter's use of the term) but a kind of container of change, describable after the fact. There is nothing in phylogeny that tells us how development should proceed, and even in ontogeny, deviations from the "normal" might just as well be mutations or adaptations to new conditions as they are aberrations or defects. In other words, recognizing that sociogeny is a way of describing human development that links the social with the biological does not in itself suggest that existing social structures have evolved to maximize the fit between organism and environment, nor does it suggest any specific formation in the future that is either morally or prudentially optimal. What it does describe is the situation in which maximal creativity and fecundity can be realized, which is the situation of diversity and equality. As with phylogeny and ontogeny, even though we cannot say what an optimal species or life-form looks like (since we cannot predict mutation and change), we can tell the conditions of stress, illness, and extinction. The same is true for sociogeny.

This is, as far as I know, a unique approach to that question (most have either searched for the equivalent of Descartes's pineal gland, the point of intersection between matter and mind, or argued for some form of eliminativism), and this is because she is trying to answer a different question than most of the cognitive scientists. When the question of consciousness is raised in cognitive science (and it often is not addressed at all, preferring to focus on neurological structures or on more operationalizable concepts such as intersubjectivity, self-consciousness, experience, etc.), it often remains as Chalmer's hard problem, as something to be explained. Wynter is interested in something more than "consciousness-of," or intentionality—the point of Fanon's "Look, a Negro!" story is not that he was not conscious of being Black, and then after the child pointed at him he became conscious. It is not access to an interpretive framework of the world or the realization of one's place in a framework in the eyes of others. Consciousness is not just a capacity of the individual to apprehend self or world, or to focus on some aspect of it. It is, rather, a feature of the world itself. Does this mean that there is some panpsychism happening? No. Sociogeny means that consciousness is extended into social relations and cultural content, dependent upon these relations and one's embodied existence and practices within them.

"As Fanon points out, for us it is 'normal' to be anti-Negro, within the case of Negroes socialized in the terms of *Man*" (Wynter 2001: 51; original emphasis). Wynter's analysis of Fanon shows that racism is not just a matter of will, weak or otherwise, but rather it is made natural and normal. It is reinforced by pleasure and pain responses so that it feels right for those who gain from it. That does not, of course, make it right, but the sociogenic principle is a developmental one, and this means that changing the results of sociogeny will take more than efforts of education, policy, or law.

Wynter anticipates the discussion among enactivists about social cognition. For the most part, cognitive science research has focused on finding accounts for cognition, and enactivists have focused on alternative explanations and models to computationalist ones. Questions of things such as ethics and larger social narratives, for instance, have largely been seen as downstream issues, following far behind the more basic questions about fundamental structures of cognition. Wynter's use of the sociogenic principle, alongside the discussions of consciousness and cognition, are unique in placing questions of race and gender, along with their experience through history and their differential impact on different groups, at the center of her approach to cognition. She is not providing an alternate theory of cognition of the sort that most cognitive scientists might recognize, but she is prioritizing what might be considered by some "higher-level" or downstream forms of cognition and arguing that they suffuse all levels of cognition. Racism is not just something that comes along after the more basic cognitive functions have done their work, as an interpretive layer or "socialization" over the more universal functions of cognition. Because of the sociogenic principle, it informs every level.

Fanon, and Wynter, see the payoff of the sociogenic as providing a diagnosis, the "sociodiagnostic" (Wynter 2001: 60). This will, in Fanon's terms, "set man free." But how? The description we have to this point is of organisms at every level embedded within their own conditions of production and emergence. Does setting us free mean giving us agency, of a sort that allows control of the sociogenic? No, no more than we would be free in being able to control the phylogenic or ontogenic. But the current situation is one in which there are already attempts at control, and the result is the lack of freedom, both for those who become the "other" in a dominant narrative and also for those who believe they benefit from it.

The importance of the sociogenic principle for Wynter is not just as a diagnostic frame to make sense of the lived experience of racism and sexism. It is also forward looking, interested in adaptation and emergence, particularly when linked to the concept she develops elsewhere: autopoiesis. She finishes her essay on sociogeny by quoting Fanon:

> "I should remind myself," Fanon wrote in the conclusion of his *Black Skin/White Masks*, "that the real leap consists in introducing invention into existence" … I am a part of Being to the extent that I go beyond it" (BS: 229). (Wynter 2001: 61)

Autopoiesis

By the time of "The Ceremony Found" in 2015, Wynter talks less about the "sociogenic principle" and more about "sociogenic causality" and the "sociogenic replicator code" (modeled, it seems, on DNA replication, which is part of emergence in ontogeny). In other words, sociogeny moves from being a layer of emergence for any consciousness to an account of how consciousness happened in the "first emergence" (217). It moves to being an account of the past. This happens, I believe, to make room for another concept that moves us into the future: autopoiesis. The classical theory of autopoiesis, though, is not an obvious conceptual tool for Wynter to use. There are aspects that put it in some tension with the project of rethinking humanism.

- For one thing, the concept answers very different questions and provides an alternative for different kinds of models for Francisco Varela and Humburto Maturana than it does for Wynter. Varela and Maturana are moving from a model of reproduction and evolution as an account of the unity of life to one that depends on interconnections and the unpredictable organization that comes of them (Varela, Maturana, and Uribe 1974: 187).
- Furthermore, as Maturana and Varela formulate it, there is little concern for history (Di Paolo 2018: 79), while Wynter's project depends on a clear thinking of both the problematic history of the formation of Renaissance humanism and the reformulation that should have happened and still can.
- Autopoiesis is a function of the relations and emergence that happen in complex at a fine-grained level—the quantum interaction, the atom, the molecule, the cell, while Wynter is interested in complexity at an entirely different level—the society, the race, the gender.

- Autopoiesis happens without agency or intentionality—there is no consciousness rethinking or shaping the creative space in order to produce results. It is, after all, an account of order without an orderer. For Wynter, there is a sense that intentional action can make possible new forms of life, once the fundamental problems of the existing order are understood.
- With autopoiesis, there is no wrong turn—there just is the order created by complex systems at a particular time within an environment. Clearly, for Wynter the Renaissance version of humanism was a wrong turn.
- And finally, the autopoietic version of life, at least in its early formulations, is a coherence theory. There is not and cannot be fundamental instability, or the conditions of life in that form would be violated. Change is evolutionary, not revolutionary.

Autopoiesis as a concept evolves as it serves to ground elements of contemporary enactivism as an approach to cognition. The focus has been on nonrepresentational or minimally representational accounts of cognition.

For Wynter, autopoiesis is a function of our sociogenic replicator code, a code that (as we shall see shortly) issues in a set of genre-specific terms. As with sociogenesis, Wynter's use of autopoiesis evolves across her writings. By the time of "Ceremony Found," it is no longer just autopoiesis but "the Autopoietic Turn/Overturn." Wynter adapts concepts by taking them out of their original conceptual ecosystem and allowing them to travel (Bal 2001) into a new space, to be used for related but different purposes. In this case, the turn/overturn conflates two modes of change—the incremental change of building on the past, and the revolutionary change of starting anew, with a new set of assumptions. These are usually seen as mutually exclusive—either one builds or one starts anew—but in autopoiesis these are not contradictories. The materiality of things means that change can only use patterns and structures that already exist, but the emergent nature of autopoiesis means that the intersection of those material structures offers potentialities not deductible or predictable from existing structures. New forms of life are possible.

The Ceremony Found

We are finally ready to ask about the ceremony now that we have unpacked Wynter's use of sociogenesis and autopoiesis. Wynter's search for a ceremony in "The Ceremony Must Be Found" starts from a quote from John Peale Bishop:

> The ceremony must be found
> That will wed Desdemona to the huge Moor.
>
> (Wynter 1984: 19)

The Othello reference is one of five epigrams that Wynter includes at the beginning of "The Ceremony Must Be Found." Each speaks to the idea of the difficulty of bringing together people deemed by some dominant narrative as outside, impure, imperfect, with those who are central to that narrative. Put this way, we might think that there is nothing more than an attempt to expand the circle, to include those who have not been included. But then, why would a ceremony be needed? And what kind of ceremony does Wynter claim to have found? Why is it a ceremony, rather than just a theory or an implementation of law or policy? Does social reform not require changes of structure that will yield better outcomes than what came before? The fact that she spends decades looking for a ceremony is significant, because what she seeks is not simply a structural solution, important as that might be. The problem lies at a different register. This is not just about inclusion or expanding the circle. This is about something else.

The quotation presents autopoiesis as a very specific kind of ceremony, that is, a wedding. Mina Karavanta elaborates:

> In Wynter's work, "wedding" signifies the reciprocity between the ontogenic and sociogenic aspects of being that found what she calls autopoiesis that she tries to articulate post the binary between the western bourgeois Man as the dominant idea of the human and his foils, all the liminal beings like the African human, the negro, the native, the subaltern, the stateless, the immigrant without documents, and the Third-World woman, excluded from the possibility of cultural and historical development. (2015: 157)

Karavanta's point is that autopoiesis is Wynter's way out of a binary, which only ever served to limit and exclude anyone who is not, in Wynter's term, Man(1), or the heir and beneficiary to Renaissance humanism. The wedding is not simply the union of two separate beings but the creation of something new. The ceremony is a kind of alchemy, not a contract, not a dialectical *Aufhebung*, and not a disguised continuation of the same power structures as had existed all along. The progeny that comes as a result of this ceremony is not predictable in advance, even though after the fact we might see that a child has the smile of one parent or the nose of the other. The ceremony puts us in a different creative space, a different logic to what Renaissance humanism by itself could offer.

Wynter's "Ceremony Found" draws on a range of inspirations and influences to chart a way of maintaining the gains of the Renaissance humanist tradition while at the same time recognizing the deep inequities and mistaken essentialisms that the tradition enabled. In the Renaissance there were two forms of negation (Wynter 2015: 188) that led to humanism. While this humanism championed reason, the negations it had to enact included the negation of race, and then later a "biocentric" line or divide, which made Black African and Afro-mixed people into the iconic embodiment of extreme human otherness (187). Wynter is pointing to a kind of existential autopoiesis, that is, a formation of our human way of being that takes us beyond kinship structures. This is accomplished linguistically and narratively (199). The ontologies of race, class, gender, and sexual orientation are instituted (i.e., experienced) as substance, in a manner not much different from what Deleuze talks about.

Wynter uses Césaire and Fanon (209) to argue for a form of science that does not lead to "impoverished knowledge," which depersonalized and deindividualized humanity. This is not a new observation—a great deal of mid-twentieth-century cultural thought critiqued the alienating nature of contemporary science and technology. What is different is the solution. Where the mid-twentieth century would argue over whether there could be a renewed humanism, or even a transcendent response to this alienation, or on the other hand we would make the best out of an atomistic existence, or some other nonuniversal state, Wynter is suggesting a different direction. This is, in fact, her ceremony. It is a request for a "new form of knowledge, a new form of science of ourselves."

> I propose, therefore, that within the terms of the *new answer* or response that the Ceremony Found gives to the question of who-we-are as that of a hybrid and uniquely auto-instituting mode of living being, *we humans cannot pre-exist our cosmogonies or origin myths/stories/narratives* anymore than a bee, at the purely biological level of life, can pre-exist its beehive. Seeing that if such cosmogonies function to enable us to "tell the world and ourselves who we are" (Leeming, 2002), they also function even more crucially to enable us autopoetically to institute ourselves as the *genre*-specific *We* or fictive mode of kind that each of us will from now on pre-conceptually experience and, therefore, performatively enact ourselves *to be* as an always-already symbolically encoded and cloned *I/We*. (213–14; original emphases)

We are self-creating. This much is true of everything, including the bee. Wynter's Ceremony Found is the event of creation at the edges of the multiple physical and symbolic systems in which we find ourselves. This Ceremony Found is temporality—it is experienced time, significant time. It is vitalist in the sense of being emergence engendered by the processes of life. It is a ceremony able to "emancipate humankind's knowledge of the physical and purely biological levels of reality from our order-stabilizing/legitimating symbolic codes" (204). In other words, while the sociogenic replicator codes are inevitable in our development, they initially led to the Western-bourgeois order through the birth of Renaissance humanism. This led to Man(1), that is, rational Western man, at the center of all structures of meaning, which served as the model for all. This initial result of the sociogenic replicator codes in effect froze temporality, putting in place a model of development that had reached its philosophical pinnacle, even if it had not yet worked out all the implications of that genre.

The Ceremony Found is in essence a "new science of the Word," made available by the Autopoietic Turn/Overturn (207). The Ceremony Found is the rebirth of time, the restarting of the engine of creation that had been functionally stopped (even while seeming to be running at full tilt) by the instantiation of Man(1), a static view of human life. The Ceremony Found is the move from deductive logic to abductive, that is, from the establishment of some (dubious and highly contestable) premises and the inferences that come from them, to the exploration of new potentialities based in existing flows and patterns rather than premises. It is the return to the centrality and fecundity of the question, rather than the narrowing comfort of the premise or claim.

One central aspect of the Ceremony Found is the recovery of what happened in the "Third Event" (217). The first event is the emergence of the physical universe, and the second event is the emergence of biological life. The Third Event is the "different route" that our early ancestors took in solving ecological problems, which was (in the words of Juan Luis Arsuaga), to use our "unique capacity to … tell stories and create fictitious worlds" (Wynter 2015: 217). These stories are not just about looking back and narrating origins, although they are also that. They are, crucially, about looking forward. "Our species has been enabled *autopoietically* to *institute itself* as a now symbolically encoded mode of living being" (217; original emphasis). This does not just mean that we can draw future conclusions from present data or imagine a desired situation and work toward it. Autopoiesis specifically argues that the future is unexpected and unwritten. We do not control it. We can plan, yes, but what we actually do is have an idea of the future, take a step, look at what happened with that step, reevaluate, collect more data, and do it again. We improvise. This is what our stories have to be able to bear. They are not just moral lessons for the future or prudential tales. They are stories about how creation happens bit by bit.

The tendency, though, is to try to control. We do this by making these narrative into genres. We imagine that stories have morals, which are timeless truths or rules to live by. Why does this happen? First, because as our stories started emerging in our past, they only were able to be replicated if they activated "the opiate reward and punishment biochemical implementing mechanisms of the brain" (218). There was, in other words, a physical feedback loop. Second, the stories invariably end up defining groups: "*We/Us* as over against *They/not-Us*" (220; original emphases). Because of this, we experience the world through these narratives that have in effect been captured as genres, and we begin to think that the genres are the only possible stories we can tell. "The way each organism knows and experiences reality through its species-specific 'perceptual categorization system,' in turn, *can therefore in no way be concordant with the way that reality is outside that species-specific viewpoint*" (221; original emphasis). These captured views from the inside, these genres, become the only stories we can see. These captured stories are what become the "macro Western world-system" (222), extending its bourgeois configuration to the entire world.

It is this capture that the Ceremony Found is meant to move us past. Since the issue is in the meeting of narrative and scientific order or structure, the Ceremony must recover the earlier fictive nature of narrative, not in the sense of making up false or fanciful (or worse, self-serving) stories that supersede scientific ones but in the sense that scientific stories do not stand alone as interpreters of human meaning, nor are they captured by linear causal forms of emergence. The sociogenic principle is a mode of replication but also a mode that introduces layers of complexity and unpredictability into any story we want to tell. So, the stories from the European Renaissance, while opening up a particular mode of thinking, at the same time closed down other modes that now must be addressed. And, it must also be noted, those who benefitted from the success of the Renaissance capture of narrative are unlikely to be the ones to be at the forefront of moving past them. The opiate reward and punishment system is very strong.

A superficial reading of Wynter might lead one to think that she is arguing for the reintroduction of folkways, myths, and other kinds of cultural narrative back into contemporary life. That would be to misunderstand what it means to move past the genre established in the Renaissance. She is arguing for something much more radical than that. She is arguing that the mode of scientific reasoning established in European modernity is inadequate to account for human life. And in fact science itself is coming to recognize this. The fact that we think in terms of self-organization rather than divine teleology or a natural code that exhaustively governs its expressions and phenomena means that we realize the irreducible complexity at the basis of all things. And nothing—not science, not myth, not religion, or cosmic belief—can control and predict the emergence of things, much less chart the potentialities of human action and becoming. The point here is not to substitute something else for Western science but rather to usher in a new way of living in the face of these creative uncertainties.

Wynter uses a powerful example to illustrate this. In 2007 the authors of the Fourth Assessment Report of the Intergovernmental Panel on Climate Change (IPCC) won the Nobel Peace Prize (Wynter 2015: 231–40). Wynter argues that this report, along with the subsequent report in 2014, is evidence of a "continued misattribution/misdiagnosis by even the most rigorous of scientists of the origin/cause of the ongoing crisis of global warming and climate change" (231). The problem is that "while rightfully attributing the etiology of the dually related crises of global warming and climate change to non-natural (and not merely natural) causes, nonetheless also systemically misattributes such activities as having purely originated from 'anthropogenic forcings' or generically 'human activities'" (231). This has led to proposing solutions framed in economic terms, which start from our current paradigm of knowledge production.

Wynter argues that until we move away from thinking that a particular mode of science is the only way we can account for phenomena such as this, we will continue to make specious distinctions such as those between "natural" and "non-natural" causes for climate change (as if we could keep the social world apart from the natural and base an ethics and a politics of the environment on whether or not "we" are directly responsible). We will continue to mistake the history of climate change, seeing it as coextensive with the rise of Soviet and Chinese industry, and recognize that it also coincided with the anti-colonial struggles after the Second World War, which modeled themselves on the economic successes of the industrial West. (233) The real conclusion to draw, Wynter says, was seen by Sven Lütticken: "the truly terrifying notion is *not* that [global warming/climate change] is irreversible, but that it actually might be reversible—at the cost of *radically changing the economic and social order*" (Lütticken 2007: 118; Wynter 2015: 235, emphasis is Wynter's). The real question is not how to remedy climate change using the logic of Man(2), the *homo oeconomicus* that is the endpoint in the genre-logic of Renaissance humanism, but rather how to ask a new question, one made available by the Autopoietic

Turn/Overturn, or what I will call, following Gaston Bachelard (1966), a new problematic.

The Ceremony Found enables human Second Emergence (Wynter 2015: 243). If the First Emergence was the human spread out of Africa two hundred thousand years ago, the Second Emergence

> marks a break this time not from the Primate-type mode of total subordination/restriction of eusocial, inter-altruistic, kin-recognizing behaviors to a level of cooperation whose narrow limits have been preset by the species-specific replicator DNA code. Instead, this rupture will be from our hitherto subordination, normally, to our own autopoetically and, thereby, genre-specifically invented and cosmogonically chartered, pseudo-speciating sociogenic replicator codes of symbolic life/death. (243–4)

We will, in other words, be able to ask questions about human existence that truly come from the encounter of humans, across the borders of race and culture, and that therefore enable a form of both scientific and cultural advancement we have not yet seen or experienced in our existing models of human thriving based in Renaissance humanism. Wynter's dream is that we will "no longer need illusions—such as those which now *inter alia* threaten the livability of our species' planetary habitat—in order to now remake, consciously and collectively, the new society in which our now existential referent 'we ... in the horizon of humanity' will all now live" (245).

Literature and the Genre

In "The Ceremony Must Be Found" in 1984, Wynter focuses significant attention on the function of literature. Her image of literature there is of something that reinforces authority in most circumstances but has the potentiality to support different narratives as well. It is a form of mindshaping (Zawidzki 2018), the social and bodily reinforcement and generation of narratives in a particular manner to achieve particular ends.

By the time the ceremony is found in 2015, literature is not mentioned at all. What takes center stage is the genre or rather, "genre-specific" reality. Genre supports particular constructions of the human, specific ways of telling the story of being human. It has conventions, and once a logic is established for the human, it tells that story using the sociogenic replicator code. Every retelling reinforces the initial assumptions about being human and at the same time the metaphysics of those stories. It is not just narrative, it is character—the *homo oeconomicus* becomes a real character in this genre. We might think of it as a superhero genre, in fact, and that character saves the world, every time. In doing so, it instantiates the symbolic life/death border, along with racialized and gendered borders. We congratulate ourselves, when instantiating the superhero tropes, that we have "kick-ass women," and mistake that for the true engagement of women's wisdom to write new stories. We see Black faces on the screen or in the comics, or some other nonwhite characters, and congratulate ourselves on our diversity, not realizing that the genre has just been reinforced yet again and *homo oeconomicus* has triumphed in the end.

Genre is not in itself to be avoided. Indeed, it becomes inevitable, since narrative has tropes, rhythms, and patterns. The problem is less about genre in itself and more about genre specificity. And so, I will recover the term Wynter used earlier that she moved away from, in order to distinguish the replication of genre from the space in which genre can emerge and evolve under new conditions: a literature. Wynter is, in effect, asking for a new literature, a new space of writing, one that does not just orient us toward replicating the same genre conventions with slight variations. She is in search of a new origin story and a new trajectory into the unknown.

Wynter's literature depends on genre. "The term genre derives from the same root etymology as gender, meaning kind. I use genre here to denote the fictively constructed and performatively enacted different kinds of being human, of which gender coherence is itself always and everywhere a function" (Wynter 2015: 196n20). Genre is a potentiality within what I am calling a literature, one that is "fictive" but one we can come to see as real. Potentialities of human life manifest as genres; the problem comes when we forget (or when the incentive exists among those who benefit from a genre) that they are fictive. Literatures manifest in genres, that is, sets of conventions that "performatively enacted roles/identities of class substance (including rich/poor and, at the world-systemic level, developed/underdeveloped substance), of sexual orientation substance, and, of course (and centrally so), of race substance" (195).

It is not simply being human but becoming human that this literature must be able to support. This is why autopoiesis is so important—it suggests a literature that looks forward, not just backward, but that at the same time is not constructing a utopia or laying out a path toward emancipation, as important as those might be. The barriers to emancipation do not lie in not having a plan to reach it (indeed, plans abound) but in not having a sufficiently rich literature to support it and imagine its potentialities. No emancipatory project is a straight line, and resistance to those projects reconfigures itself based on the new environments in which they find themselves. Almost every racist and sexist resistance to change today has plausible deniability about its grounds and goals. And so, a rich literature is crucial to provide the creative flexibility that autopoiesis requires.

Humanism, Post-Humanism, Ahumanism

The problem with using a term like "humanism" is that it tends to be interpreted through the lens of individual agency. Classical Renaissance humanism saw the individual will and intellect as the height of human creative capabilities. The religious versions of this humanism saw the same will and intellect as the greatest manifestation of the creation of God, the true Imago Dei. Enlightenment humanism keeps the individual will and intellect at the center, adding the implicit model of the European adult male property owner as the highest form of the human. Romanticism gives us the human as a more complex figure having irrational as well as rational capacities. The individual may, in Blakean fashion, be the flashpoint of cosmic thought, the realization of all the currents of energy brought into focus as the mad genius, the one who sees beyond the existing structures of matter that we mere mortals take for granted.

Part of the baggage of using a term like "humanism" is thus this implication that the individual will and intellect are, in the end, in some sort of control. The individual is the productive force, the locus of creation, the thing that makes the new possible and without which nothing new would happen. It is this baggage that Wynter explicitly rejects.

What then, if not the human? We have a blizzard of edge-terms—post-human, nonhuman, trans-human, antihuman, ahuman, cyborg. We have diagnosed the problem, or so we think—we (whoever we think we are) center ourselves, and in so doing decenter, marginalize, disregard, diminish, and use that which is not at the center for our own ends. Or, we see into the future of technology, and the lines blur between ourselves and our systems, tools, and toys. But it is one thing to have defined the problem and another to chart a course out. And it is very difficult to stay true to the course, whatever we have decided it is, because the impulse to recenter the human, or some humans, or even a human, is so embedded in our language and habitus that we hardly know how to think from elsewhere. In the end, we still master the world or some part of it, we still dominate a body of knowledge, make our cases for our positions, collect true beliefs like prized possessions, or even just try to give a new interpretation of things that is closer to the truth. We cannot avoid being at the center of our stories. We still transcend. Telling a story about expanding the circle of value or standing is still me the human telling that story, imprinting on all other things an idea of value that I already have and now recognize that nonhuman things might have. As Christopher Peterson says, "According to scholars of the nonhuman turn, the scandal of theory lies in its failure to decenter the human. The real scandal, however, is that we keep trying" (2018: 23).

Wynter is not arguing for post-humanism. The title of her earlier "ceremony" essay is "The Ceremony Must Be Found—After Humanism" (1984). After humanism—her response to humanism is an event, not an essence, not a "post" that is the next thing that will correct the mistakes of the last thing, only to itself require its own correction sometime down the road. J. Paul Narkunas makes clear the limits of the post-human:

> How can we be "posthuman," or discuss taking the human off its anthropocentric pedestal, rendering it as simply another object, when so many *homo sapiens* have never even been treated as human over the scales of deep time due to colonialism, imperialism, gender, race, and economic inequality, and the technologization and instrumentalization of life by capitalism? And what politics are possible in a post-anthropocentric world, given the emphasis of posthumanism on the autonomy of things and animals on the one hand, and the continued institutional pervasiveness of Enlightenment and humanist ideas of freedom on the other? (2018: 17–18)

By the time of the Ceremony Found, years later, she comes to describe Renaissance humanism as "monohumanism"—a global homogenization around a particular neoliberal Man—the *homo oeconomicus* (194). And the purpose of the Ceremony Found is to finally answer the question of the earlier essay: after humanism, what (192)?

Her vision of the new human, the "full cognitive and behavioral autonomy" of humanity. We have seen in the concepts already addressed in this chapter that she has built a thoroughgoing critique of the limitations of the logic of humanism as we have known it. What she desires in its place is

> the functioning of the human brain's natural-opioid behavior-regulatory system (i.e., its executive PFC or prefrontal cortex (Stein, 2007)), itself lawlikely activated in the terms of the specific positive/negative system of meanings of each pseudo-speciating genre of being human's sociogenic replicator code, then implemented as a living entity as that of the code-made-flesh. This telos

will therefore call for its praxis of the Autopoetic Turn/Overturn to function in a hitherto unsuspected, trans-disciplinary, trans-epistemic, trans natural-scientific cum trans-cosmogonic modality. (245)

Narkunas, again, gives us another version of this:

> Ahumans are acentered forms of sentient life in the process of becoming that emerge through connections with objects, concepts, sensations, technologies, and other nonhuman entities that previously went unrecognized due to the givenness of the species form. I argue for the humanist and Marxist idea of changing the world because these ideas are historical human inventions, subject to the foibles and failures of the human mind, and because the human, as posthumanists have documented, is no longer essential to its operation, from a position that is more readily identifiable as posthuman. Yet I introduce the premise of the ahuman as a way to bring the human back—not into the center, but as a sensibility of indeterminancy, a figuration machine. I argue that the ahuman, rather than constituting a focus that should be shunned given the reappreciation of ontological reality, should be attended to as a messy network of actual and virtual images that reorient affective and sentient perception around a shuffling between regimes of truth. Ahuman processes are transindividuated, immanent figurations of life that offer alternatives to the market-centric economic ontology that consumes, conducts, and controls life. (18–19)

The ahuman is the becoming-human (although in some other configurations, it is to face the loss of the human rather than its recreation; see MacCormack 2020). It is the version of the human that recognizes it is not the center of everything, that recognizes that transversal systems intersect with human life so as to render the future in principle opaque, and that therefore requires tools of adaptation, including narratives and mythological structures that can enable becoming-human in unanticipated conditions. It requires a shift in how we think about temporality. The Ceremony Found is an enactment in time of a potentiality of the human. It is a move from linear time, progressive in some limited sense but ultimately only working out the logic of a particular genre, to a rich, creative time in which truly new possibilities might become available, reconfiguring our sense of temporality in new terms.

The ahuman, Wynter's Ceremony Found, depends on a literature, a meaningful inscription that sets up a space of thought, one that is open-ended and about to create and replicate meanings as they become available or necessary. The skills of the ahuman are based less in deduction and more in abduction, less in the making of maps meant to control territory through vision and more in the making of charts that listen to the experiences of those who travel the land and adjust to the changes as they come.

Wynter's concepts will prove to be foundational for the rereading of African philosophy in the rest of this book. She gives us a guide for a different way of reading central texts, and with this guide we can see other potentialities. In some cases, these potentialities were secondary to the authors' intentions, and in some cases they are, I would argue, closer to what the authors actually were trying to do. But authorial intention is perhaps beside the point—what we get is a space of thought within African philosophy that does not gain its legitimacy or relevance from answering a metaphysical or definitional question such as "Is there an African philosophy?" We can instead see evidence of a rethinking of both time and literature that leads to the creation of the new as a necessary function within African philosophy, rather than just the interpretation of the old.

2

Vitalism and Bantu Philosophy: Placide Tempels and Jamaa

Tempels in His Time

In the story we tell about the history of African philosophy, Placide Tempels stands as a problematic and vexed originator of the modern study of African philosophy. He does not originate African philosophy as such—that lies in the hands of Africans and dates much further back. Rather, for philosophers, he originates the discussion within a European context of the existence and nature of African philosophy. The context of the book's appearance was that Africans had largely been written out of the story of the development of philosophy. The story we tell has Tempels establishing a version of philosophy that lies in the practices, language, and everyday thoughts of people. Paulin Hountondji (1996a) famously rejects this as a location of philosophy, calling it "ethnophilosophy." Others, such as Alexis Kagame, develop Tempels's insights in other areas of Africa, in order to flesh out the nascent thought within African cultures.

Tempels's publication of *Bantu Philosophy* (1959) was, at the time, a brave act in its context. It spoke back to a Catholic Church and an academic establishment that had rejected the very idea of Africa as having an intellectual life and heritage. The church at the time assumed an assimilationist approach toward Africans, that is, that there was little or nothing within African culture itself worth saving or developing and so the best that Africans could do was to abandon their own culture and become as much like Europeans as possible. They would never, of course, truly *be* Europeans, but it was considered to be better than their current state.

Tempels started out his time in the Belgian Congo as an assimilationist but came to realize that there was something more within African culture. He never abandoned his goal of converting Africans to Christianity, but he came to realize that that did not have to come with cultural obliteration. There were, in fact, elements within traditional African culture that led directly to the core truths of Christianity, he believed, and enabling Africans to realize their own true nature would simultaneously mean that they would come to recognize that Christianity was the ultimate fulfillment of that nature. *Bantu Philosophy* was written in this spirit.

Part of the question about *Bantu Philosophy* comes down to what we think the book is doing. The title suggests to philosophers that it is sketching out a philosophy that Bantu people hold, or perhaps even one that they must hold in order to be truly Bantu. Using a word like "Bantu" already suggests a linguistic orientation or gateway to this philosophy—the most obvious thing that binds together up to six hundred ethnic groups across Africa is a shared root for what, over the years, became dialects and then independent but partially mutually understandable languages.

So, from a philosopher's point of view, many questions arise if this is what we imagine is happening, and many of these have been raised over the years. But was Tempels's goal really to produce a work of academic philosophy? It is not clear that it was. He was not himself a philosopher. His book had few links to academic philosophical discourse at the time—there were few footnotes, and few named figures. We can see the influence of Henri Bergson in the book, despite the fact that he is never named and that his "élan vitale" appears under several related but distinct terms such as "force vitale," "la puissance vitale," "les influences vitales," "la force de la vie," "la force vivant," and "l'energie vitale," and even some terms that seem to draw on this concept, such as "élévation vitale." However, despite Bergson (and possibly Teilhard de Chardin) framing Tempels's view of the world, there is little evidence that this was meant as a contribution to philosophy at all, at least not as academic philosophers understand it.

This does not, of course, mean that the book is not of philosophical interest or importance, or that it has not played a role in the philosophical conversation. All it means is that if it had been intended as a contribution to philosophical literature, it would have been written differently. Subsequent writers such as Alexis Kagame recognized this—while he thought that Tempels was on the right track in trying to identify elements of philosophy in traditional African culture, he thought that his method was insufficiently precise.

So, if he is not intending to engage the philosophical world, is he instead interested in anthropology, perhaps? There is little evidence of that as well. Tempels walks a similar path to someone like Claude Levi-Strauss in that he argues that non-European intellectual life is as complex as European (on this, see Levi-Strauss 1966). Having said that, there is little evidence that he is adhering to any of the disciplinary methods or structures of anthropology or of philosophy. He does quote some anthropological studies but only of the ethnic groups he is directly interested in. If this was a work of anthropology with as wide ranging a title as it has, we would expect more to be done to connect the linguistic analysis with other aspects of lifeworlds across the range of Bantu peoples.

So, if *Bantu Philosophy* was not intended as a contribution to either the literature of philosophy or anthropology, what was it intended to be, and what difference does it make to establish the problematic outside of the disciplinary narratives of these areas? That is the story of this chapter.

Tempels's Problematic

Tempels asks that we "seek out and define the fundamental thought underlying Bantu ontology, the one and only key that allows native thought to be penetrated" (1959: 15). This metaphor is clearly one of translation—the point is to find the single idea that allows a philosophy of life to be "penetrated"—but by whom? By outsiders presumably, because those who currently hold this philosophy would already feel it in their bones and not need this kind of summary. He goes on: "This ontology exists; and it penetrates and informs all the thought of these primitives; it dominates and orientates all their behavior" (15).

This is clearly an approach to philosophy that does not have its roots in African spaces of thought. How do we know, from an African point of view, that there is such a thing as a single "key" that allows an entire philosophy to be understood? This approach looks much more like a Catholic version of philosophy and theology, rooted in Aristotle and Aquinas, a search for first principles and ultimate causes. It is the question that Tempels proposes to Africa and as is so often the case, it is the wrong question. It is not wrong because it does not have possible answers but rather because it sets up the problematic in a particular way. The range of thought is governed by the question of what the single idea or concept might be that illuminates everything, and allows the non-African to "penetrate" Africa and its thought (the violent and sexual imagery hardly needs commenting on). Tempels confirms that the central question is one posed from outside of Africa:

> It is our task to trace out the elements of this thought, to classify them and to systematize them according to the ordered systems and intellectual disciplines of the Western world. (15–16)

So, the central problem is not that nothing Tempels comes up with really represents any African culture but that the initial question posed defines the problematic. In this problematic, there is a central concept that sheds light on an entire body of thought, and the goal of the inquiry is to systematize the thought as it appears, using that concept and with a view to translating it into the ordered systems and intellectual disciplines of the West. It is not, in other words, to understand African thought in its own terms, in its own complexity, or using any indigenous approaches to knowledge. It should not be a surprise, therefore, that it fails to serve the purpose of explicating African philosophy in its own terms. It was never intended to do that.

Once we identify the question and its resulting problematic, we have the ability to assess a document in its own terms. But more than that, we can also ask a different question. It may be that Tempels, in working out his problematic, also provides the elements for another kind of inquiry. In fact, I think this is exactly what happens here. In his attempt to make an African intellectual lifeworld available to the European mind, framed in such a manner as to give access to African life for the purposes of conversion to Christianity or to make Africans' complaint with colonial rule, Tempels also gives us some tools for a very different kind of inquiry. It is not the inquiry that most people picked up on when they thought he was dealing with a different problematic than he actually was. If the point was never to work out an African system of thought for Africans, in an African place, then the resultant discussions about ethnophilosophy miss the point. Tempels was not looking for the source or foundation of African philosophy but for a core concept. Criticisms of Tempels having to do with the over-expansiveness of his claims about "Bantu" philosophy likewise miss the point. He is not doing an ethnography; he is engaged in an imaginative creation for the purpose of finding a single point of interpretation that will be recognizable in Western categories for conversion and governance.

Tempels located African thought in language, but if the problematic is to find the single point that would allow translation into a European system of thought, for a particular range of purposes, then language may or may not be the point of departure for a different problematic, for instance, the problematic of explicating African thought in an African place.

The lines of criticism against Tempels are understandable if we assume questions that he was not asking. And it is easy to assume those questions. While he is explicit about the question he is asking, most of his study can easily be seen to be answering different kinds of questions.

So, is he successful in answering the question he has posed for himself? We have the benefit of decades of history at this point to answer that question. At one level, he was successful, if his answer using the "ntu" linguistic form is judged by its later success in adoption. Muntu, Ubuntu, and the other words stemming from this root are indeed a central part of African philosophy for many people at this point.

His question, though, was about finding a single idea or concept that would enable translation into Western terms. Does he succeed in this? It seems less likely. The path he takes from African systems of thought to Western systems travels via Teilhard de Chardin, Bergson, and other French philosophers who are interested in life force in various ways. His depiction of ontology, in other words, is of a specific kind in the Western tradition and one not exactly mainstream at the time of his writing. He did not, for instance, find a concept that translated Bantu philosophy into something that looked Aristotelian (and, indeed, others have taken this route—see, e.g., Shutte 1993). The hostility of Tempels's superiors to his work is not surprising. They understood the problematic he worked with, and whatever they might have thought about the viability of an African philosophy (and there surely were racist assumptions about the capabilities of Africans to have a philosophy at all), Tempels translated Bantu philosophy into a form of Western philosophy that would have been seen as heterodox at best in the Catholic tradition.

It is important to note that, although Tempels is looking for a translational point, he is also looking for a feature of Bantu ontology that is, for lack of a better term, determinist. When he reflects on "Why does not the African change?" (1959: 19) he concludes that even those who have taken on Christianity, as well as those who have become modern (the "évolué") are still committed to an ontology that belongs "to his essential nature." Tempels's goal, then, is not to change what he sees as a fundamental ontology but to "add new nobility" to it. As far as he is concerned, very few Africans truly change to a new way of thinking at a deep level. Better to understand this hard-wired (as he sees it) worldview than fight against it.

The agency here is clearly on the side of the colonialist and European. It is the colonialist who makes the translational move, not the African. Tempels sees himself as intellectually generous—"whose fault is that?" he asks about the supposed inability of Africans to move out of a way of seeing the world.

The irony is clear, of course. Tempels is just as unable to move outside of his way of understanding the world as he supposes Africans to be. He is committed to a particular kind of agency on the part of white colonists, and that too is an inevitable part of their system. And yet, it is an agency of translation into terms he is already familiar with, a form of ontology developed by thinkers he is familiar with.

Rather than castigating Tempels, though, I am more interested in what a new problematic might afford for us, out of his efforts to find a single translational concept. It is important to note that the problem of understanding Tempels does not lie in the fact that he wants to put European and African thought in conversation, but rather that he assumes that European thought is the standard for understanding all thought. To suppose that we must find some "pure" African thought, untainted by other cultural influences, will be virtually impossible (for more on this, see Janz [2009], in particular the chapter "Culture and the Problem of Universality").

This does not mean that language is irrelevant to thinking about African thought, just that Tempels's explicit problematic was to find a single concept that allowed translation. Language is the site of philosophy, not as has often been understood, the source (or evidence of the source) of philosophy. So, what if we were to reassemble the tools he creates but in the service of a different problematic?

At the end of his introduction, Tempels mentions in passing that his investigation of Bantu ontology "is perhaps that common to all primitive people, to all clan societies" (1959: 26). He footnotes this with comments from Melvin Herskovits and Jean Capart, both of whom suggest that the philosophical principles that Tempels has found are very close to those held by other people, not just in Africa but around the world and also in ancient times. It is noteworthy that Tempels does not draw what seems like the obvious conclusion from this, that he has simply identified the "other" of European modernism. Instead of seeing these principles as being roughly the same across many unrelated cultures and throughout time, it seems more likely that the issue is the vantage point from which the analysis has been done.

Tempels's study tells us much more about European thought and its shadows than it does about African thought. Having said that, it is still possible to see elements of what he discusses as starting points for philosophy, not just in Africa but anywhere.

Lines of Flight from *Bantu Philosophy*

There are three parallel conversations that arise from *Bantu Philosophy*. Two are among philosophers, and one is among anthropologists and religious studies scholars.

1. Some see *Bantu Philosophy* as a template for how to engage with traditional Africa. This includes especially Alexis Kagame but many others as well. Senghor, for instance, recognized the significance of Tempels's sketch of vital force and before it Bergson's use of *élan vitale* and connected it to Négritude (1956: 24–5); it is probably too much to say, as J. Obi Oguejiofor (2009: 88) did, that Senghor "borrowed the basic structure of his metaphysics from *Bantu Philosophy*," since it is just as likely that Senghor was also reading Bergson (Diagne 2011). John Mbiti's work on time and religion explicitly looks back to Tempels, as do some versions of Ubuntu.
2. Others regarded the project of *Bantu Philosophy* as fundamentally flawed. This includes Franz Crahay (1965), Okot p'Bitek (1964), and especially Paulin Hountondji (1996), in his charge of "ethnophilosophy." It might be strange to see opponents of Tempels as a line of flight from his work, but it is in the sense that his work encapsulated for many a problematic way to think about African philosophy. Other versions of ethnophilosophy existed at the same time as Tempels, of course, usually written by anthropologists, that tried to capture a worldview of some particular African group. Marcel Graiule's *Conversations with Ogotemmeli* (1965), for instance, preceded Tempels, and for most critics would fall into a similar category as *Bantu Philosophy*.
3. Proponents of these two lines are, of course, well aware of each other, and among philosophers the debate between these has animated a great deal of the development of African philosophy. There is, however, a third line of flight that comes out of *Bantu Philosophy*, and it is one almost entirely unacknowledged by philosophers (it is mentioned in passing by a couple of philosophers, but probably the most extensive treatment in the context of philosophy is in Deacon [2002], relying on De Craemer but not Fabian). It is the line that Tempels himself directly pursued, as long as he was still in Africa, and that continued after he was forced to leave. It was the Jamaa movement in the southern Democratic Republic of Congo.

Jamaa has been chronicled and discussed in several books and articles by anthropologists and religious studies scholars (e.g., De Craemer 1977; Fabian 1969a; Fabian 1971; Mataczynski 1986, among others), and was the subject of some concern among Catholic Church officials and state functionaries in Zaire from the 1950s to the 1970s. Jamaa worked out a particular trajectory of Tempels's work and explicitly looked back to *Bantu Philosophy* for inspiration and guidance, but it is a trajectory that depends not just on the book itself but also on Tempels's own interpretation of the book for his communities. Tempels's own religious and social work among the people of Katanga brought forth the Jamaa movement.

We have two paths to think about this one text (if we think of the first two as the philosophers' conversation, and the third as devotional and religious conversation as described by anthropology): one focusing on the claim that there is a philosophy that exists in the cultural and linguistic heritage of African societies, and the other focusing on the claim that activating particular social patterns and ideals will lead to coherent and fulfilled lives, both within African society and within the Catholic Church. The first approach looks back and the second forward. In a few cases, anthropologists writing about Jamaa acknowledge that there is the discussion among philosophers but deem it irrelevant not only to the ethnography that they are engaged in but also to Tempels's own project (e.g., Fabian 1969a: 46). Very few philosophers acknowledge that the Jamaa movement arose from the same work that is seen as the foundation of ethnophilosophy, and they too seem to regard the philosophical/religious community that arose from the book as irrelevant to the philosophical discussion.

What might we learn if we brought these two paths together? Is it necessarily philosophically irrelevant to note that a group formed around this philosophical work, with the explicit purpose of living by its guidance? Why would it be irrelevant—because there is a tradition of ethnography whose task it is to analyze African social formations? What if this happened at the same time in Europe or North America? We might see groups who followed the teachings of Sartre or Dewey as more or less true to their thought, but we would likely still see them as relevant to working through the potentialities of that thought.

If we think of philosophy as a deductive practice, that is, grounded in its assumptions and bound by rules of inference, we might think that the pragmatics of actual lived experience might be irrelevant, even in direct relation to what seems to be a philosophical text. If, though, we are making claims about the nature of culture (as Tempels is), it seems entirely relevant to look at cultural groups who put into practice a philosophical approach to culture. An enactivist approach, that is, one that does not see thought as always and necessarily coming before action, but rather that lines of influence can run both directions, would take seriously the fact that putting Tempels's work into practice might be relevant to the ways in which it is understood.

None of this assumes that the Jamaa movement necessarily did a good job of understanding Tempels, although it is worth noting that this is one relatively rare occasion in which the person who wrote the book was also the guide and leader for the movement, and so we might expect there to be some fidelity to the original vision. If there was ever a time when a pragmatic working-out of a philosophy is likely to be of interest, in other words, it would be this time. But the question of whether they understood Tempels's work is something that would have to be determined by looking at what they did and what they taught. This is something that almost no philosophers have done.

The two major accounts of Jamaa are by Johannes Fabian (1971) and Willy de Craemer (1977). Later work critiqued the approach of these two, including a published student essay by David Mataczynski (1986) under the direction of V. Y. Mudimbe. We do not have very many first-hand accounts from participants outside of the anthropological studies, and this is a problem in making sense out of Jamaa, since a movement that is supposed to draw from one's own cultural background should have those rooted within the culture to speak for it. (Wyatt MacGaffey [1979] recognizes this issue in his review of De Craemer's book.) So, at best, what we can do here will be to raise questions that further research (especially by those from this intellectual and cultural place) could expand upon and refine, or even fundamentally change. I will sketch out some of the elements of Jamaa here based on those works, so that this line of flight can be better understood, and we can be in a better position to think about the nature of Tempels's vitalism and what, if anything, it might still have to say to us today.

Here is Fabian's account of what *Bantu Philosophy* is about:

> In its origin and spread, the Jamaa is similar to other prophetic-charismatic movements operating in the same geographic area, but certain of its characteristics make it an exceptionally interesting case. The founder was not an African, but the Belgian missionary Placide Tempels who first became known as the author of *Bantu Philosophy* (published in French in 1945). The book was widely acclaimed and wildly criticized. From the later development we know now that it was misunderstood by most of its critics. The book must be seen as Tempels' first manifesto in which he laid down the basic elements for the message which later be- come the doctrine of the Jamaa movement. *Bantu Philosophy* (which should be read together with the essay "Catéchèse Bantoue") was at the same time the "discovery of the Bantu soul," a critique of sterile, rationalist Western thought, and, for Tempels personally, a symbol of his conversion from a colonizer to a prophetic rebel. Its central idea was that the

gap between Christianity and paganism can be bridged once it is recognized that both are basically concerned with "man," his innermost desires, and his aspirations. However, it is essential to know that, for Tempels, this constituted not so much a theoretical task as a practical step: "encounter" between Christian and Pagan. Encounter, which became one of the key concepts of Jamaa teaching, implies, above all, *recognition* in the two connotations of the term: recognize that which people have in common, and acknowledge its validity and importance as a basis for reconciliation and ultimate "unity." (Fabian 1969b: 46; original emphasis)

The message about *Bantu Philosophy* that "we know now that it was misunderstood by most of its critics" clearly never made it into philosophical circles, judging by the majority of the critical work on the book among philosophers. And, of course, they would likely disagree that it has been misunderstood. But what is important here is that *Bantu Philosophy* activated a different world among those closest to it and to Tempels than it did for philosophers. What was that world?

The most important thing to recognize about Jamaa is that it is first and foremost a movement, not just a set of beliefs. In other words, it drew people to it, and it was a set of practices. It was not first a doctrine or set of propositions to which one assented. It was more like an emergent connection between aspects of life that made sense of a world for those who were part of it. It is important to see this because it might be tempting to think that a movement that grew out of a book called *Bantu Philosophy* is simply implementing a set of principles set forth in that book. This is not the case.

The fact that a movement like Jamaa emerged out of *Bantu Philosophy* means that Tempels is not so much a philosopher, scholar, missionary, or even a priest but a prophet and an organizer (Fabian 1971: 32–48). Those who followed Jamaa regarded him this way. He was the conduit of a truth that existed in their own past, the truth that led to living a fulfilled life. The driver for the adherents of Jamaa was not that they believed in ethnophilosophy but that they saw possibilities in Tempels's approach that leveraged their past to allow them to build a future. From Tempels's point of view, those who had converted to Christianity had done so superficially (de Craemer 1977: 18), and the only way to connect peoples' past with their present and future was by understanding that past and showing them a way of constructing their future that was true to the past but creative and hopeful.

It is worth keeping in mind that just as it is possible to shift our view of how Tempels characterized Bantu life, it is also possible to shift our view of how he thought of Christianity. Normally we think of the goal of a missionary as being conversion of the people who are the target of the mission activity. This relies on a conception of Christianity that is propositional, that is, a set of beliefs to which one assents, and once one has assented, it precludes other sets of beliefs. It involves the abandonment of previous beliefs, especially cultural ones. For the purest versions of missionizing, not only must one assent to a set of beliefs that are laid out in a creed or some other belief statement but one must also not be syncretistic, that is, one must not combine elements of those former beliefs with the new ones.

This understanding of the mission experience is, in fact, more or less the case for many missionaries, and it might well have been the case for Tempels in his early days in the Congo, but as time went on it seems to have been less true for him. Specifically, it seems that the propositional and doctrinal content was less important, and what was more important was the kind of life made possible by understanding the connections inherent in the vital force. It was not, in other words, a belief that there was such a thing as a "vital force" but the ability to think about this force as a creative element, rooted in past cultural successes as embedded in things like family connections and other kinds of social ties. This affective engagement is something Tempels seems to have realized lay at the base of both Christianity and Bantu life, even if the specific nature of that creation differed in different places.

It is possible that Tempels's characterization or understanding of the creative moment in a place was wrong. It is still possible to see Tempels's prophetic role as doing violence to traditional culture and possible too to see him as still deeply indebted to a neo-Thomist view of the world. But what matters here is how the people of Jamaa experienced it. They clearly saw something significant, and not just as a cargo-cult type strategy of copying practices in order to enhance one's standing or curry the favor of the gods or the colonizers. These explanations diminish the agency of those who were part of Jamaa. That Tempels's presence and *Bantu Philosophy* were incursions on life in the region is true and uncontroversial. The question is, though, what kind of incursion was this, and can it be completely accounted for under the general banner of colonial violence and missionary indoctrination? Fabian, in the above quotation, characterizes the incursion as an "encounter," which does not diminish the potential for colonial violence and misunderstanding, but which does suggest that the point was not to examine the "savage mind," to use Levi-Strauss's term, as a disinterested observer and chronicler. Whether Jamaa succeeded in being a real encounter is, of course, still an open question, but at the very least, it is not a philosophy in the sense of being a set of beliefs about the world.

The nature of the vital force becomes clearer (perhaps ironically) in a place where the term does not show up. In "Catéchèse Bantoue" (Tempels n.d. [1948]), Tempels shifts from using the term "vital force" to writing about love or charity. This is not a change of ideas but a clarification of what he means by vital force. In particular, it clarifies that vitalism is not about a metaphysical system of life forces that flow through all creation but rather about how to live well. Tempels's frame of reference is, of course, Catholicism, but Catéchèse Bantoue is about the connection between what he considers the essence of Christianity and the essence of Africanity—the ability to live in love. It is an enactive version of vitalism, one that addresses "the total life of the Bantu, as they think and how they feel" (262).

It is important to note that one might reject Tempels's equivalency between Christianity and Bantu existence, while still understanding how he is thinking about vitalism. He certainly has a metaphysic in mind, not only one for Bantu thought but also for Catholic thought, and he clearly sees the essence of these two as similar. For the purposes here, though, that is merely the space that allowed a question to be asked about the nature of African existence.

Jamaa was both an approach to a vital force and, as the movement developed, a set of social structures. As is the case over time with any structures of this sort, power relationships emerged and instabilities became manifest. Fabian (1971) gives the most complete account of these. Jamaa as a movement was not a utopian space but rather one in which material forces both leveraged the best of what was possible for the (mainly) miners in the copperbelt of Kolwezi and made possible the lust for power and influence that often accompanies movements. The point here is not to suggest that Jamaa is the "real" or "true" meaning of *Bantu Philosophy* in all the ways it worked out historically but to recognize that the patterns of creativity that Tempels argued for found resonance among people in a particular place, and that resonance bore little resemblance to the philosophical discussion around what become known as ethnophilosophy.

Jamaa focused on familyhood, as the name suggests (it is the same Swahili word, "ujamaa," as Julius Nyerere used to designate his nationalist philosophical project). Jamaa took seriously the idea of family—the first adherents were seven couples, each joined in a "union of love" that was a symbol and outgrowth of a deeper tie that binds people together. It was also an image of the relationship between Jesus and the Virgin Mary, which was one of purity that washed away sin (de Craemer 1977: 59). Marriage was almost universal among adherents apart from, of course, the priests who were involved.

The importance of marriage was more than symbolic. Marriage is an act of love, and the vital force is, above all, love. Love is a principle of unity, and of creativity. The focus on love is, in a sense, an alternative to a creed or other codified doctrinal forms. The Catéchèse Bantoue is a catechism but a very different kind than most since it focuses on love. If a typical catechism is a series of questions and answers designed to communicate and instill doctrine, this catechism instead makes clear that there are no "ready-made instructions" (as Tempels says in the first sentence): "The solution is not found in theories or formulas, but simply in the soul of the living man, whether he is white or black" (1959: 260).

The full belief structure of Jamaa is too extensive to recount here, and it has already been done well in both Fabian (1971) and de Craemer (1977). The references and imagery are very much Christian—if we were to look at Jamaa from the point of view of its symbolic and doctrinal content, we would conclude that it is simply a sect of Christianity, and it would be difficult to see how it connects to *Bantu Philosophy*. And yet, that book is the single most important document for this movement. The answer to this seeming incongruity is that the symbolic content does not capture the vital force. The contrast with charismatic Christianity is instructive:

> In terms the two movements themselves use to define what they are about, the Jamaa *thinks*, charismatics *pray*. Jamaa gnosis (a possible translation of *mawazo*), however hermetic and introverted, has been conceived as a philosophical vision with humanist perspective. Jamaa often defined itself, collectively, as searching for a way (*kutafuta njia*). Charismatics do not search for the Holy Spirit; they wait and pray to be "filled" by its power. (Fabian 1998: 112; original emphases)

Jamaa, in other words, despite its Christian frame, searches for creative forms of life, and this can be seen well beyond religious doctrine. Fabian sees a trajectory from *Bantu Philosophy* to Jamaa to thought as embedded in popular culture. The religious/humanist nature of Jamaa established patterns of thought that would later become evident in history (such as the *Vocabulary of the Town of Elisabethville*), visual art, and other aspects of culture (Fabian 1998: 116–20). "A striking convergence can be observed between Jamaa teaching, poetry in popular music, the recording of colonial memories in the

Vocabulary, and their translation into painted images and narrative in the history of Zaire" (121).

The Context of Tempels's Vitalism

It is worth thinking about the space of thought in which Tempels was working, not just to understand why he analyzed African thought as he did but also to think about what his space of thought affords to us. It is facile to simply reject him as too indebted to Catholicism or to mid-century anthropology, which he surely was. We might simply see him as having "got it wrong," and as such, we can move past him.

But there are a couple of reasons why that would be too hasty. First, the history of African philosophy since his time has been strongly influenced by him, both in terms of those who follow his example and in terms of those who argue against him. Second, no space of thought is created from nothing, and the fact that his has formed part of the vocabulary and conceptual architecture of contemporary African philosophy means that moving further requires attending to the spaces we already find ourselves in. If a problematic is an epistemological break, it is also true that breaks leave their traces on what comes after.

The question I want to think about here is Tempels's relationship to his intellectual forebears, as well as to the immediate effects of his work. As far as the forebears are concerned, there is a kind of tension between his debts to Henri Bergson and to Pierre Teilhard de Chardin evident in his work, and that tension gives us a sense of how to move forward. From Bergson we get the vitalism evident in Tempels's account of Bantu thought, and from Teilhard de Chardin we get the evolutionary sensibility, of a particular sort. It is worth noting that these two do not coexist easily—vitalism of Bergson's sort is non-teleological, whereas Teilhard de Chardin's evolution has a sense of "higher" development.

V. Y. Mudimbe does not think that it is likely that Tempels encountered Bergson (2005: 28), while Souleymane Bachir Diagne sees a closer connection (Diagne 2016: 15–18). Tempels does not, in fact, cite very many academic sources at all in *Bantu Philosophy*. There is no index or list of references in the earliest Dutch, French, or English editions, although the later "Critical Edition," produced in 2001 after Tempels's death, has a reference list (mostly consisting of other works of Tempels's) and extensive endnotes (mostly consisting of textual variants) (Tempels 2001). The lack of references was likely deliberate. Tempels would have known that his depiction of Africans would be controversial with his superiors in Belgium. Furthermore, his education would likely not have included such heterodox thinkers as Bergson and Teilhard de Chardin, and including them would have given all the more ammunition to critical church officials.

Absence of evidence of influence is not, of course, evidence of influence. But the point here is not one in the history of ideas. I am not trying to establish that Tempels is really giving us a disguised version of Bergson or Teilhard de Chardin, based on having read them himself. The point is one of family resemblance, and further, to think about the range of potentiality within Tempels's thought. His vitalism tends to be read as both an old-style version of an animating life force or spirit that inhabits everything, and as a culturally progressive force, or at least one that accounts for different levels of cultural evolution (along the lines of Levi-Bruhl, who is likely his most direct intellectual target).

We are faced with an ambiguity in Tempels's version of vitalism in part because his debts are unclear. As noted earlier in this chapter, he does not actually use the term "élan vitale," which would be a clear indication of a debt to Bergson. He uses a host of other similar terms. Why is this important? Because vitalism itself has an ambiguous history, with both classical forms (see Driesch [1914] for a history of these) and several versions of modern forms (Lash 2006). It has also been taken up in the context of Négritude (Jones 2010; Diagne 2011).

Relatively little has been done on Tempels's version of vitalism, but Diagne has done so in *The Ink of the Scholars* (2016; "The Force of Living"). Diagne's focuses on the "living force," as he calls Tempels's various formulations in which "vitale" appears, and he links this explicitly to Bergson, as well as seeing Tempels's work as a response to Levi-Bruhl's insistence that Africans had a "prelogical" and "primitive" mentality. Bergson too rejected Levi-Bruhl's depiction of Africans, most notably in *The Two Sources of Morality and Religion* (1935), his last work.

Diagne goes on to trace this version of vitalism through Alexis Kagame and to the aestheticism of Senghor. His goal is to think about translation: "[*Bantu Philosophy*] is at once neocolonial and postcolonial in the way that it treats the question of translation" (Diagne 2016: 17). One of Tempels's goals in writing his book was to find points of dialogue between Africa and the West, particular Western Catholicism. Since he rejected an assimilationist approach, he needed to find a basis for dialogue. The vital force was that basis, as it was not just a feature of the African world but one of human existence itself.

The dialogue that Diagne is interested in, though, is the one that starts from the relationship between thought and language. "The words which philosophy uses," Diagne says, following Barbara Cassin, "are *words* first before they are *concepts*" (24; original emphases). Tempels's strategy follows this pattern—it consisted in "opposing the Bantu *dynamic* ontology of living force to Stagaritic ontology, considered as a *static* method of posing the subject/substance and then attributing to it various attributes/predicates" (25; original emphases). Catholic theology had, in other words, become static because it had become propositional. The significance of translation and dialogue become apparent:

> The philosophical object defined in the seven theses [Leo Apostel's summary of *Bantu Philosophy*] and named *Bantu Philosophy* has ended up freeing itself from its specific and exclusive incarnation in the Bantus' view of the world in order to become a sort of *universal monadology* where a truly *first* philosophy expresses itself, where being-force is not yet frozen into substance. The effort of translating it from a language where it gives itself to be read immediately into a language becomes, in Europe, that of philosophy; ultimately signifies the task of guiding this latter back towards a retrieved childhood where it (re)discovers itself as a philosophy of life (and therefore, according to Tempels, a Christian one). (27; original emphases)

While it might be somewhat reductive to rely on Cassin's formulation that concepts only exist because of the prior existence of words (do the words not also inevitably exist in a conceptual space, a problematic, in which language is able to express meaning?), Diagne is surely correct that being-force is prone to be "frozen into substance." Translation renews the life of thought. For Tempels there are challenges for both Bantu philosophy and Western philosophy—the first exists as vital force and is in need of articulation, whereas the second is frozen and is in need of remembering its own vitality. Both of these can be addressed by translation.

There is a critical view about vitalism, which is that it is a mystical ascription of life to all things. It is analogous to pantheism and has its roots in Romanticism and earlier nature mysticism. This version of vitalism is certainly common among Tempels's critics, as well as among the critics of Négritude. It looks like there is an essence, an alternate way of being that stands in contrast to modern or Western ways of being that rely on reflective reason.

It is opposed to mechanism, which is the view that the organization of something is externally caused. In this version of vitalism, organization is internal. What problem has vitalism historically proposed to solve? It was the problem of inert matter and its emergence. It was the problem of mechanism in science and its perceived limitation as an account of life. It was the problem of accounting for meaning in the physical world. It was, simply, an account of life that was not reducible to its components. The solution with early versions of vitalism involved teleology and transcendence—we see hints of this in Newton's interest in alchemy and clearer versions in figures such as Jacob Boehme (1575–1624). It required a mind, an intentional consciousness of some sort, even in the form of an emergent intelligence. Vitalism fell out of favor in the nineteenth century in part because it offered no clear causal accounts. It seemed to add little to our knowledge of the physical world. When many readers see a phrase like "vital force" in *Bantu Philosophy*, they think of this quasi-mystical Romantic sense of vitalism.

Tempels's vitalism is usually assumed to owe its intellectual heritage to Bergson, but as we have noted, he never exactly uses the term that Bergson uses, "élan vitale." The fact that he does not use this term could lead some to believe that he is, in fact, advocating something like a Romantic spiritual essence that flows through and animates everything, and which has a special relationship to Africa. Bergson's "élan vitale" is not Romantic at all, and for that matter not metaphysical in the sense of being an entity that flows through anything. It is, rather, a process of emergence and creativity. It is what we might now, in the wake of scientific work on complexity, see as the emergence of order in the immanence of disorder rather than a teleological principle of life underlying its emergence. "Bergson rejects the idea of a Life Force at work in evolution precisely because it fails to pay attention to the empirical details of evolution (this differs from the élan vital in that it works as a transcendent principle, not one that is immanent to an evolutionary movement)" (Ansell-Pearson 2018: 106).

D. A. Masolo argues that Tempels's vitalism differs from Bergson's (1994: 49). The fact that he uses terms other than "élan vitale" seem to support this. Masolo's reasons for seeing a difference, though, do not quite get to the point, nor do they create a new problematic for readers of Tempels. Masolo sees Bergson as a dualist, based on the idea that we see life and matter mentioned in his work. But Bergson does not separate these out. His vitalism is precisely that matter organizes itself, and the act of organization is life. Bergson is, in fact, a monist, as are most vitalists. While Masolo is correct to recognize the differences between Tempels and Bergson, those differences lie in his terminology rather than the concepts themselves. It is useful, in fact, to collapse the distinction between the two and bring Bergson closer to *Bantu Philosophy* by seeing vitalism in his terms rather than the earlier quasi-mystical terms.

It is worth thinking about what might happen if we are willing to bring Tempels even closer to Bergson than we have already. There is evidence of this even in *Bantu Philosophy* itself. At the very end of his book, where he considers the question of whether the life force is material, he contrasts the "earthly and materialistic" to the "higher things—moral, religious, humanitarian" (Tempels 1959: 122). This is a contrast not between immanence and transcendence but between parts and whole, or structure and meaning. He is not asking whether African philosophy leads toward something like the Christian God (which is often the way that missionaries argue—all systems have a hint of revelation in them, which is what the missionary must use to convert the people to Christianity). The last section of the book focuses on whether there can be a system of meaning within material life:

> Instead of our being able to say that the Bantu ideal remains materialistic even in its loftiest forms, it seems to me that we ought to say, rather, that even in their most material cares, the Bantu point of view is dictated by a lofty wisdom in regard to life, linking on to their philosophical principles. (Tempels 1959: 122)

In other words, for Tempels there is a kind of wisdom evident in all of life. His answer to the question of whether materialism exists at the highest levels of thought is that that thought guides life at the mundane levels. Is this a statement of transcendence? It does not have to be. It is not a statement that the wisdom of life was arrived at by any other means than the actions of the mundane. Nothing divine or spiritual broke through into mundane life to give it meaning. The system of meaning is therefore transcendental, not transcendent.

Of course, in other places it is clear that Tempels's goal is to convert the Bantu to Christianity. We assume that this is a particular version of Christianity, one in which a transcendent God gives meaning and order to the world. For the most part, that assumption is well-founded. And yet, there are times when we see something more like an immanent, materialist faith, rooted in the emergence of life itself.

Diagne's insight, that there is a component of translation in vitalism, is useful here. It would be tempting to see vitalism in Romantic terms, as a transcendent, shared spirit flowing through everything. In that case, no translation would be needed, only an excavation of the common meaning that the spirit bears. In fact, this is often how we think about dialogue—the point is to exchange viewpoints until a common understanding is reached. In this vitalism, though, there is no discursive underpinning that can be shared. The manifestations of life are multiple. Under those conditions, translation is itself a philosophical act, in that it draws attention and structures thought that might otherwise be either unreflective or solidified. As with something like speciation in nature, there might well be commonalities of solution to sets of existing conditions, but there might also be surprisingly different solutions to what seem to be identical conditions. "Evolution" in this example does not designate anything specific about what is shared by organisms, nor does it suggest any teleology. It is a name for the space of creation.

Tempels, Jamaa, and the Creation of the New

The point of recounting the history of Jamaa and how that relates to vitalism in African philosophy has not been to suggest a reexamination of Jamaa by philosophers. That could be done, but it is enough for the purposes of this chapter if we can simply see another line of flight available from *Bantu Philosophy* apart from that taken up by champions of ethnophilosophy on the one hand and critics on the other. If we understand the vital force as something that led to a movement rather than a philosophy among those most directly influenced by the author of the book, and also see Tempels's vital force as being closer to Bergson's "élan vitale" rather than as a metaphysical and transcendental entity, we end up with a very different problematic than what has happened.

Is this new problematic more correct? That is not the right question to ask. Correct to what? In what terms? Correctness is representational, and it asks us to think that there is a reality out there that our intellectual systems are meant to properly mirror. It leads us straight back to thinking that the most important things we can have are accurate propositions or claims, rather than good questions. A new problematic is the potentiality for a new event. Instead of asking about whether any version of ethnophilosophy really accurately captures a set of beliefs of an African group, Jamaa leads us to ask how the lived experience of Africans can lead to new ways of living, as the inevitable friction between the past and the present make possible new and unanticipated ways of thinking about life.

One of the charges of anti-ethnophilosophers against Tempels was that he proposed a version of philosophy that had no philosophers, that is, that had no individual responsibility for arguments and positions. This assumes that philosophy lies in its arguments and the propositions that are defended by those arguments and the people who hold these propositions as beliefs. This model of philosophy depends on a model of progress within philosophy that can come out of greater clarity of ideas along with greater fidelity of philosophical models to the world, in this case the world of Africans. It is no accident that Hountondji saw science as the proper model for African philosophy, and that philosophy in Africa did not yet exist because it was not yet formulated in those terms (1996: 66–7).

What Hountondji's model of philosophy does not address is the place of the creation of concepts. It assumes that concepts are produced from within the brilliance of the individual philosopher, a figure outside of history and culture, who can stand back and reflect on it all dispassionately and objectively and produce considered opinions on how it should be modeled. While any human individual is necessarily limited in the scope of his or her knowledge, the ideal of the philosopher is to rise above that and touch the universals.

This model, whatever its merits, does not owe its heritage to any African culture or thought system. It is in fact Platonic in origin and modern in ambition, but its form and method have little basis in its place. Taking the line of flight from Tempels's book through the Jamaa movement, though, suggests another route to African philosophy, one that does not depend on individualism and progressivism. Science itself, since Hountondji first presented his paper "African Philosophy: Myth and Reality" in Nairobi in 1973, has moved away from a mechanistic structure and recognizes that the emergence of new forms in complex reality does not depend on a straightforward cause-and-effect relationship between entities. Knowing about evolution, consciousness, the genome, biological development, and a host of other things means knowing in part about regularities and causal structures but also in part about intervening forces that do not easily fit a mechanistic or linear causal pattern. Evolution, for instance, has often been thought of in terms of descent and speciation based on natural selection, but there are other transversal forces that can make the story of descent far more complex. If we are to model African philosophy on science, it should be the kind of science that recognizes the embeddedness of all things in their networks, places, and ecosystems, and the virtuality of the interventions that networks make upon each other at different levels and in different ways.

African culture and intellectual life is this kind of complex structure. It is easy to think, based on reductionist anthropology of an earlier era, that cultures can be modeled, structurally or functionally or in some other way, and therefore that philosophy based on that culture can represent the intellectual and symbolic aspects of the culture. This tends to stabilize culture and make the philosophy that results from it lacking in a creative impulse. It is a philosophy that looks back, only asking whether it adequately represents the past from which it came.

The Jamaa movement shows us something else. It shows us that living into the future, in our place, requires an understanding of the past, and of patterns of behavior, at a fundamental level but also that nothing about the future is guaranteed, and therefore philosophy has not accomplished its task by modeling the past in the hope that it will be a guide for the future. A philosophy can emerge, neither as the chronicle of past cultural beliefs nor as the product of mechanistic science but as the creator of concepts adequate to a place. The vital force, understood as "élan vitale," is a space of creation and a space of thought.

The philosophical significance of Jamaa is not in the details of its belief structure but in its attempt to create something new that used two disparate vectors of thought. One vector was Christian practice, which used the vehicle of doctrine and symbolism, but which searched for a visceral, intellectual Christianity that was embodied in love. The other was the "vital force," not to be understood in essentialist terms but as a creative impulse that relied on connections between people. The vital force and love showed a potentiality in each other that, at least in its initial formulations, suggested new ways of living.

While the existence of Jamaa raises the question of creativity in philosophy, it also raises questions about power. In Johannes Fabian's 1971 study of Jamaa, he focused on giving an account of the movement in terms of a Weberian theory of charisma. Later, he shifted to looking at the effects of Jamaa in popular culture, as well as questions of power within the movement (Fabian 1998). If, as I have argued here, Jamaa's interest for philosophers comes when we place it alongside of the philosophers' discourse about ethnophilosophy and see that there is an enacted version of *Bantu Philosophy* that takes a very different path, we also need to consider questions concerning power, that is, how it is that some concepts and social forms emerge and others do not. The emergence of Jamaa happened within a different set of forces than the philosopher's discourse. The core of *Bantu Philosophy* is of course all about force, vital force, which is usually taken as something apart from the immediate, as something buried deep within culture. Fabian does not connect vital force to the immediate directly, but he does come to realize that popular culture was part of the constellation of cultural currents that laid the groundwork for the emergence of Jamaa. The focus on marriage, for instance, might be seen as something derived from Catholic doctrine, but it was at least reinforced by popular music on the radio in the area at the time (Fabian 1998: 48–9). There was also another kind of power at work—the control over information, particularly information about Jamaa itself (55–7).

The anthropological observations about power and the formation of Jamaa can be useful to philosophers, at least by raising questions about power and the formation of philosophical concepts. The sense philosophers often have about their own work is that they simply follow the logic of an argument to its natural conclusion. As I have argued elsewhere (Janz 2009), African philosophy itself has been motivated to answer a non-African question, and this has shaped a great deal of what has happened in the field, even if indirectly at times. If the central concern is to demonstrate that African philosophy exists, before any engagement with concepts that emerge from a place, this skews the discussion away from examining concepts that actually matter to those in Africa while foregrounding those that matter to someone outside of Africa.

This is about power within the formative discourse of philosophy (and of social movements as well), but the emergence of these discourses and practices is as much about desire as power. The vital force is a form of desire, and understood as such it is a partial response to the criticism that Tempels's discussion of vital force is an imposition of an external metaphysic upon Africans. If vital force is seen as desire, the question then becomes, what kind of desire exists within African society, both at an individual and collective level, and how is it realized, can it be co-opted, and what might emerge even in the presence of its co-option? Jamaa's success is, in part, due to the fact that it appealed to a group of people at a particular time and place. It would be easy to ascribe bad faith to that group, to see them as having been duped or brainwashed by a Catholic missionary, but that does not line up with the facts and reports of the situation. A more responsible question would be about the nature of desire on their part.

Both power and desire are actualized by a set of relations existing in a place and time. This is true both for Jamaa and for the discourse among philosophers about *Bantu Philosophy*. They are virtual, in the sense that they come into existence because of a set of relations and emerge only when the conditions are right. The tendency is to analyze Jamaa as the product of desire and power but analyze the emergence of philosophers' discourse about ethnophilosophy as an exercise in the success or failure of reason. It is more useful to see all of these as operative in both cases. There is a rationality within the Jamaa community, an ability to see that the vital force, as explicated by Tempels, has a translational ability for something that they already knew as a potentiality within their own culture. And, at the same time, the conditions of power and the impetus of desire existed as well.

Among philosophers, the same is true. The emergence of those who looked for ethnophilosophical work across Africa is, in a sense, the philosophers' Jamaa, the potentiality that presents itself and is realized through the examination of language, the discussion of Négritude, and so forth. That realization is, of course, also the occasion for covering-over the potentiality, and the line of flight of ethnophilosophy can also be a trap. It can capture vital force as an essence, turning it into just another artifact of African life that can be dispassionately examined.

It is this capture that the critics of ethnophilosophy see all too clearly. But it is also possible to see that those critics are also driven by a productive desire. This desire is not a response to a lack, as it has been framed (i.e., the lack of a philosophy in traditional Africa, and the resultant need to construct one), but rather desire as a positive force of creation. The contemporary story about African philosophy among many critics of ethnophilosophy is that there was an absence of African philosophy as a reflective, sustained endeavor. Tempels and others did not demonstrate that philosophy existed all along, but rather started a conversation about what African philosophy could and should be (negatively, of course, by demonstrating what it was not).

This story, of course, overlooks the sustained and disciplined thinking that existed within African communities since ancient times. To say that ancient Kemetic texts, for example, or the work of Zara Yacob, or the oral thought passed down among the Yoruba is not philosophy is to circumscribe what counts as philosophy. We are faced with definitional problems—does a philosophy have to have a sustained critical conversation? Does it have to be attached to specific individuals? Does it have to come in a particular rhetorical form? This is the problematic that is opened.

Jamaa opens a different problematic, one that raises the question about what kind of philosophy is or can be enacted. We need not be committed to Jamaa's success as an enactive philosophical project in order to see the new directions of thought that are possible.

3

Sasa, Zamani, and Myths of the Future: John Mbiti, Memory, and Time

What Is Mbiti Asking About Time?

John Mbiti's main impact in the philosophical world is his theory of time. His approach to time is a perennial inclusion in most courses on African philosophy, and when philosophers in the West want to include a passage from Africa, many turn to Mbiti. Since he is African, he is taken as a reliable narrator of African ontologies, and since he is a religious studies professor, he is taken as knowledgeable about the contrasts in religious practices and their intellectual underpinnings.

It is worth revisiting such a well-known milestone in African philosophy because it provides a useful and interesting example of the self-imposed limits that philosophers put on their activity. To some extent, these limits are understandable. It is almost irresistible to look at such a well-written and compact chapter as Mbiti's central exploration of time as an example of the difference between African thought and that of others in the world. It provides, for many people, a ready response to the classic (and as I have argued in the past, problematic) question: What is *African* about African philosophy, and what is *philosophical* about African philosophy?

Mbiti's own reason for offering an account of time is somewhat different. In his chapter on time (1969: 15–28), he spends the first two pages making the case that an African worldview is essentially religious. He offers an "ontology," as he calls it, one that looks more like an anthropological account of a traditional system of knowledge than what a philosopher might recognize as an ontology. It has five components:

1. *God* as the ultimate explanation of the genesis and sustenance of both man and all things.

2. *Spirits* being made up of superhuman beings and the spirits of men who died a long time ago.
3. *Man* including human beings who are alive and those about to be born.
4. *Animals and plants*, or the remainder of biological life.
5. *Phenomena and objects without biological life.* (16; original emphasis)

Mbiti's expressed reason for outlining a version of time is as follows:

> To see how this ontology fits into the religious system, I propose to discuss the African concept of time as the key to our understanding of the basic religious and philosophical concepts. The concept of time may help to explain beliefs, attitudes, practices and a general way of life of African peoples not only in the traditional set up but also in the modern situation (whether of political, economic, educational or Church life). (16)

So, he is offering this theory of time to explain how Africans live. It is left unclear as to whether the phenomena (that which requires explanation) is something observed by Africans, by outsiders, or by both, and how that observation was collected. It seems that he thinks of African life as something generally observable to anyone and uncontroversial in its broad strokes.

This is significant because this standard of explanation does not live up to either philosophical or anthropological standards. Observations need to be established more clearly if we are to have any faith that an explanation is adequate. And this is not the only classic question people have about Mbiti's account. There are also these:

1. Is Mbiti right about the nature of time in African cultures?
2. Is he right about the linguistics that support his account?
3. Does Mbiti's account apply to all Africans?
4. Is this model a plausible reason for the supposed lack of development in African cultures?

These are not, though, the questions I want to pursue. More interesting, I think, are the following:

1. What does Mbiti himself plan to do with his explanation?
2. What is Mbiti asking about time? To what question is this account of time an answer?
3. What is left out from this explanation?
4. What if this is not an explanation at all, but despite Mbiti's claim, it serves a different purpose?

These questions are not an attempt to determine what Mbiti is really thinking. Mbiti might be seen as an unreliable narrator on temporality, at least to some extent. Mbiti himself was limited in the ways he could question time. His limitation becomes apparent in the rest of his book—the goal is to give an account for African culture, and in particular for some of the barriers within African culture to conversion to Christianity. Furthermore, it is to try to show (as is the case for Tempels, in a different way) that the philosophical assumptions embedded within African culture, properly understood, inevitably lead to Christianity.

This is instead an argument that the elements are present for a different understanding of temporality in Africa. If we recognize the problematic within which Mbiti is working and find a different problematic that reconfigures the elements he presents to us, we have the potential to see Sasa and Zamani entirely differently. The place to begin is in thinking how exactly we might describe the kind of theorization of time he is engaged in. We usually think of his project as one of presenting an African philosophy of time, and this is how he frames it. And yet, what exactly does that mean, and what might the other options be? He might, in fact, be doing one of several things in his discussion of time:

1. He might be providing a *concept of time* or a belief about it. The chapter in which he initially works out his version of time is, after all, titled "The Concept of Time as a Key to the Understanding and Interpretation of African Religions and Philosophy." In this case, it would be a theory of how this concept interacts with other concepts to produce an African philosophical worldview.
2. He might be providing a *philosophy of time*. This is what many take him to be doing and arguably what he sees himself as doing—arguing that in Africa time works differently, and the theory he presents is simply an account of Africans recognizing and living by this reality.
3. He might, on the other hand, be giving us a *philosophy of temporality, or time-consciousness*. In other words, he might be telling us about the individual and collective experience of time and how it affects various features of African life.
4. He might be giving us a *phenomenology of time*. By this I mean that he might be doing something more than observing the subjective experience of time among Africans. He might be trying to think about how time is constitutive of all experience, that is, how it is that we could not have

experience without time, and that in Africa time constitutes experience differently than elsewhere.
5. It is possible, given how he structures his evidence, that he is attempting an *anthropology of time, or of temporality*. He is, after all, using African languages as evidence of his theory of time. This might, in other words, be an empirical theory rather than an ontological one, describing contingent reality about Africans rather than transcendental conditions of experience.
6. He might be proposing a *pragmatics of time*. By this I mean that he might be proposing a theory of time that is little more than a way of helping Africans to get through their daily lives. The theoretical aspects are secondary to the question of how people successfully navigate their cultural, symbolic, and material spaces. This would necessarily involve elements of a philosophy of temporality but would differ in that it would include the symbolic and shared aspects (e.g., modes of reference to time for coordination of action).
7. Finally, he might be sketching out an explanation of *time as part of a cognitive process*. This means that the analysis is not, in fact, of time itself but rather of time as an element within a process of decision-making, knowledge construction, and action within African cultures.

Of course, the intention of his theory might be one thing and the effect something else. And it is possible that more than one of these ways of thinking about time are at work at the same time. And finally, it might also be that he really does think he is doing one thing, but in fact he is relatively unsuccessful at his intended goal but can be seen as more successful at a different goal.

So, the Sasa/Zamani model bears traces of its others, just as it is meant to represent the experience of African people. The contrast to Western time is apparent in Mbiti's occasional comments in the book that some Africans, due to their contact with the West, are "discovering the future dimension of time" (1969: 27). Mbiti's account also stands in contrast to other variations that might be proposed within Africa. Euphrase Kezilahabi, in his doctoral dissertation, suggests a number of these (1985: 120–3):

1. Ruch Omi and K. C. Anyanwu use Gabriel Marcel focus on the importance of mythos in African time. Myths are "more than history. They also point out that the African concept of time is existential and practical" (121).
2. Diana Axelsen analyzes several African thinkers such as Nkrumah, Nyerere, Cabral, and Fanon and shows the importance of African values and emancipatory politics in a conception of African time.

3. John Ayoade adds a sense of time-future, extending beyond the end of life, and sees time as a liberating force rather than just a limiting one.
4. Finally, John Murungi uses the example of the Ameru in Kenya to argue for a conception of time based on event rather than span.

These variations on and alternatives to Mbiti at least suggest a range within cultural experience of time within Africa. While some of these erode the strong contrast between Sasa and Zamani, none of them opt for a version of time that is about control, either of the future or of temporal spans themselves (i.e., the more and more precise calculation and synchronization of time for the purposes of organizing behavior—he calls this the "commodification" of time). All have an existential character to them—they are about the engagement with time practically and are woven into the practices of both individuals and groups.

Kezilahabi sees a different discourse about time that comes out of literary figures (1985: 128). While these pertain mainly to how temporality is used in literary work, it is nevertheless useful to think of these as variations on or alternatives to Mbiti as well. Briefly, they are:

1. Atiboroko Uyovukerhi's conjunctive form. This refers to the idea that inner and outer forces are conjoined within a literary or theatrical moment. This is accomplished through the use of images, ritual, participation, and rhythm. These do not represent a reality that is not present but are "the thing itself."
2. Wole Soyinka's cyclical theory. In *Myth, Literature and the African World* (1976), Soyinka argues that there are ritual archetypes, along the lines of Jungian archtypes, that writers work with to draw out intuitive content. Time in his account is cyclic and does not move only in one direction, as, for example, names are used for babies that call forth the past and, in effect give a new birth to the ancestors. The artist "has taken the place of the deities and chief priest as the organizing center of perception" (Kezilahabi 1985: 137), and this allows the artist to allow the person, social, and mythical to bleed into each other.
3. Emmanuel Obiechina's syncretism. Obiechina synthesizes elements of African and European time by using the formal requirements of the European novel while still using a cyclical sense of social time.
4. Kunene's cyclical theory. This theory uses the journey motif at three levels, "physical movement, psychological movement which leads to intellectual movement, and narrative movement which moves along with the plot"

(138). The cycles are more like spirals in that change happens while cycles happen.
5. Isidore Okpewho's mythical time. Here, tradition is the central element. Okpewho ties myth, tradition, and orality together in four stages of development: (a) tradition preserved; (b) tradition observed; (c) tradition refined; and (d) tradition revised (143).

I recount Kezilahabi's survey for several reasons. First, he shows that time and narrative are inextricably linked. This is something that Mbiti does not emphasize, even though in places it is implied. Second, he shows that Mbiti's account of time in Africa is not the only possible one. Third, he raises the question of how philosophy and literature might relate to each other in the construction or presentation of temporality (about this we will hear more in a later chapter). And fourth, he raises the question of how something might be created within the temporal space described by Mbiti and others, and whether other aspects of temporality will need to be explored in order for that creativity to happen.

The task of this chapter will not be to join in the assessments of the faithfulness of Mbiti's depiction of time to African experience or to philosophical reasoning. It will be to investigate whether the question he thinks he is answering is the right one to be asking, and whether the normal understanding of his answer within African philosophy is the only way to look at his text. He creates concepts here, for a purpose, and so our goal will be to both see how and why he does this, and to see what else might come out of his lead.

Fourteen Pages

African Religions and Philosophy is a book of almost three hundred pages, written while Mbiti was the head of the Department of Religion at Makerere University in Kampala, Uganda (Peterson 2019). Most commentators focus only on the fourteen pages of chapter 3, in which he explicitly works out a theory of time. The problem with focusing only on that chapter is that he is working that theory out in order to provide an intellectual framework for the rest of the book. And he regularly comes back to his central terms, Sasa and Zamani, later in the book, and those passages illuminate his meaning. Even within the fourteen-page chapter, there is context that gives his argument a different complexion than it usually gets. We will look first at what he does in those fourteen pages, then what happens outside of those pages in the rest of book. We will think about the concepts and questions he does not extensively address or that are disguised as other questions.

Most commentators ignore the context that Mbiti gives for his discussion of time and move straight to his fundamental distinctions about time in an African context. Most of the versions of time commentators assume (and perhaps Mbiti also assumes this) are versions in which we experience time as a separate thing or as a relation between things (Russell 2003: 90).

One central issue for many commentators is whether Mbiti's depiction accurately represents African existence, either as experienced or in an ideal or metaphysical form. Tied to that is the question of what the implications would be for social life in Africa if his depiction is accurate, as well as whether this African view, if accurate, can be sustained in a modern world.

Mbiti himself tells us that he is explicating an African concept of time because it "may help us to explain beliefs, attitudes, practices and a general way of life of African peoples not only in the traditional set up but also in the modern situation (whether of political, economic, educational, or Church life)" (1969: 16). In other words, Mbiti's version of time is initially proposed as an explanation for observed phenomena, specifically that of actions in the present that have connections to the past. This is the question he thinks he is answering.

Time, for Mbiti, must be experienced. It is event. But in what sense is it event? Any person engaging the material reality of the world recognizes that some things are figured in one's temporal structure and some are not. Some fall below the level of significance. Some are not understood, and therefore do not matter.

> *Actual time* is therefore what is present and what is past. It moves "backward" rather than "forward" and people set their minds not on future things, but chiefly on what has taken place. (17; original emphasis)

This is usually taken as a representation of time. But what if it is a description of a reaction to existing conditions? What if the lack of future orientation is not about a lack of realization that there is a future but the recognition that the future is complex and cannot be predicted, whereas we can look to the past to understand how our reactions have had particular kinds of results? The description of time here, in other words, might be closer to a description of cognitive process than metaphysical reality or phenomenological experience. To suppose that there is a future that stretches out in advance is to claim some knowledge about it, at least schematically. The picture we get here might be the more epistemologically humble approach than versions of time that make claims on and about the future.

There is also often a confusion about the register that Mbiti is trying to describe. Is he describing the individual's approach to events in the world, or is he describing a cultural shared attitude, embedded in institutions, laws, and political practices? It seems that it must be the first, because the culturally shared institutions and the rest are necessarily future-oriented. There can be no legal system without a sense of the future, a sense of the consequences of actions, the desired outcome of legislation, and more generally the kind of society one is trying to create by engaging in these shared activities. And yet, in traditional Africa at least, there is not a liberal sense of the desirable state or the good society.

So, if Mbiti is describing an individual's approach to the world, the conclusion most people come to is that they engage in the world with little or no sense of the future as a guide. But does that mean that they have no sense of desire for a particular state of affairs? Of course not. People plant, they plan, they engage in things that they expect will bring outcomes. In other words, people act with the future in mind, both collectively and individually. Sasa reflects this, for Mbiti—it extends out no more than six months (on the chart on Mbiti [1969: 18]; it is closer to two years in the text [17]). But some actions clearly depend on an idea of the future stretching beyond that. They simply might not be planned for in an abstract sense, even though they might be part of the potentiality of any action.

At the level of metaphysics, then, it is hard to know what to make of the claim that for Africans there is little sense of the future. Mbiti derives his picture of African temporality from linguistic sources, mainly, first in Gikuyu and later in Kiswahili. Behind the linguistics, though, there is a description of common practice that is more interesting. He says that time is not a commodity, as is the case in Western or technological society, but that it has to be produced, and that people can make as much time as they want (19).

The day, he says, is reckoned according to it significant events (20). Just as maps prior to lines of longitude and latitude mapped significant places (and thus, to modern eyes look out of proportion), days are marked not by minutes and hours but by significant things that happen. Mbiti's example is from traditional Ankore people in Uganda, who would reckon their day based on when cattle needed to be milked, when they needed to be watered, grazed, and so forth. There is, in other words, a kind of ritualized life, a day regularized by events. Of course, this does not mean that nothing else can happen, or that no change is possible. It does not mean that if a cow went missing, they would not stop the regular process and look for it. It means that given the world in which they live, this method of living allows the world to be a predictable place. If the world were to change, the process (and hence the sense of time in a day) would also change to meet that, within reason.

The same logic applies to the month and the year, Mbiti argues, although those cycles involve different kinds of events (21). Months are related to growing cycles and the rainy/dry season cycle, and years can vary in length because they are collections of events. Apart from the reckoning based on things that happen in peoples' lives, Mbiti says, there is little or no sense to talking about years.

From this description, Mbiti moves to the concepts of the past, present, and future (22–3). This is the part that most commentators start with. Sasa, he says, has a sense of "immediacy, nearness, and 'now-ness.'" Its sense of the future is extremely brief—it is about understanding the events that happen. Recall that this comes after the description we have just seen about the nature of days, months, and years. This is a way of understanding how that system works, as opposed to a general statement of metaphysics. Or rather, there is a metaphysics here, but it need not be the one that many commentators bring to the discussion.

Sasa has a fast decay in its ability to see the future: "If the event is remote, say beyond two years from now ... then it cannot be conceived, it cannot be spoken of and the languages themselves have no verb tenses to cover that distant 'future' of time" (22). Mbiti again works from linguistic evidence here, but the important issue is that Sasa makes no knowledge claim on the future. Why is that? Because the future is, by definition, unknowable. It is no different from someone in a capitalist society making claims on the future of the market—a person might try, but it is complex, chaotic space, and those claims cannot reliably be made by anyone. The same is true of any chaotic system—the weather, future evolution, or neural activity. This does not mean that no action is possible but rather that we depend on what seem to be regular cycles in the past to act into the future. We do not see the future; we cognitively act so as to bring about the future and then react to what we have brought about.

Mbiti's notion of Sasa describes action in a complex system. Zamani is, for him, a larger scope of time. He describes events as happening in Sasa and disappearing into Zamani. "Zamani is the graveyard of time, the period of termination, the dimension in which everything finds its halting point" (23).

Mbiti's depiction of time in an African context has often been understood as something that stands in the way of African societies developing into modern societies. Understood as just described, though, there is in fact little difference between the cognition of time in the societies. It is not that a long future cannot be imagined but rather that it cannot be guaranteed, and we are foolish to imagine that it could be.

Indeed, arguably, the African cultures that Mbiti describes have a stronger hold on a sense of a long future than Western societies do. Do we really imagine that a society that destroys the climate and the environment the way technological societies have done really understand the cycles of life that lead into Zamani? If one looks at actions, it seems far more likely that Western societies are the ones that have an inability to imagine a long-term future, and instead live only for an immediate future. In other words, the lack of an abstract plan for the far future could be the best way to ensure the existence of a far future, by respecting the limits of human knowledge about that future and therefore not acting in a manner that would compromise it through arrogance and unintended consequences. Sasa, then, is the recognition of the complexity of culture and its place in the material world, and Zamani becomes a set of regularities that are not guarantees but guides.

Mbiti does argue that history moves backwards, not forwards. Recall that his book in general and this chapter in particular has as one major goal to think through how an African of the world does or does not cohere with a religious, that is, a Christian, understanding. His concern is whether there can be a teleology and/or an eschatology. If things are as he describes, then the traditional understanding of Christianity as offering a roadmap to the future seems difficult to maintain.

Beyond the Fourteen Pages

Mbiti regularly comes back to Sasa and Zamani throughout the book, when he is accounting for various cultural phenomena that have made establishing Christian churches in Africa difficult. If Christianity preaches a futuristic hope of paradise, this is difficult to translate into a temporal worldview, which he sees as one without much concern for the distant future (Mbiti 1969: 234–5). "They need to see it realized 'immediately' for it to have real meaning. They cannot conceive the possibility that the end of the world is an ultra-historical myth which cannot be fitted into the immediate conceptualization of individual men and women" (235). It is worth noting that Mbiti's religious conviction means that he does not consider the following possibilities: (1) that it is indeed possible to plan into the future, and the only thing at jeopardy is an eschatology rooted in a different cultural space and maintained, interpreted, and mediated by the church in Europe and North America; and (2) that one option here would be to not worry about the growth of the church but rather have a version of

Christianity that started with listening to the people first, with no agenda at all, in order to understand the cognitive practices rooted in centuries of life within Africa.

Mbiti's approach to time comes up again in the final chapter of the book, when he is discussing Négritude. This is a chapter that, as its title says, looks at various "new values, identity and security" in African society. By this, Mbiti means to catalog alternate religions and thought systems that might compete with Christianity. Négritude is one of these. He is very dismissive of it, depicting it as an "ideological point of reference for a few elite particularly from French-speaking countries of West Africa" (268).

> Nobody in the villages understands or subscribes to its philosophical expressions. It is a myth of the Zamani when it means "the sum total of the values of the civilization of the African world." It is also a myth of the future when it aims at contributing to the macro-mythical "civilization of the universal." Negritude is, then, a comfortable exercise for the elite who wants, seeks and finds it when he looks at the African Zamani and hopes for an African future. It has neither dogmas nor taboos, neither feast days nor ceremonies. You only need to imagine it and you will be able to identify it; be lucid about it and you will be able to see it. Negritude is because it is said to be. (268)

This is a scathing account of Négritude and, it should be noted, a different kind of dismissal than we normally see of it. Mbiti does not dismiss it because it appeals to emotion rather than reason or because it is a version of ethnophilosophy. He dismisses it because it imposes upon Zamani a "myth of the future." A myth of the future is, in some sense, a long-term vision or goal of exactly the sort that Africans are often criticized for not having. Notably, though, it is not a long-term vision or goal that looks at all like what might have emerged in the West—a goal involving incremental economic and material development, based in or requiring things such as property rights and resulting in things such as a higher standard of living for most individuals, an established middle class, and a higher GDP for African nations. In other words, the demand for a sense of the future, which Mbiti assumes that Africans do not have and his theory of time is meant to explain, might just be based on the inability to recognize other kinds of futures than what is recognized and accepted as a future in the West.

More interesting for our purposes, though, is the idea that Zamani can be co-opted. We need not subscribe to the idea that Négritude actually does co-opt it, to recognize that Mbiti admits that it is at least possible. It means that Zamani is not simply the addition of the events experienced in Sasa but is a narrative.

Mbiti does not explicitly say that the reason Zamani is co-opted is because it fails to maintain a close link to the events of Sasa, but that is at least one possibility here. The narratives of Zamani are not free-floating but rather must be tied to the material, that is, the events that happen in the real world. Other kinds of narratives are simply too abstract and lose their legitimation because of that.

He comes back again to Zamani at the very end of the book (271–7). By the conclusion, Zamani almost functions like a worldview. And it is a worldview that is easily hijacked—"attempts are underway to relate modern ideas to the values of our African Zamani" (271). The problem is that "the strength of this argument is simply that these ideas are 'good,' 'valuable' and 'honourable' because once they were practiced in the normal life of our forefathers. They are valid for today, therefore, because once they were part of African traditional life."

The problem for Mbiti is that "it is extremely difficult to demonstrate that these ideas can or cannot be traced to the African Zamani" (272). Religion, in Mbiti's ontology, does not purport to hijack Zamani. He argues that Christianity and Islam especially (as well as indigenous religions) can practically be considered indigenous African religions, since they have been there almost as far back as their founding. They are, in other words, embedded in African culture and practice in ways that other intellectual systems are not. Their challenge is to find new ways to evolve for a current world.

> Traditional religiosity ... is rich in Zamani myths but absolutely devoid of future myths. Through the current religious turbulence and ideological movements, future myths have begun to dawn in tropical African societies. The direction and centre of gravity of the myth have now begun to shift from the Zamani to partly the Sasa and partly the future. There is a Sasa and a future in Negritude, African personality, African socialism, Christian ecumenism, Muslim brotherhoods and nationalism; and there are purely futuristic expectations like Christian and Muslim paradise and messianic hopes, African unity, economic bounty and the collapse of apartheid. So now, religion is deeply involved in the shift of the myth, partly and chiefly because it has its own myths of the "now and hereafter," and partly because by its very nature the myth is fundamentally a religious creation. (273)

Zamani has a fundamentally religious nature. Interestingly, there is a reciprocity between Zamani and Sasa that Mbiti has not previously discussed. The image we had earlier was that Sasa was the immediate experience, focused on the present and the past, and this provided the basis for Zamani's broader outlook. Clearly now Zamani affects Sasa as well.

Mbiti's ultimate goal in this book is to set the stage for the triumph of Christianity in Africa, or at least a recommendation from him that Christianity is the only path that can give Africa the focus and purpose for the future.

> The main strength and contribution of African traditional religions lie in the Zamani. It is in that period when each society evolved its own religious system and in turn the religion shaped the evolution of the society in which it was embedded. Traditional religions then became dangerously institutionalized and part of every department of human life ...
>
> But precisely because religion became so deeply entrenched and institutionalized in all the different forms of African life, it lost its ability to continue exercising supreme control and holding a position of absolute authority once new challenges and radical changes came upon African societies ... This is not the inadequacy of religion as such, but simply because its form, its mode of expression, its structure of beliefs and its thought pattern, all belong to the solidarity which evolved in the Zamani in response to historical and environmental circumstances different from those which define the man of today. (272)

Losing the ability to "continue exercising supreme control" suggests that Mbiti regards his version of time in Africa as a kind of regime of control. His view of a philosophy in Africa (or presumably anywhere else) is of a system of thought, consciously arrived at or not, that is a kind of control mechanism for action. This is an understanding of ontology that does not itself derive from African lived experience (or any other lived experience, for that matter) but rather is brought to it, as a way of explaining it. It comes along with the justifiable conviction that there is philosophy in traditional Africa, and it stands as a kind of abductive demonstration, that is, a form of reasoning to explanation from observation. While it is understandable why one would look for a unique African philosophical cause that would account for unique African lived experience, it is also not something that can be justified from that experience itself. An enactivist approach is at least as likely, that is, the idea that our conceptual systems are worked out in direct connection with action in the world, and as embedded and extended into a material world of practices and objects.

There is some irony here in that Mbiti throughout the book seems to hope that the Christian version of Zamani would prevail. Négritude stands as an alternative story about the future, one that does not include Christianity in any central way. Christianity, then, in his mind, brings a true sense of a future, whereas something like Négritude does not. More than anything, and despite Mbiti's comments to the contrary in the book, this aligns Christianity with the West. He would, no doubt, want to argue that in fact traditional African culture actually aligns with Christianity, as a proto version of Christianity, but to do that one would have to dismiss much of contemporary African intellectual culture that does not start from the assumption that Christianity is fundamentally correct and true. The account, in other words, in both form and content, is loaded in favor of a particular conclusion, and this becomes apparent later in the book when he looks at alternate ways of thinking about the future.

An alternate way of thinking about how Christianity fits within Mbiti's structure is that it is a form of capture. This is a term used by Deleuze and Guattari (1987: 424–73. For Mbiti, the problem with his structure of Sasa and Zamani is not that Africans cannot conceive of a distant future and plan for it but that it offers no path from "the slavery of formal religiosity to the freedom of self-hood" (276–7). The "long mythological route" might get Africans there, but there is a "shorter path" to "mature manhood and self-hood" in the figure of Jesus. There is, in other words, a single story that makes sense out of African traditional and contemporary experience, and its natural conclusion is in the success of Christianity.

On the final page of the book, Mbiti says the following:

> I consider traditional religions, Islam and the other religious systems to be preparatory and even essential ground in the search for the Ultimate. But only Christianity has the terrible responsibility of pointing the way to that ultimate Identity, Foundation, and Source of security. (277)

It is a "terrible responsibility" in the same way that Africa is the "white man's burden"—it is a rhetorical way of giving credit to those who, in the end, have a single story about Africa that they will recognize and cannot imagine another way to understand it. This is capture—all data and all experience become part of one narrative. And for Mbiti, Sasa and Zamani are the vehicle for that capture.

If we stop at this point, though, we lose what might be creative in Mbiti's text. The reality about capture is that nothing remains captured, no matter how dominant its narrative or how airtight its logic seems. The molar structures of capture always make possible the molecular lines of flight and potentialities. There is always a minoritarian literature within these stories of capture. What is it in this case?

Responsibility to the Past and Memory

Mbiti's depiction of the deep past is of a God who stands both inside and outside time. It is the realm of Zamani. The image he gives us is of a large number of ethnic groups, all of whom basically have a monotheistic God of a vaguely proto-Christian variety (Mbiti 1969; see chapters 4–6). It is "proto-Christian" because the variations we see on the expressions of God all have elements of the Christian God but not variations that would be opposed to Christianity. In this, Mbiti follows Tempels's lead in seeing African religion as being on a path to Christianity (and hence, the work of missionaries is justified in showing them the logical endpoint of their own religious assumptions).

The depiction of God, though, is not the most interesting part of Mbiti's working out of Zamani. One thing that is left out when Mbiti's approach to time is discussed is the nature of memory. He does talk about the past, and about history and pre-history, and ancestors, but these are not the same as memory. Memory is tied to engagement in the present, the stories we tell about the past that enable us to make sense out of the present and the future. Memory is sometimes treated as a subjective feature of consciousness, but it is clearly more than that. We memorialize as a collective act. We build and narrate and eulogize in order to remember in a particular way. We repeat things, not as rote unthinking acts but as adaptive strategies, and this carries the past into the present as memory. What we mis-remember can be as important as what we remember, for it can point out desires or emotions that exist but are difficult to admit.

To see the place of memory in time, it is worth trying to imagine what time would look like without memory. It is not easy, especially if we rule out thinking about time as an objective fact of the universe standing apart from human engagement, as Mbiti does. We might imagine that time without memory would be life without meaning. Or, perhaps, the meaning would lie in the immediate and nowhere else. And yet, how could the immediate have meaning at all? We might think of human existence the way a liberal economist might, as a set of actions done in the moment in response to opportunities and constraints. Economics itself does rely on memory (without it, we would have no efficiencies because there would be no way of improving anything, and we would find it difficult to price anything because there would be no history of successes or failures in previous transactions). But that version of memory could be excised, for the sake of this example, and we could imagine just being faced with opportunities and constraints and the option of acting or not acting.

It would seem difficult, under those conditions, to construct a symbolic world. We might be the *homo economicus*, with the capacity of means/ends rationality that would always optimize utility, but that optimization would seem to require a great deal of extra psychological and social capacity to account for what we see currently in the world, whether African or otherwise.

This example is, of course, unrealistic as a model for human activity (despite what some might think about the usefulness of economics as a model for life). One thing that makes it unrealistic is its inability to think about memory as anything other than data for the next market decision.

One approach to memory is to think about how Mbiti himself handles it. He does not discuss it directly, but he does discuss its mechanisms. We can see this scattered throughout his book. For example, in the chapter about the worship of God, he says, "These then are some of the ways African peoples worship God. They have no creeds to recite; their creeds are within them, in their blood and in their hearts. Their beliefs about God are expressed through concrete concepts, attitudes and acts of worship" (67). In other words, the model of God is a lived one, embedded within mundane actions. The rhetoric and thinking about God is woven into day-to-day action rather than contained within a thought system. This means that engaging with God is part of one's way of thinking about the meaning of any given situation or person and does not stand as an intellectual system worked out in the abstract and then applied to lived experience.

Another example comes later in the chapter on the worship of God. Mbiti depicts African existence ontologically as hierarchical in a manner that involves Sasa and Zamani. The ontology is organized along the lines of who has access to God and in what manner. Priests, prophets, oracles, and leaders have various forms of access. Elders have another form: "Elders are the people with the longest Sasa, whose Sasa extends deepest into the Zamani period and hence they are ontologically 'nearer' to God than are ordinary, and therefore younger, people" (69). Then there are the "living-dead," that is, those who have died but are still remembered. They continue to function as intermediaries. "Thus, there is constant and heavy traffic from the Sasa into the Zamani" (70). Mbiti notes that it is rare that animals serve as intermediaries, and no inanimate objects serve as intermediaries (70–1). This explains, he argues, why there are no idols in African society or other intermediaries from the natural world.

The trajectory of the human world, though, runs along the Sasa-Zamani continuum but also exists in rhythm.

> In the rhythm of birth, procreation and death, man is moving "backwards" along the Zamani dimension of time, "approaching" God in a way that neither animals nor natural objects and phenomena are drawing "nearer" to Him. This is man's history in rhythm, and in that rhythm of passing from the Sasa into the Zamani, man must needs go through the stage of the intermediary, whether individually or, more often, corporately ... It is not the means but the end that matters most. Sometimes that end is sought or attained, not by the individual alone, but corporately with or on behalf of his wider community of which he is a member or whose religious functions are entrusted to him. In reality, religion is not, and cannot be, a private affair: it must involve two or more parties. (71)

It is important here to separate out the observations about African existence from the ontology. For the purposes of Mbiti's book, he interviewed people from many African ethnic groups. There is no reason to doubt the information he collected. There is, though, reason to question the ontology. More specifically, it is not necessarily the case that the spiritualist ontology that Mbiti assumes is the only possible one. One feature of thinking of philosophy as a space of thought rather than a mode of thought is that single accounts of phenomena or of intellectual spaces (metanarratives, in Jean-Francoise Lyotard's terms) are resisted.

Mbiti's account of both worship and of the various functions of beings along the Sasa-Zamani continuum could instead be seen as something more like an enactivist account, in which the central question is not about access to God but about acting in this world. The figure of the divine can be seen functionally in terms of moral authority, ideals and values, and so forth. The host of intermediaries can be seen as repositories of earned wisdom about acting in the world, both in the physical and the social world. The fact that wisdom fades as an intermediary recedes into Zamani suggests that the wisdom needed for coping in the world needs to be kept up to date, and so more recent figures are important. However, the significance placed on the recent dead suggests that wisdom does not need to be relearned with every person—there is a social and cultural repository and not just an individual transmission.

It is, in other words, possible to construct a different kind of ontology around the observations provided, as long as one does not assume one particular kind of ontology to begin with. In a sense, this is the most serious issue with Mbiti's book—not the framing of time as a continuum of Sasa and Zamani, nor the observations he has collected, nor even the fact that Christianity is part of the mix. It is that a particular ontology that supports one version of Christianity is assumed as operative, rather than interrogated. The ontology, in other words, does not provide a problematic but instead covers over the possibility of a problematic.

What does it meant to think of Mbiti's account as enactive? It means to think of temporality embedded in a decision-making process. Thought of in these terms, the structure makes sense. We do not, in fact, know much about the future. We observe the present, and memory allows an interaction and a narration of the past in the present. It cannot help but be selective, based on a host of different things, but under most circumstances it is grounded in bodily habit, a habit that is informed by the individual and collective memory of intermediaries. Our lives are virtualized, that is, brought into being through the interaction of our cognitive systems and the material world around us. The regularities exist in such a manner that we think we can plan into the future. But of course, there are limits and we know that, because all conditions do not remain the same at all times, and all actions change conditions. And, the further out we look, the greater the accumulation of variables and unexpected components there are in our temporal stream.

Because of this, time is not, in fact, linear, but consists of a set of potentialities that we actualize through action. And the past too is not one but a multiple—a new sound, a different scent, and a different memory can reappear. Our present becomes constructed by the variations from both the past and the future.

It is therefore no surprise that Sasa degrades as we move into the future. We do not and cannot predict it. It is not a matter of lack of planning but lack of knowledge. The use of this model to support racist depictions of Africans as lazy or as unable to plan is, therefore, unsupported. What is clearer, in fact, is that if something like Sasa and Zamani hold for traditional African experience, they were ahead of the West in thinking about how knowledge about the past and future might exist and what its potential and limits might be. The so-called planning for the future in the West is more like domination of the future, or wishful thinking, guesswork, and luck disguised as bold decisions and deep insight.

Shifting toward something like an enactivist ontology could, of course, be just another all-encompassing frame for the phenomena. It is therefore worth noting that the argument here is not one in which a materialist ontology is substituted for a transcendentalist one. The issue is actually about how, or whether, a new problematic can be opened up. Under what conditions might one see new questions and new concepts become available? Any ontology that proposes to explain or interpret reality will be faced with this issue, not just the quasi-Christian ontology that Mbiti finds in traditional Africa. Using a materialist ontology, therefore, just opens the door to the possibility of the new, rather than making a claim to a new explanation of the phenomena. To put it another way, in a field of various candidates for theories of being, this is a theory of becoming.

Myths of the Future and Becoming

One implicit charge against Africans since the time of Hegel is that African culture does not plan for the future. This is meant to be a dividing line between Western culture and African—in the West, people envision and plan for a distant future, which is why there is a built environment of large, organized cities, technology, and so forth.

This dividing line is a deeply problematic one. The supposed evidence of the lack of material culture is, in many cases, really the evidence of a colonialism that obliterated the traces of civilization when it overtook the land. There is clear evidence of highly advanced cultures, with extensive trade, technology that rivaled any in the world for the time, and a built environment that was highly developed. It is clear, in other words, that for most of the history of Africa (and certainly the period in which Sasa and Zamani were developed within culture as an understanding of time), African cultures were no different from any others in the world in terms of long-term planning. The real dividing line, then, comes between Western modernity and traditional cultures in general (including traditional cultures in the West), if it comes at all, rather than between Europe and Africa.

More interesting, though, is the general attitude that Western philosophy has had toward Africa's way of facing the future. Mbiti's work reinforced this stereotype, but as I have tried to show, Mbiti was in fact more interested in temporality than time, and in the kind of cognition that develops in the face of uncertain reality. It makes sense to think of this as reaching only a short distance into the future.

What of future plans, then? To the extent that Mbiti is talking about traditional Africa when he talks about Sasa and Zamani, he could be talking about traditional forms of cognition in many cultures around the world, including those in Europe. Of course, Mbiti wants to say that this attitude toward time is buried within the cultural consciousness of Africa even today. But what does this mean? Does it mean that no one thinks about the distant future? Of course not. It means that phenomenologically there is an approach to time that has some humility toward what can be known about the future.

Mbiti's model of temporality is linear. Sasa and Zamani exist in a continuum (albeit one that has circular or cyclical elements), and one shades into the other. If time is considered in these terms, and if we assume that Mbiti is describing time and not temporality, then it does look like planning for the future is difficult in this model. But these assumptions are not required, or at least, it is possible to think of the potentiality of Mbiti's model in different ways. We have already seen that leaving out any discussion of memory and becoming renders this model difficult to take seriously. Mbiti is constantly appealing to something like the experience of time and the structuration of time symbolically within African culture. This is, in other words, more than just an account of time apart from the human experience of it.

Mbiti's reason for proposing this theory also does not stand up well under scrutiny. If he is trying to find an explanation for African existence (and, as we have noted, an existence that does not have very much empirical or other data to support it), he is not giving the reader much to support the claim that there is a causal effect here. Is it the belief in this version of time that has effects in behavior? If so, where do these beliefs come from, and what happens if someone in Africa changes beliefs? He points out that this version of time holds even within urbanized and modern Africa (16). So, the causal account must exist beyond a set of beliefs. This is why it is framed as an ontology. But simply calling something an ontology does not in itself tell us much about why it is there, where it came from, and how it exerts causal force on behavior.

So, what if time is not linear, what if the causal/explanatory model that Mbiti depends on is not sustainable, and what if we reintroduce memory and becoming? The account of Sasa and Zamani, and Mbiti's discussion of how time is manifest within culture, remains relevant. Mbiti can be understood not as offering an ontology of time but as describing time as a cognitive structure that allows experience to be manifest. For this to be the case, he would have to be seen as an unreliable narrator for African ontologies—unreliable because the overall structure he brings to it is not, in fact, from Africa as such but exists in contrast to non-African, European ways of thinking about time. The lack of a distant future within his account exists in part because of the contrast to the perception of European models of time, which (he assumes) do have a way of thinking about the distant future.

The conclusion to draw from this is that Mbiti's approach to time is not simply characterizable as ethnophilosophical but offers the possibility of a new problematic. That becomes available only if we set to the side some of his unexamined assumptions and his reason for formulating the structure of time in the first place. Setting those aside, though, allows for new questions to be asked and offers the possibility that we can see time as embedded within African thinking in a deeper manner than even Mbiti thought possible.

Sawyer's *Homo Liminalis*

Some of these possibilities become apparent in Michael Sawyer's (2018) treatment of temporality, which uses entirely different sources and influences (and indeed, he does not mention Mbiti at all) to explicate *homo liminalis*, humans in/as liminality, at both the temporal cusp and the point of frustration of new problematics (my terms, not his). Like Sylvia Wynter (in fact, inspired by her), Sawyer sketches out a far more structured, nuanced, and schematized approach to temporality than we see in Mbiti, and to an entirely different end, which is to both resist any linear account of time (something that Mbiti remains committed to if he is taken metaphysically but less so if he is taken cognitively) while also positing a temporality imbued with dialectical tensions and production that arises from them. His argument is that

> the productive legacy of something like post-colonial theory, in order to take up the project of centering concerns of the subaltern (race, gender, the colony, sexuality) in thought, must be prepared to take up the same questions that preoccupy Western philosophy but understand that the subject themselves is constantly changing its form and content to elide detection and definition by the very hegemonic technologies that created them. Finally, the argument made here is that the *homo liminalis* is abstract enough to be employed to address concerns of race, gender, ethnicity, and sexuality in that the resistance here to understanding sovereignty as an "on or off" condition but rather as a continuum of interlocking relations across a number of registers allows for tracing the instability of these subjects without forcing them into a position of static definition that destroys identity through identification. (319)

This is, then, a subject emplaced in its own historicity, one that is not just a linear set of causal elements or the subject produced by a narrative that has been cast back upon the past using the lens of present-day concerns and questions. Sawyer's approach here is close to my revision of Mbiti's sense of time—he argues for a "continuum of interlocking relations across a number of registers," which does not describe a linear or causal sense of time, but which enables the agency, resistance, and shared meaning that arises from these things.

The figure that Sawyer uses for this temporality is *homo liminalis*. The liminality here has to do with the border between nonbeing and being, between the existing and the not-yet. This is inflected with much more than just becoming in the sense familiar in Western philosophy. There is an energy, a simultaneous attraction and repulsion between what Sawyer terms the "Abject" and the "Exalted" (6). These do not (and cannot) interact directly and so require an intermediary, the Elemental (7). These are states of being, subject-positions that have integrity but also desire. Humanness lies in the middle mode, the Elemental, but can be pulled or forced in either direction. The humanness of the middle mode takes on the role of the citizen when another axis to this ontology is recognized, that between the Divine and the Profane (11). Between these two there is also an intermediary mode, which Sawyer calls the "Common." Taken out of the religious imagery, the Common is the State (14).

In setting up this ontology of tension and opposition, Sawyer draws on a dialectical tradition in Western philosophy that we can see in Hegel, Derrida, and Foucault. But philosophers such as W. E. B. Du Bois, Frantz Fanon, and Sylvia Wynter are more central to his account. Sawyer draws from Wynter an attention to a new notion of the human, not rooted in Renaissance humanism but in a creative space, a liminal space, in which temporality is an oblique vector moving from the Abject (the slave) to the Exalted (the sovereign). Temporality, in this formulation, is not time. It is not simply the measurement of the passage of events. It is lived experience, but the lived experience of the Black subject that exists closer to the Abject than to the Exalted due to a configuration of subjectivity that maintains exclusion. The temporalities (or, following Husserl, the "internal time signatures") of the Abject and the Exalted are different. Temporality and self-consciousness are inextricably linked (indeed, at one point Sawyer simply substitutes temporality for self-consciousness in Hegel's master-slave dialectic [147]). His goal is to account for abjection and understand the reasons why it is not overcome in as straightforward a manner as Hegel thinks will happen in his dialectic.

Sawyer's central question is different from Mbiti's. He is interested in an account of the genesis and maintenance of racism in particular, and Black life in a hostile and indifferent world more generally. Mbiti, in my reconfiguration of him as a theorist of temporality rather than time, is interested in the ways in which humans can act into an uncertain future using the resources they have at their disposal. He hardly mentions the history of race or colonialism at all, and that is because he thinks he is reaching to something more primordial and older than that, buried within African consciousness and social organization.

Sawyer is also a theorist of temporality, but for him the central question has to do with the alienated state of Black life. The sources he draws on all focus on that question, and there is little if any speculation on a primordial state.

Sawyer's project is far more sophisticated and analytic than what Mbiti engages in, and his central questions are different, but my argument here is that it is on the same continuum, once we understand Mbiti to be advancing a theory of temporality rather than a philosophy of time. Sawyer does not mention Mbiti anywhere, and that makes sense if we understand the trajectory of interpretation philosophers have given to him in the past. He has been seen as providing an explanation of the difference between African and Western cultural structures of time and has therefore been seen as a representative of ethnophilosophy. Mbiti's project does not have the analysis of alienated temporality that Sawyer provides, and there is little about the fundamental damage of colonialism, slavery, and racism. But Mbiti takes the first steps toward that possibility if we see his account as closer to enactivist than has been seen in the past.

What Mbiti might add to Sawyer is the one thing that he ironically lacks—a sense of what action into the future might look like. With Sylvia Wynter, we have a reconfiguration of humanism that suggests a cultural direction. With W. E. B. Du Bois, we have the talented tenth, and a theory of education and other things that are suggested by his analysis (problematic as some of these might be for other reasons). With Fanon, we have the necessary and cathartic response by Black consciousness, which has been individually and collectively crushed by colonialism. Sawyer's analysis leads in part back to Hegel (and given the dialectical nature of his model, this should not be a surprise).

Mbiti can have a contribution here, whether or not we are willing to take his explicit direction of Christianity as the ultimate answer for living into an uncertain future. His struggles to articulate Sasa and Zamani as forms of memory open the door to a new problematic, and Sawyer's work on time as liminality takes us a step further.

4

Oginga Odinga as Sage Philosopher: H. Odera Oruka and Historicity

Gail Presbey, in her *Internet Encyclopedia* article about sage philosophy, thinks of Oruka's work in three stages (n.d.: section 4), mainly based on the evolving way that he used terms such as "sage philosophy" and "philosophical sage." She identifies Oruka's third stage as running from 1984 to 1995.

Presbey's staging of Oruka opens interesting doors, especially to his late work on Oginga Odinga; moreover, it raises questions about a productive sense of sage philosophy that I think has not been pursued in a significant manner to this point. Furthermore, rethinking sage philosophy's trajectory and potentiality raises questions about how African philosophy can engage its place and, more than that, engage its memory and historicity. If one of sage philosophy's earliest reasons for being was for Oruka to answer Hountondji's charges about ethnophilosophy, and the difficulty of a true African philosophy to emerge from African culture, we may see Oruka's development of that program toward the end of his life as opening sage philosophy to something new, something that opens a new problematic within the field.

In this chapter, I will focus on Oruka's final major work, his set of conversations with Oginga Odinga. This works represents a shift of methodology of sage philosophy for Oruka, one that makes it possible to see sage philosophy as something other than just an answer to Hountondji. It always was more than that when it came to the products of the interviews, that is, the thoughts of the sages, but if we can tease out those products from the method of sage philosophy itself, we can see that it remains an answer to the charge that traditional Africa is not in itself a source of African philosophy. Oruka, in the Oginga Odinga interviews, introduces new elements to the sage philosophy method that allows it to evolve into something richer than it had been in its earliest iterations. Some of this I have already unpacked in another place (Janz forthcoming), and so here the goal will be to connect the *Oginga Odinga* (1992) book more strongly to a mutation in sage philosophy methodology and how this connects to enactivist African philosophy.

Sage Philosophy and/as Method

It certainly seems that Oruka's sage philosophy method differs at different times during his research career. These differences do not correlate to whether or not he knew his subject well, as his interview of his father in *Sage Philosophy* (1991) is like an early method, whereas *Oginga Odinga*, based on interviews with another figure he knew well, represents a later method. Oruka does not precisely date the interviews, for the most part, but we can date some by the deaths of the figures (e.g., his father died in 1979). He does date the interviews with Oginga Odinga—the first were done in 1982 and the second set in 1991–2.

So why does this matter? Sage philosophy method is not ethnography, and indeed Oruka throughout much of his career argued against sage philosophy as being ethnographic or anthropological, but it nevertheless has some of the same characteristics as ethnographic research. One similarity is the relationship between theory and method. In some respects, the questions that arise are more similar between sage philosophy and anthropology than they are between sage philosophy and other areas in academic philosophy. While we might superficially think that ethnography is untainted by theory (i.e., the method is simply one of description, and theorists come along later to build on that, arguing for competing theoretical structures that make the best sense out of the observations), that is not actually how it works. If we think that ethnography is giving us a window on a functionalist account of culture, particular kinds of questions will be asked in the ethnographic interviews that will be germane to that theoretical framework. If it is a Marxist window, or a phenomenological one, or a structuralist one, the mode of questioning and interaction will be different. Some of the data might be generated through explicit dialogue and others through participant observation, analysis of texts, and a host of other techniques.

Philosophy is not anthropology, but its modes of questioning bear some similarities at points. Is sage philosophy a method? It seems that it is, and if so, it raises the question of what kind of window it gives us to a world. It is worth noting that no window is complete. All windows are partial, all windows are tinted in some way or other. All windows are frames, and as such they include some things and leave others out. Sage philosophy appeared at a particular time, as part of an agenda, which was to demonstrate that traditional Africa really did have a philosophy. More specifically, it appeared after the charges by Paulin Hountondji against ethnophilosophy, charges originally published in Kenya before they gained widespread fame by being published in book form. Oruka wanted to demonstrate that (1) *contra* both Western philosophy and Hountondji, there was philosophy in traditional Africa that was not reducible to culturally held and anonymous worldviews; (2) oral tradition was sufficient to represent and communicate that philosophy; (3) oral tradition was reliably accessed by talking to present-day sages; (4) there was a difference between simply representing the wisdom of a culture (Oruka called these "folk sages") and doing philosophical analysis based on cultural wisdom (these were the "philosophic sages").

The way these goals are laid out, it does not look like there is a specific theoretical orientation for the method. Oruka seems to want to simply uncover whatever philosophy happens to be in the culture. And yet, we also know that every method makes choices and decisions about how data or material is uncovered, framed, and presented. There is no reason that sage philosophy should be any different.

One might object that sage philosophy, at its core, is about dialogue. I addressed this issue in an earlier paper I wrote (see "Wisdom Is Actually Thought" in Janz [2009a] for a revised version of that paper). If sage philosophy is about dialogue, we need to consider what kind of dialogue is actually happening, and whether that dialogue can lead to anything like what we see in Plato, or in forms of dialogue that have a dialectical aspect to them (for more on the general conditions of dialogue, see Janz 2015; Janz 2018a). It does not appear, at least in Oruka's early version of sage philosophy, that we have that kind of dialogue. It is very formulaic, it begins from concepts that have their roots in Western metaphysics, and it tends to be static, that is, it tends to simply ask a question and elicit an answer, without revisiting the original question for revision or following up a line of thought. This might in part be because of a lingering ethnographic sensibility in this form of question, which assumes that the subject is a representative of a more or less pure culture, and to follow up questioning might be to taint that purity with Western (i.e., "professional philosophical") content and thus dilute or warp the cultural expression that is contained in the sage's thought. But if one is already starting with philosophical categories that have their provenance in the West, and their most ready exemplars as well, it is hard to see how the enterprise is not tainted right from the start.

But my criticism in that chapter was never meant to suggest that sage philosophy should not be pursued, or that it is itself tainted in principle. At the time, my goal was to introduce a more explicitly hermeneutic approach to sage philosophy, which would allow for a reciprocity of questioning, which would lead to the uncovering of the position of the questioner and the horizon of the questioning itself. The hope was to produce better sage philosophy through better questioning, not to suggest that the method was fundamentally flawed.

The question of the relationship between method and theory or philosophy does bear further examination though, especially in the case of sage philosophy (for more on the question of method, see Presbey [n.d.], Kazeem [2012], Etieyibo [2018], and Janz [2018d]). This is somewhat unusual territory for philosophers, because philosophy usually does not think that it has a method separate from theory. If philosophers have a method, we might think, it is logic, since the objects of our analysis are concepts, propositions, questions, and arguments. Or perhaps it is "reflection," a looser term that usually encapsulates questioning, self-criticism, contextual awareness, and other virtues. Philosophers are not like anthropologists, who have theoretical constructions or explanations for the phenomena that present itself, which is accessed by similar methods, and there can be different theoretical constructions that people argue for. Of course, philosophers argue for different positions all the time, but it is not generally on the basis of the uncovering of data, its interpretation, and its inclusion in an overall explanatory structure. Explanation itself might be alien to most philosophical projects (even if, like hermeneuticists, we might want to reserve "understanding" for what we do).

There is, though, this longstanding heritage of dialogue (Janz 2015). At least as far back as Socrates in the Western tradition, and as far back as oral culture in Africa and elsewhere, dialogue has been prized as the context of philosophical reflection. Is it a method? Not in the sense that there are steps that, if followed correctly, will lead to a guaranteed or highly likely outcome. Dialogue in philosophy has become somewhat attenuated. It is often not literal dialogue between two people, as much as the dialogue between "positions" or "schools." There is rarely anything like a "proven" and "disproven" philosophical position—at best, positions lie dormant, sometimes for centuries, only to be taken up later and explored further. To the extent that philosophy tries to explain phenomena in the world, there can be better and worse explanations. To the extent that it tries to understand human or other existence, there can be more or less adequate understandings. None of this implies proof or disproof of anything.

And yet, sage philosophy uses a more literal version of dialogue, one that looks far more like what the social sciences might engage in, and for that reason, we are faced with the question of the relationship between theory and method.

Part of the point of sage philosophy is empirical and is a response to Paulin Hountondji's perceived position that there is no philosophy in traditional Africa. Sage philosophy sets out to make the empirical point that there is, and that it is not reducible to ethnophilosophy since it has a critical edge and can be represented in individuals known as sages.

That is not the only purpose for the project, though. Merely answering back to the charges against ethnophilosophy would not take us very far, and as Oruka proceeded in his research, this purpose seems to be less central. At least some of the time, sage philosophical research aims to uncover some interesting aspect of traditional African philosophy from the sages. When it engages in this agenda, it starts looking like social science. Sages start to look like informants, although of course as philosophical informants, part of their task is a critical one. In other words, they are not just mute texts, waiting to be read by a researcher. They are meant to be engaged as philosophers.

Sage philosophy explicitly looks to sages, and the means of accessing those sages is typically the interview. It need not be that—one could conceivably access sages through writings, but the act of writing itself, on some versions of traditional culture, might be seen as disqualifying a sage from truly representing that traditional culture.

The more serious question about the relationship between theory and method has to do with what kind of philosophy might be made available using the sage philosophy method, and what might not. Is the sage philosophy method of Oruka really philosophy-agnostic, able to turn up any philosophy that happens to be there, or is it already oriented by its very nature toward finding some kinds of philosophy rather than other kinds?

One implication of my earlier work on sage philosophy is that I think the method is not, in fact, philosophy-agnostic. It does lead to specific kinds of conclusions. Some of this is because of the way the method was executed by Oruka. Having a simple question-and-answer method, without the possibility of real dialogue (i.e., the subject questioning the questioner, in particular the questioner's questions), means that the metaphysical assumptions of the questioner remain in place. It means that the answers to those questions will tend to be mostly static, philosophically speaking, even if they are at the same time dynamic in a social or cultural sense. They will be presented as values of a culture that do not change much over time, even if the culture itself is dynamic in how it enacts those values (e.g., through internal discussion or debate of various forms). Oruka's own method in his early interviews is strongly oriented toward a version of philosophy focused on propositional content—all questions lead respondents to give definitional answers for abstract concepts, within a static space.

But the inability to uncover existing presuppositions in the questions, while a significant problem, does not in itself mean that sage philosophy method leans toward some specific philosophy. The method as it stands, though, does tend to reify concepts and make them into relatively static things. If you ask someone "What is truth?" it does not really matter how they answer, what they will say will have a perennialist ring to it. And as with most perennialist wisdom, the only thing that can happen to it is corruption and compromise. In other words, there is a kind of philosophically conservative core to sage philosophy—identifying perennial wisdom implicitly means comparing ourselves and our present to it and finding that our present does not measure up.

As already mentioned, of course, the sage philosophy interview process is not exactly the same as an ethnographic interview, because the sages are regarded both as repositories of cultural wisdom and as philosophers and therefore critical thinkers. One might expect the first role to look like an interview and the second one to look like dialogue. However, as already noted, there is in fact little real dialogue within Oruka's record of his encounters with sages. The questioning goes one way. There might be some follow-up questions for clarification, but there is not an exchange of equals, in which questions are directed two ways, and in which both the sage and the interviewer are challenged on the coherence or viability of their philosophies. Very rarely, Oruka might raise an issue of consistency between things that a sage says, but that is as far as the critique goes.

One might see the sages occasionally pushing back against the interviewer, but this is always subtle. There is a kind of cultural sensitivity being shown here by the sages—none is willing to get into an actual argument with Oruka. But sometimes, they do not exactly answer his question but rather another one. This might be read as an implicit statement that the question that was asked made no sense but another related question did, and so they will answer that one.

Oruka and *Oginga Odinga*

Odera Oruka's *Oginga Odinga* changes the model of sage philosophy from what has just been described. The book does not read like most of the sage philosophy interviews he has done elsewhere. Or rather, while the early interviews he includes superficially look like the classic sage philosophy methodology, the later interviews, conducted in 1991–2, do not look like the earlier ones at all. The earlier interviews have Oruka starting by asking the classic philosophical questions he asks in all sage philosophy interviews, about truth, power, and so forth, but quickly the discussions go into specific events in Oginga Odinga's life and career. This does not happen in any other sage philosophy interviews that Oruka does—they all remain at a general cultural level, whether Oruka is dealing with what he calls "folk" sages or "philosophical" sages. (For more on this, see Janz forthcoming.)

The later interviews diverge even more from the established sage philosophy method. They make no pretense of investigating abstract philosophical concepts. They look more like political histories than anything else. Odinga talks about Kenyan and international figures he has known and gives his opinion of their place in history. He explains his actions during particular historical events and gives his views on what needs to be done in Kenya to bring about freedom in the sense that he understands it. Oruka does, in places, ask him more philosophical questions about freedom, the nature of humans, and so forth, but the bulk of the latter interviews focus on Odinga's political past.

The point here is not that the discussion does not have philosophically interesting aspects, because of course it does. The point is that this is a long way from Oruka's pattern of sage philosophy interviews. This is significant, I believe. We might want to assume that *Oginga Odinga* represents a development in sage philosophy method. It comes later in Oruka's career (although of course he did not know that he was going to die in 1995). Or we might see this as an aberration in sage philosophy method. Either way, this volume raises questions about the philosophy that the sage philosophy methodology leads to, and whether changes to that methodology change the philosophy that arises from it.

One might argue that the later interviews with Odinga begin from sage philosophical wisdom and then proceed to use it to analyze events from his life. That might be the case, but then we have a further methodological question. How do we tell the difference between sage philosophical wisdom and Odinga's personal views on things? Does everything that Oginga Odinga say count as sage philosophical wisdom? Is a view only sage philosophy when he links it to some cultural source? If so, there are almost no examples in this book where he does that. Oruka does this in his introduction, when he makes a case for Odinga to be a sage and outlines different kinds of honorable people in Luo society (1992: 22–5). But these are general categories, rather than justifications for specific beliefs that Odinga holds.

This is a significant question, because it is entirely possible that any sage holds a combination of cultural wisdom and personal views on things. Those views might have come from study, or from observing the world around, or from what Aristotle might have called "phronesis," the knowledge gained from experience. Whatever its source, it is not clear that this is the same thing as sage philosophical wisdom. Oruka's method does not easily distinguish between these different kinds of wisdom, but throughout Odinga's interviews there are many times when his statements seem more likely to come from his political experience than from the cultural wisdom passed down to him.

This again has implications for Oruka's sage philosophy methodology. If there is no clear way to tell the difference between sage philosophical wisdom and personal experience, the door is left open for the interpretation of the interviewer to make that determination. In the Odinga book, it seems as if Oruka is implying that everything he says is sage philosophical wisdom. How far might this extend? I do not have in mind trivial examples, such as Odinga's shopping lists or something like that. I have in mind examples in which the figure is not a widely admired one such as Odinga. What if the "sage" turns out to be a murderer? What if the sage leads the country, or the people, to their ruin?

There is an answer to this, of course, which is that sage philosophy is always connected to the recognition of the community, and so the community would never authorize someone like that to be a sage in the first place. Being a sage is not just about what one says, but it is about the connection between ideas and actions and takes effects into account as well.

And that is a legitimate response. But the door remains open to ask about the dividing line between sagacious wisdom and personal experience. If a community authorizes the sage, this might keep the morally odious person from being a sage (in fact, it certainly would), but it might also keep the iconoclast or the contrarian from being a sage.

This is an inherent tension in Oruka's approach to philosophy within culture. The difference between a folk sage and a philosophical sage is that there is critical ability in the philosophical sage. This usually manifests itself as a divergence of opinion on the part of the sage toward cultural wisdom. But how far can that go? If a sage diverges enough, they will not be authorized by the community as a sage and likely never interviewed by a researcher. If they diverge very little, they are not philosophers. So, there is a sweet spot of divergence, a room-for-maneuver, that a sage has in his or her approach to cultural wisdom.

These tensions are the result of approaching sage philosophy methodology in a fairly analytic manner. The point here has been to think about what happens with philosophy in general and sage philosophy in particular when we see method as part of the philosophical process (apart from the philosophers' usual sense of method, which is logic in particular and reasoning in general). There are, of course, other considerations when we introduce method—how do we deal ethically with research subjects, how do we move from the descriptive to the normative (if we so desire), how do we represent the world in which philosophical claims are made without doing violence to it in the process of translation and representation—but those will have to wait for another time.

What is perhaps more interesting is the question of what might come to be, in the context of sage philosophy. It has largely been seen as an archeological project, a recovery of fading cultural memory. While one goal has been to answer back to those who would say that there is no philosophy in traditional Africa, another goal has been to reconstruct some of that philosophy. It has been a task of representation, in other words, and it has all the hope and peril of any task of representation—the promise of memory, the reintegration of a cultural self, and at the same time the potential to do violence to that which is being represented, even if inadvertently.

Coming to be is a different impulse than the one to represent a culture. Coming to be assumes that philosophy lies in the present and future and uses the resources of the past in order to accomplish its tasks. What would sage philosophy look like in this mode of thinking?

Sage Philosophy as Creative Space

As I have argued, there are questions raised about sage philosophy method if we consider this text produced late in Oruka's life, both about the trajectory of Oruka's own thought and about sage philosophy as a method and as leading to philosophical positions, theories, and so on. We might, though, take a further step and think about sage philosophy as philosophy itself, that is, not as a method to something else, for some other reason, but as the production of concepts within a place. It is, as Diagne argues about African philosophy in general, fundamentally related to language (2016: 24). While he is surely correct about one foundation for the creation of concepts (even if there are other possible sources as well), he tends to focus on concepts as represented by words, in specific languages that render concepts related to their places.

Oruka suggests another place for language, not as an alternative to Diagne's account but in addition. Oruka focuses on dialogue. As we have discussed to this point, there are limits in this method, some of them rooted in Oruka's relatively unreflective approach to his own store of concepts that provide the basis for dialogue.

But we might ask a more productive question about sage philosophy. What if this is not a practice that simply recovers philosophy that exists in traditional Africa, and thus represents traditional Africa in modern philosophical terms? What if it is the production of philosophical concepts out of the encounter between traditional practices and academic structures of thinking? Moreover, what if this dialogue is not a cooperative event, as it is presented to be, but there is a productive space in the ways that the traditional sages and the modern philosophers walk out of step with each other?

If we think of sage philosophy as method, potentially supporting diverse philosophies, we would expect to see a deep diversity of philosophies actually uncovered. This is not what we find. This is not a problem with sage philosophy in itself, but with African philosophy in general. The fact that it was born, in its academic version, as a philosophy of resistance means that it has always had a tendency toward uniformity. There are, to be sure, differences between people at the level of specific beliefs. We see this in sage philosophy as well as other areas of African philosophy. But this does not mean that there is a fundamental difference in philosophies.

Of course, I overstate the case somewhat—there are always exceptions to every sweeping statement like this. But I overstate to make a point. The tendency has been toward a kind of uniformity of thought. When the modern birth of a philosophical movement is in struggle and resistance, the tendency will be to orient thinking toward the external threat. Even though African philosophy has largely given up explicitly asking the question of "Is there an African philosophy?" a question I have argued is not an African one but one posed by a skeptical West, implicitly its resources continue to be oriented toward answering that question. Social theory in African philosophy ends up looking collectivist, in one way or another. The overall worlds discussed by the sages end up largely looking like each other, even if they differ in detail. The metaphysics, the epistemologies—all of these look far less diverse than one would expect in a continent of over one billion people, which can trace its cultural roots further back than any other place on earth.

Diagne follows Barbara Cassin in observing that all concepts start off as words, and so it is important to think about how language works and what words mean in their original context, in order to understand concepts (2016: 42). He is correct about this, but this tells only half the story. All concepts start as words, but all words are activated by conceptual spaces. Of all the words that are possible, some matter, and they matter because they activate conceptual systems and connections. There is, in other words, a reciprocity, and only half the story does not allow a philosophy to develop and flourish. As I argued when I sketched out what real academic freedom looks like, the investment we make is the freedom we make (Janz 2016). In other words, even as we can establish the specific provenance of concepts by attending to the words they use, we can understand why words are activated the way they are by attending to conceptual structures. And, more importantly, we can use this reciprocity to move forward and create new concepts (and, in some cases, new words), rather than seeing this as only an archeological exercise.

There was a time when women's experience of harassment in public and private spaces was rampant, but it was impossible to talk about this except in a piecemeal fashion. A number of women essentially invented a phrase "sexual harassment," which became a concept, which opened up a range of new things to talk about (for more on this, see Fricker 2007: chapter 7). No longer was every specific example simply a "he-said, she-said" situation. There was a conceptual space. More recently, we have the Me-Too movement in social media and journalism, sparked by the revelations about many sexual predators and abusers in positions of authority and influence. There is a space of thought, a way of changing a conversation to address human experience that was widespread but not put into words.

Another example: As Keeanga-Yamahtta Taylor (2017) demonstrates, the history of the concept of "identity politics" has its roots in Black feminism and in the Combahee River Collective in particular. It came about as a way of articulating oppression based on one's identity rather than on questions of doctrine or belief. And it was not just about who one was as an oppressed person; it was also about "what you could do to confront the oppression you were facing" (Taylor 2017). The potency of the concept can perhaps be measured in the myriad ways it has been co-opted, captured, diluted, turned on its head, and misunderstood by all sorts of commentators, both foes of Black flourishing and even potential allies of it. Put bluntly, Black women's agency was seen as such a threat to the existing political and social order that a concept like identity politics had to be brought under control, made safe for the continuation of that order. Now it has turned into a shorthand for self-interest, special treatment, and self-absorption, and most politicians run away from it. But the fact that it has been so corrupted does not mean that we cannot see the space of thought that was created initially by its introduction.

Is this about words or concepts? It is both. Is it philosophy? In some cases, it is. It is certainly a reflection on the phenomenology of present life or lived experience. And it shows the dynamics of concept production—there is a moment when a problematic is created by the introduction of a concept that articulates experience in a manner that was previously impossible or difficult. That problematic develops, it is explored, and at the same time it experiences external threats, attempts at capture by other networks of thought to which this new concept stands as a threat. The point is that this is a way of leveraging existing language to create conceptual systems that can deal with existing problems. And this is the turn that sage philosophy might take, a potentiality worth exploring.

When Oruka thinks about the ways that sage philosophy might be relevant to the contemporary world, he usually thinks in terms of the application of general principles to specific circumstances. His questions to the sages, when they deal with present-day issues, tend to be framed in those terms. We can, though, imagine other ways to proceed, given the argument to this point in this chapter. If sage philosophy is a method, and there is a difference between methods and philosophies, we might ask what philosophy is supported by not only a particular sage but by a group of sages. A group might not be an ethnic group but something else. So, we can imagine that there could be a group of sages arguing for some version of a materialist position in metaphysics, for instance. We could imagine general worldviews that have little or no resemblance to those found in Western or other philosophical traditions, but that nevertheless have a coherence, in that the sages work with a similar body of concepts, or phenomena in the world, or something like that.

More significantly, though, we might ask about how sage philosophy could help us explore conceptual space, as opposed to looking for propositions held by sages. Instead of looking back, and trying to faithfully represent thought as it exists in traditional Africa, is it possible to look forward and ask about a range of possibilities for existing questions within African culture? Can sage philosophy as philosophy (and not as the application of philosophy) look forward, or only backward? Can it be more than a set of principles for action, a set of ethical standards that can be applied to specific circumstances? Applications, principles for action, and ethical standards all assume a philosophy in advance of the world as given. Nothing new is derived from the contingencies of the world. But what if this transcendent sense of philosophy is itself little more than a belief, a commitment within classic forms of philosophy, which itself comes from somewhere other than Africa?

It would be ideal if we could find an example from Oruka, even from his book on Oginga Odinga, that would illustrate what this kind of creativity would look like. This does not exist. Oruka's orientation was strongly toward representing the past, first to answer back to Westerners and to Hountondji about the existence of philosophy in traditional Africa, and second to explore the thought that existed in culture. While he recognized that sages could diverge from culture, he did not emphasize a version of culture that changed in significant ways, in particular in ways that philosophy might have a hand in shaping. When we see him thinking about the future, he says things like "We cannot pretend to know what history and the future have for people of Odinga's type. The future may assess them positively, but it can equally be negative … For Odinga personally, history will assess him as a great personality" (Oruka 1992: 14). Since *Oginga Odinga* is mostly a political history of a significant figure in Kenyan history, this sort of speculation is fine, but it has little to do with thinking about philosophy as future oriented.

But we can see elsewhere what more philosophical versions of traditional culture might look like. Eduardo Viveiros de Castro, for instance, in his book *Cannibal Metaphysics* (2014), argues for an anthropology that can truly deal with an "indigenous practice of knowledge" (42). He calls for "a new anthropology of the concept capable of counter-effectuating a new concept of anthropology, after which the descriptions of the conditions of the ontological self-determination of the collectives studied will absolutely prevail over the reduction of human (as well as non-human) thought to a *dispositif* of recognition: classification, predication, judgment, and representation" (43; original emphasis). In other words, he is arguing for an anthropology that can take ontological categories in their own terms, that can take not just the static concepts and beliefs within a culture seriously by freezing them in the form of propositions but can understand the dynamic nature of thought in culture, the ways in which culture is a becoming, not just a being. My suggestion for Oruka here is not to have a philosophy that mimics Viveiros de Castro's anthropology but rather one that runs parallel to it, one that moves from examining the dynamics of existing culture to asking what it would mean for a culture to recognize and honor its past and at the same time to become something new, as all cultures do and must do.

Viveiros de Castro cannot be mistaken for a sage philosopher or for depicting his subjects as sage philosophers. He is not interested in the same kinds of questions that Oruka was interested in. There are no interviews with individuals, no posing of philosophical questions. What there is, though, is an attempt to unseat the metaphysic with which most anthropologists approach their subject matter and suggest a new way to look at a living culture. Viveiros de Castro's conclusion is that there is a kind of perspectival account within Amerindian culture that he researched. He wants to engage in an "anthropological fiction," which consists in "treating indigenous ideas as concepts and then following the consequences of this decision: defining the preconceptual ground or plane of immanence the concepts presuppose, the conceptual personae they conjure into existence, and the matter of the real that they suppose" (187). This is a fiction not because it is untrue but because it defines a trajectory that these indigenous concepts take, assuming their own ontology and their own motivating questions.

Treating indigenous ideas as concepts means that they can be seen as "carrying a philosophical meaning or a potential philosophical use" (189). Philosophy is, in other words, where you find it, and not packaged in a discursive format that signals its philosophical nature. More than that, though, Viveiros de Castro wants to affirm "the equivalence, in principle, of anthropological and indigenous discourse, with the same going for their 'reciprocal presupposition' of each other, which accede as such to existence only by entering into relation with knowledge" (189). In other words, the encounter of anthropology and indigenous discourse is a virtuality, an event of thought. In such an event, when the dialogue is real and not simply the search for a set of truth claims about an indigenous culture or a set of projections onto those cultures by anthropologists, there can be the emergence of "a certain relation of intelligibility between two cultures" (190).

Sage philosophy is not anthropology, but it owes a debt to anthropology, despite Oruka's longstanding antipathy toward the field. More than that, though, what Viveiros de Castro shows us is a potentiality of sage philosophy, a way that sage philosophy might move from excavating an African past that it sees itself as having no direct hand in creating, to recognizing that the event of dialogue between the indigenous and the research method of sage philosophy shows forth what was already there. What Viveiros de Castro says about anthropology could just as well be said about sage philosophy: "In the end, doesn't the inventiveness of anthropology reside there, in this relational synergy between the conceptions and practices of the worlds of its 'subject' and 'object?'" (190). This too is the space that sage philosophy, at its best, opens up. Viveiros de Castro gives some examples of how this works:

> We could say in this respect that the Melanesian concept of the person as a "dividual" (Strathern 1988) is just as imaginative as Locke's possessive individualism, that deciphering "the philosophy of Indian chiefdom" (Clastres [1962] 1987) is of as much importance as understanding the Hegelian doctrine

of the state, that Māori cosmology is comparable to the Eleatic paradoxes and Kantian antinomies (Schrempp 2002), and Amazonian perspectivism a philosophical objective as interesting as Leibniz's system ... And if the question is to know exactly what is important to evaluate in a philosophy—its capacity to create new concepts—then anthropology, without at all pretending to replace philosophy, proves itself to be a powerful philosophical instrument capable of expanding the still excessively ethnocentric horizons of "our" philosophy, and liberating us, in the same move, from so-called "philosophical" anthropology. Let's not forget Tim Ingold's powerful definition (1992: 696) of anthropology as "philosophy with the people in." Although what Ingold means here is "ordinary people" (everyday people or common mortals), he is also playing on the political sense of a "people." A philosophy, then, with all the people(s) in: the possibility of philosophical activity maintaining a relationship with the "non-philosophy"—the life—of the other peoples inhabiting the planet and not just our own, and where the "uncommon" people are those outside our sphere of "commun-ication." (191–2)

Viveiros de Castro brings anthropology closer to philosophy and in so doing shows a potentiality of sage philosophy. He borrows the trope of the friend from Deleuze and Guattari—they famously said that the philosopher is the friend of the concept, the expert in concepts and the lack of them (1994: 3). Oruka's sage philosophy interlocutors were not usually friends of his, but in the case of Oginga Odinga, he was. We have here a case of sage philosophy in a different register, and it shows in the kind of dialogue that emerges. But the philosopher is not simply the friend of the interlocutor, but the friend of the concept, and also the potentiality of the concept. Viveiros de Castro, in fact, is interested in "*the immanence of the enemy* specific to Amerindian cosmopraxis" (193; original emphasis). The enemy is focused on difference, not sameness.

This brings Viveiros de Castro to ask an "impossible" question: "what happens when one takes indigenous thought seriously?" (2014: 194). It might seem strange to call this question impossible—is that not the goal of any anthropology, and for that matter any sage philosophy worthy of the name? But he quickly takes away that which we usually think of as serious engagement. "Taking it seriously means not neutralizing it—it means bracketing, for example, the question of whether and how such thought might illustrate human cognitive universals, explain modes of transmission of socially-determined knowledge, express a culturally particular worldview, functionally validate a given distribution of political power, or confirm other of the myriad ways that the others' thought is neutralized" (194). Furthermore, it does not mean "'believing' what the Indians say, or regarding their thought as the expression of some truth about the world"—this is another "poorly formulated question." Nor should indigenous thought be "related to in the mode of belief, whether by suggesting with goodwill that it contains a 'wealth of allegorical truth' ... or, even worse, by imagining it to be the bearer of some inborn esoteric science divining the inner, ultimate essence of things" (195). None of these really takes indigenous thought seriously—but why? It is because each of them undermines the "cannibal metaphysics" of the book's title. Each of these moves merely translates indigenous thought into something safer, more Western, more part of the tradition of the researcher.

What Viveiros de Castro has done here is, in effect, undermine the majority of reasons scholars have tried to use sage philosophy as an access point to indigenous African thought. I have recounted elsewhere (Janz 2009a: 99–119) how Oruka's approach in his interview methodology relied on categories of Western philosophy, ones that we can sometimes see the sages resisting in their answers. I argued that using sage philosophy to try to accomplish goal of answering the question "Is there an African philosophy?" will not succeed, both because the question is illegitimate, and also because sage philosophy cannot demonstrate that some ideas or body of knowledge is both truly African and truly philosophical. This does not, of course, mean that there is no African philosophy—far from it. But the project of demarcating it cannot in the end succeed because the question that demarcation is based on is ill-formed. Furthermore, other possible goals, such as those of accessing "real" African philosophy that might be used as the basis for African praxis, politics, or life in general will also not succeed. Again, this is not because there is no African philosophy—there is. It is because that move, of trying to define and isolate, is the move of taming indigenous thought and making it presentable in colonial or nonindigenous terms. Defining it takes away its creative potential.

What, then, do we do with sage philosophy? Even as I have critiqued it, I have always maintained that its real creative potential lies elsewhere than the project of answering a non-African question or preparing and packaging African knowledge for consumption by others. We start to see some glimpses of this in *Oginga Odinga*.

Temporality, Historicity, and Becoming

As I have already argued (and outline further elsewhere; Janz forthcoming), *Oginga Odinga* has two features that stand in opposition or tension with each other. First,

Oruka is very clear that the book is an exercise in sage philosophy. He spends most of the first chapter arguing for Odinga as a sage, their conversations as sage philosophy conversations. The second feature is that this book is completely different from any sage philosophy interview he had conducted before. If we had to give it a character, we might say that it looks more like political biography than anything else. Oruka's mode of questioning here is radically different from anything we see before this. While he occasionally asks the "classic" sage philosophy questions ("What is truth?," "What is God?," etc.), he quickly returns to a more personal discussion, which asks about events in Odinga's life, people he met, what he thought of them, and what the significance of his actions was to the development of Kenya as a nation.

How do we reconcile these two things? It is not enough to say that the interviews for this book were done later. There were, in fact, two sets of interviews, one in 1982 and the other in 1991–2, and the first set, at least, coincided with other interviews he was doing with other sages. It is also not enough to say that he knew Odinga while he did not know other sages and, therefore, took a more formal approach with them. Oruka also interviewed his own father, and those interviews look more like the standard sage philosophy interviews, even though his father also had an influential life and could have been interviewed in a more biographical fashion.

It is more fruitful, I think, to look at what Oruka adds to the Odinga interviews that changes them. The new element that he adds is temporality. He gives us an account of becoming, of how Odinga got to where he was in the world and in the nation. Rather than primarily searching for timeless truths, as he does in most of the other interviews (what we might call "being"), he looks for emergence, or becoming. Now, this becoming might be handled simply as a set of causes and effects, and sometimes Oruka does look for that. But more often he is looking for a perspective, a new layer that might help to flesh out our understanding of significant events.

Along with the becoming of temporality, there is the being of historicity. If temporality expresses the flux of event, that which happens based on both anticipated and unanticipated elements, historicity looks back to express the structure in which that takes place. Events are embedded in history, but as events they are not reducible to history. Historicity is temporality textualized, or at least, it is one mode of textualizing it. Temporality can also be textualized imaginatively (we see this in Afro-futurist work), although it is worth noting that this temporality is both cathartic and preparatory for new problematics to emerge, rather than predictive or utopian. All the forms of textualized temporality together form the basis of a literature, which we will be addressing in upcoming chapters.

Oruka's specific introduction of historicity comes in the wake of his decontextualized method (at least to this point) of sage philosophy. The historicity he investigates with Odinga tends not to be an attempt at causal explanations for present conditions. In other words, he is not trying to determine the events that happened in the past to lead us to the present circumstances in which we find ourselves. The discussion he has with Odinga is rather more like the rehearsal of the formation of spaces of thought and action.

The interviews from 1991 to 1992 read like an elderly retired politician's reflection on who he was and what he had done (for a fuller account of these, see Janz forthcoming). He was eighty at the time, and it would only be a couple of years until he passed away. He talks a great deal about important people he knew (on Oruka's urging) and gives an assessment of who they were and what it was like to deal with them. Some of his answers read like he is burnishing his legacy (and indeed, Oruka throws him some softballs on occasion that make that especially easy), but if we can look past that, we can see someone who was a political survivor, someone who both witnessed major national and international events and had a hand in creating them, someone who was trusted and loved by many and mistrusted by many others.

Oruka lays the foundation for a history of Odinga here, but if that is all he was doing, Odinga could hardly be called a sage. Sagacity exists in a penetrating understanding of culture and of how to operate within its vicissitudes. Without that, a figure is merely a Zelig, an ever-present watcher without any real engagement or inner understanding. But that is not how Odinga is presented in these interviews. This is not just history, but also historicity. It is an investigation not just of what happened but what it takes to get something done. It is an investigation of the psychology and the on-the-ground politics between people and their leaders, between Africans and colonial powers, between parties, between nations. Oruka is enough of a classical philosopher to periodically fall back into representational and causal thinking in his discussions—he looks for the principles that lead to action and to particular results, and the character traits that make good leaders and citizens—but he also does something else. He opens a space for Odinga to think about the events, the moments that allowed a new problematic to emerge and a new set of questions to be asked.

The key is to remember that Oruka sees Odinga as a sage philosopher. That means that he sees him as a repository of wisdom among his people. He is, furthermore, a philosophical sage, not a folk sage, which means that he does not simply recount that wisdom but creatively finds ways to use it or, if necessary, diverge from it.

So, what is this wisdom? Even though Oruka asks Odinga about philosophical concepts, at least some of the time, he spends most of his time delving into a much more applied and emplaced wisdom than he had explored with most of his other interview subjects. In most other cases, it was enough to ask a sage what he or she thought about a particular concept, or what he or she would do in a particular situation. With Odinga, Oruka explores the details of specific circumstances. There is nothing abstract about these discussions, even though universals or generalizations are invoked on occasion. The wisdom Oruka extracts from Odinga is sometimes culturally situated (indeed, on occasion, Odinga will explicitly talk about his experience as a Luo). But the wisdom also looks more like Aristotelian phronesis at times, the knowledge that comes from experience and from understanding the subtleties of human interaction. It is no accident that Aristotle used the figure of the statesman as his exemplar of the person with phronesis. Odinga is given every opportunity to demonstrate this kind of wisdom (and it is worth noting that for Aristotle wisdom is not the same thing as phronesis, but for our purposes here we can make a connection).

Historicity as Textualized Temporality

Oginga Odinga's account of the figures and moments in his political life are a textualization of the past. They are, in effect, rehearsals of the moments when a new problematic emerged, or almost emerged, or could have emerged under different conditions.

The point here is not just that Odinga is historicizing but that for Oruka, we have another model of the sage. Arguably, in fact, we could see a third figure of the sage, adding to the folk sage (the one who is the repository of cultural knowledge) and the philosophical sage (the one who inquires into the reasons for that cultural knowledge and, where appropriate, diverges from the received approach). Odinga is what we might call a *pragmatic sage*, not in the sense that he applies wisdom already established by the philosophical sage but in the sense that wisdom is enacted within a cultural context, makes itself apparent in the contingencies of life, and shows forth potentialities of thought, new spaces of thought, that could change the meaning of all discourse and action in a domain. (For more on this, see Janz forthcoming.)

The clearest example of this is something that Oruka and Odinga come back to several times—Odinga's book *Not Yet Uhuru* (1967). This book was presented as an autobiography (i.e., in fact, the subtitle of the book), which suggests that it is a personal account of a person's life. It is more than that, of course, coming at a time after Kenyan independence when there was still a great deal of dispute about what the government of this country should look like. It is a country established by colonial borders, set up at the time of the Scramble for Africa and shortly after, and these borders do not make much sense as far as the traditional areas of ethnic groups are concerned.

Not Yet Uhuru was a provocation at the time, a statement that freedom (*uhuru*) had not yet been realized, despite the fact that independence had been declared from Britain in 1963 and the Republic of Kenya was declared in December of 1964. Odinga had been a close friend of the first president of Kenya, Jomo Kenyatta, but this relationship had soured, and both Odinga's book and his later discussions with Oruka give evidence not only of why they soured but also of what opportunities were missed at the time. Particularly in the interviews, Odinga points out that some people thought he was talking absurdity and called him a mad man for saying that independence had not delivered freedom (Oruka 1992: 115). His point was that these critics were indeed enjoying the fruits of freedom, given their status as well-paid ministers, but the conditions for the realization of freedom had not been set. Kenyatta had given in to demands of Kenya's former colonizers, the British, to remain involved as advisors (74–6).

I previously argued that sage philosophy, like Viveiros de Castro's version of anthropology, lies in the encounter between the theorist and the subject and focuses on "taking indigenous thought seriously." In other words, it is not simply an exercise in looking at the subject, in this case Odinga, and hearing them in a sympathetic manner. The philosophy happens in the encounter. This encounter is between Oruka and Odinga and gives an opening to see past the political program as it unfolded over a lifetime.

We can see this in the encounter between Oruka and Odinga, perhaps more than almost any other sage philosophy interview Oruka conducted. In most of the others, he was clearly the trained philosopher. He respected the wisdom of his interlocutors, but he guided the conceptual terms of the conversation. He was there to sympathetically listen to them. With Odinga, though, Oruka was always adjusting his approach to questioning in light of what Odinga said.

One example is the very last recorded question Oruka asked in the 1991–2 interviews. It starts as if he wanted to return to the standard sage philosophy format of asking a definitional question. Odinga, characteristically, did not answer with a definition. Oruka had an opening to pursue the issue further, but the discussion stops before that could happen. The exchange is as follows:

Q. You have interacted with all kinds of personalities, both young and old, famous and ordinary, men and women. May I ask you one metaphysical question? What is the nature of a human being?
A. I will answer this by referring you to what one very wise man from my clan told me a long time ago. I was then still youthful and inexperienced. He told me something about man which I cherish dearly to this day.
He told me: Look here Oginga, I want you to know what *dhano* (a human animal) is. *Dhano* is the most cruel, clever, cunning, and complicated of all animals. You can easily learn and understand other animals, but cannot fully understand *dhano*. The moment you really think you fully understand any given human being, you are in for a big disappointment. Even when you have your own baby, as soon as the baby begins to grow and talk you will discover some very different and strange habits in the baby. He will never really be exactly what you wish him to be.
So Oginga, he said, be careful about *dhano*.
Yes, I have throughout my life always found this advice to be true.
Q. So human beings are very complicated and we cannot rightly be able to comprehend and fully describe them.
A. We cannot. Anybody who claims otherwise would be wrong. (Oruka 1992: 117)

This is an open door to further explanation that Oruka did not go through. Odinga did not answer the question, but instead told a story about how unpredictable and complicated humans are. Does that mean he does not think he can know anything about them? Of course not. We see evidence here of the potentiality of a question, in other words, that was not asked. That question would involve asking about the nature of the complexity of humans.

Odinga has just regaled Oruka with his impressions of a host of figures and his analysis of events he had been part of. Oruka could have easily followed this up by asking him about the contradiction between this story and all the cases already recorded in which he either made good decisions or made bad ones and learned from them. It is of course true that humans are not predictable the way particles in Newtonian physics are, but then, no one ever thought they were. It is clearly not the case that Odinga is advocating we just throw up our hands and regard human interaction as completely random and intrinsically unknowable. So then, how do we act in an uncertain world? Odinga would likely have fallen back on accounts of traditional wisdom and political savvy, in other words, on the knowledge that comes from the community and that which comes from personal experience. It would have involved a strategy for telling true from false, better from worse, believable from unbelievable, reliable from unreliable. It would have involved history and historicity. It would have been the textualization of temporality, that is, the recognition that both individual and collective action are too complex to know anything for certain but at the same time are not so opaque as to render action, and the knowledge that stems from it, impossible.

This is the door that Oruka's revised version of sage philosophy opens, but that Oruka himself does not walk through. It is enough, though, that we can see another way to think about sagacity.

5

Ubuntu as Enactivism: Mogobe Ramose and Be-ing

Spaces, Problematics, Frames

The space of thought that the concept of Ubuntu occupies has a pattern to it. It is a concept that does some work in African thought. For some, the work that it does is primarily ethical; for others, political; for yet others, it constructs a particular version of subjectivity. Concepts can, of course, accomplish any and all of these things and more. But what is interesting is how the various uses of concepts relate to each other, and how a concept that has its roots in one space might succeed or fail in accomplishing other tasks.

The question of the space of thought for a concept is important for understanding what questions or problems it can answer and which it cannot (yet). The space of thought is made available by a problematic, a space defined by questioning, which enables some kinds of investigations and makes other kinds seem irrelevant or impossible.

Asking a question that opens up a problematic must always occur within the space of another problematic, which was opened by another question. There is no intellectual creation ex nihilo. More than that, though, the problematics in which new questions are or can be asked become a frame for those questions. A frame is more than a space of inquiry; it is a field that defines the kind of question that is asked and, therefore, the range of acceptable answers that might be given. A space of inquiry suggests a new opening, a new field for investigation, whereas a frame suggests the acceptable terms of that investigation.

So, to use examples from other traditions of thought: One might approach John Stuart Mill as a moral thinker first, in which case his theory of utilitarianism is a prescriptive account of human social behavior. It is usually seen as an ethical theory, telling us how we should make moral (and other) decisions. It provides a ready method for deciding between better and worse moral decisions. In another frame, though, Mill might be approached as a social theorist first, in which case he is telling us how action does happen in the social world, not how it ought to happen. In that case, if some action seems to violate principles of utility, the response would not be to castigate the person acting but to ask ourselves what we do not yet understand about the person's utility calculation that would make sense out of this. In other words, it is not the person who is irrational but we as the observers. This difference of frame is roughly the difference between the philosopher's account of Mill and the economist's. And, depending on one's frame, entirely different questions will be asked and concepts will perform different kinds of work.

One might tell a similar story about Confucianism. Is there a prescriptive or a descriptive system at stake? Is it an ethical system, a religious one, or a political/bureaucratic one? The easy answer would be that all of these are intended, but that answer is too easy, because it does not tell us about the frame in which something should be understood and the questions that are being asked. Each of these asks and answers different questions, and these frames are not necessarily just consecutive questions, in which one frame gets asked and answered, which leads to the next frame, and the next, and so on. And it does not allow us to examine what happens at the edges of the various frames.

One's account of Hume can have several frames. Do we read his *Treatise* beginning to end, in which case we tell the story about a fundamental skepticism that arises from elements of empiricism, and a not-entirely-satisfactory fix that is our human connections through sympathy, or do we read the *Treatise* from end to beginning, in which case sympathy is more important than anything else and the opening to a new kind of investigation of human life, which includes ethics and social thinking at the foreground rather than epistemology and metaphysics, and which forms part of the basis of phenomenology, Deleuzian thought, and other contemporary philosophies? Do we read his *History of England* as part of his philosophical enterprise, or do we think of that as a different and unrelated project?

We can see similar framing issues within African and Africana philosophy as well. Some of them are evident in other chapters in this book. In some cases, questions look like they are philosophical but are anthropological, or vice versa. Disciplinary boundaries are fluid, which in itself is not a problem, but which raises the question of the frame of the question. Disciplinarity is a history of development of methods and questioning, which suggests new questioning. That history may well be (and often is) inflected by politics, colonial assumptions, racism, and so forth, but the answer to those problems is not to assume that all frames can be ignored and we can simply develop a new set of questions without any history at all, or alternatively, look to a historical frame without asking about its provenance up to the present. This questioning of the nature, space, and affordances of questions might be seen as "metaquestioning." As much as philosophy has focused on the nature and structure of questions in multiple domains, metaquestioning still has much to be done.

It is worth noting (and we will elaborate on this elsewhere in this book) that the frame of inquiry is not the only determinant of the nature of the space of inquiry. There is also the intensity produced between the cognitive system of the knower and the affordances of the known, which enable some questions to be pursued and not others. Everything from the life span of the knower, to his/her cultural history, to his/her mode of embodiment in the world, to the specific processing patterns of the brain of the knower activates elements of the world as affordances and suggests some patterns of thought and precludes others.

Questions around the nature of problematics, the nature of frames, and intensities come into focus as we look at Mogobe Ramose's account of Ubuntu. There are many approaches to Ubuntu in the literature, and it is not the intention of this chapter to give a definitive or new definition of it. There is no attempt here to reflect on Ubuntu as a general concept. And there are other sustained projects in the philosophical analysis of Ubuntu by people such as Leonhard Praeg (2014b; Praeg and Magadla 2014), Thad Metz (2007a, b; 2011), Michael Onyebuchi Eze (2010), and many others, which also in their own ways open up spaces of thought. The purpose here is to look at a specific thinker and text in order to determine what kind of problematic he establishes and what frame he is using. The hope is to see how this version of Ubuntu allows us to ask a new and different set of questions. The text is *African Philosophy through Ubuntu* (1999), by Mogobe Ramose.

Ramose's Account of Ubuntu

Ubuntu is usually understood as either a metaphysical system or a phenomenology of African experience. In other words, its claim is either that there is something fundamentally different about African existence, captured under the umbrella of "Ubuntu," that is shared across the continent and is determinative of social patterns, values, and attitudes. Or, on the other hand, it is a shorthand for the observation of social patterns, values, and attitudes on the continent, and the argument that these characteristics have been part of African self-consciousness since time immemorial.

There have been fault lines that have emerged in the discussion. Michael Onyebuchi Eze sketches these out in *Intellectual History in Contemporary South Africa* (2010). There are lines between those who see the concept as deeply rooted in traditional culture, and those who see it as a late concept, emerging from mostly white anthropologists and figures such as Placide Tempels. There are lines between those who see it as a primarily metaphysical concept, describing the true and unique nature of Africans, and those who see it as primarily descriptive.

The goal here will be to offer a new possibility for Ubuntu, one that Mogobe Ramose points toward in several works, but which has not yet been clearly worked out. It is a transversal reading, which is to say that it is not a reading designed to supplant or argue against existing readings. It is, rather, an attempt to reask the question of Ubuntu in a new way (although Ramose would almost certainly say that this is the foundational sense of Ubuntu, from which others are derived). I believe that Ramose has reasked that question, and this chapter will sketch out what that means. He is working with a different frame for the question of Ubuntu from that often assumed, and as such he opens up a new space of thought.

Ramose's frame, I will argue, is that he sees Ubuntu as an enactive cognitive system rather than an ontological, ethical, or political one. Or put more carefully, he sees these systems rooted in enactive cognition, rather than the other way around or rather than completely leaving out questions of cognition and moving straight from the ontology of Ubuntu to epistemological claims about the constitution of African knowledge, and then on to ethical and political considerations. As an enactive system, its central questions have to do with the acquisition and maintenance of knowledge, practice, expertise, and authority at an individual, social, and cultural level.

The transversal nature of Ramose's reading is evident from the misreadings we can see of his approach. Innocent Asouzu, for instance (2007: 206–10), reads him as asking a roughly similar question to other Ubuntu theorists, and complicating matters by bringing in a foreign language (the rheomode). He sees him as still engaged in an explanatory project, one that is trying to account for African life, and his approach as lacking because it does not present an adequate model for communication and thought. As we will see, reorienting the approach to Ubuntu as Ramose does addresses Asouzu's concerns. Likewise, Bewaji (Bewaji and Ramose 2003: 392–4) reads Ramose's Ubuntu as describing an ontological force, rather than a cognitive strategy, and finds the "*onto-triadic* account of being (be-ing), based on the idea of the living-dead, the living, and the yet-to-be-born" problematic (393). And indeed, if it is meant as a metaphysical description of African reality, there may well be problems. But my contention here is that that is not Ramose's project.

Ramose's transversal approach has been hinted at by others. Abeba Birhane (2017), a cognitive scientist, in a post on the online journal *Aeon*, suggests that Ubuntu amounts to an anti-Cartesian approach to cognition that is supported by contemporary research in the cognitive sciences. Michael Onyebuchi Eze also suggests a similar path, not from the cognitive sciences but from the recognition of the kinds of questions Ubuntu is particularly suited to addressing:

> I have criticized this kind of generalizations and false proclamations of one heritage, one culture, one civilization, et cetera, as simply an illusion, a historical chimera, and abdication of facts … Ubuntu (as a heterogeneous culture) underwent change from being an arcane and obscurant philosophy characterized as it were by witch-hunting, abuse, and exploitation of women, social rejects, and pariahs to become a philosophy of humanism, espousing genuine human traits such as friendship, magnanimity. The context defines a new intentionality and meaning. In order to understand the meaning of Ubuntu, it is necessary to historicize and situate it within the sociopolitical, economic, and cultural context across periods in which it emerged, developed, and flourished. (2010: 181–2)

Where Eze's project was to debunk a version of Ubuntu as a particular articulation of a universal African spirit and place it in a historicized logic of adaptation to contemporary needs, my goal here is to think about Ubuntu as a strategy for decision-making in a complex world grounded in shared cognition and practices, with an eye to creating new forms of life that can be seen as having continuity with the past but are not reducible to it or held hostage by it. Eze's historicism ends up in a similar place that Ramose's version of Ubuntu does, that is, as a situationally and contextually emplaced form of reasoning about complex events, along with an evaluative component that does not apply universal rules to particular situations, but that does enable someone to recognize the difference between better and worse reasoning. And Birhane suggests a different orientation toward Ubuntu that we are coming to appreciate in our evolving understanding of cognition. Ramose's account of Ubuntu, I believe, anticipates and supports both of these and with them suggests an understanding of Ubuntu that is different from the dominant one.

Being as Becoming

The central aspect of Ramose's approach to Ubuntu is the connection between being and becoming. He regularly hyphenates the word—be-ing—in order to call forth the hyphenation in Ubuntu—Ubu-ntu. Ubu

> evokes the idea of be-ing in general. It is enfolded be-ing before it manifests itself in the concrete form or mode of ex-istence of a particular entity. *Ubu-* as enfolded be-ing is always oriented towards unfoldment, that is, incessant continual concrete manifestation through particular forms and modes of being. In this sense *ubu-* is always oriented towards *-ntu*. At the ontological level, there is no strict and literal separation and division between *ubu-* and *-ntu*. *Ubu-* and *-ntu* are not two radically separate and irreconcilable opposed realities. On the contrary, they are mutually founding in the sense that they are two aspects of be-ing as one-ness and an indivisible whole-ness. (Ramose 1999: 50)

Ramose here gives us an ontology of Ubuntu, but not one rooted in a set of propositions held in the mystical past or in some collective racial or cultural unconscious. He is rather pointing to a creative moment, a striving for manifestation. What strives for manifestation? The simplest answer is that it is both Bantu-speaking people as a whole and also individuals within that group.

Be-ing, in this understanding of Ubuntu, is not fragmented (53–6). This is a monist ontology—be-ing is wholeness. This does not, however, mean that this system is Parmenidean or Platonic, with change being an illusion. Rather, there is an "incessant flow of motion [that] is perceived as chaos since it is considered to provide neither certainty nor equilibrium" (55). Language necessarily makes this order appear both fragmented and as if the elements are static, but this is a distortion. Be-ing is wholeness.

The incessant flow of motion Ramose calls "pantareic": "On this view, 'order' cannot be once established and fixed for all time" (58). It is also musical—the flows within be-ing are rhythmic, and that rhythm can be understood intellectually or emotionally. These are merely perspectives on the same thing, just as a song can have a mathematical order and set of relations and at the same time an emotional movement within it and for those hearing it. It is not that Africa is emotional and Europe is rational—everyone is everything, and to suggest otherwise is to fragment being.

Since rhythm and music are central, so is dance (59). All of these aesthetic forms involve both structure and spontaneity. They are all creative without being random. Experiencing music as a passive spectator the way non-Africans do, Ramose thinks, is surprising to Africans, and that surprise uncovers an underlying "ontological-epistemological difference."

Rheology as Questioning

Ramose characterizes his approach to Ubuntu as "rheology" (1999: 56–64), following David Bohm (1980). This little-known concept is part of Bohm's inquiry into the relationship between wholeness and fragmentation. Ramose's interest in the concept is as a linguistic one, a "new mode" of language. The chapter up to the point of his discussion of the rheomode examines the nature of being in Ubuntu, which he writes as "be-ing" to reflect the fluidity in wholeness of Ubuntu. In other words, this is not Being contrasted to Becoming, a static entity that cannot admit change. It is, rather, a space of change that nevertheless has a unity, a oneness to it. Ramose uses the term "holon-ness" (1999: 57), which "speaks directly against the fragmentation of be-ing" but retains the "perpetual and universal movement of sharing and exchange of the forces of life" that is at the core of Ubuntu (57–8).

Why does Ramose see Ubuntu as being rooted in linguistics? Most writers go back to Bantu languages to find the structure of Ubuntu and conclude that it is something like "humanness." It is the recognition of a particular kind of humanness. This may well be correct, but this approach tends to misrepresent what language actually does. Language is creation. It is for the production of concepts, the framing of experience, the coordination of action, and many other things. In other words, to look for a theory in language is to solidify the functions of language and treat its productive capacity as subordinate to its metaphysics.

We might instead reverse this ordering and think about language as first a productive and creative practice, as used by humans rather than as existing apart from any humans. Considered this way, language becomes cognitive practice. By "cognitive practice" I mean more than just the means for the production of knowledge. Contemporary phenomenological cognitive science understands enactivist cognition as the range of ways that humans find to cope with the world, both explicitly and implicitly, and the ways in which our networks of cognitive practices range between individuals and groups, between nature and culture, between abstract thought and embodied practice.

It is also worth noting that the other side of language is listening and legibility. In other words, an enactive approach to Ubuntu would recognize that the regularities within the historical practices of Ubuntu serve to make culture legible and give voice to people. This might be said of any traditional social structure, of course, but what is important here is to recognize the particular forms of legibility and listening afforded by African society. And as important, we also need to recognize the shifting cognitive structures within society and ask what legibility and listening might look like now. Ubuntu is not, in other words, a static system. It is not like a specific state formation, in which specific components must be present in order for it to remain intact. It is not a philosophy, in the sense of a set of individually necessary and collectively sufficient beliefs or propositions. It is a mode of creating and of reading/listening. It is a cognitive practice.

If we understand Ubuntu in these terms, much changes, and at the same time, little changes. Here is what does change: We are no longer looking for some essence of Africanity. We are instead looking for the means of cognitive practice that have emerged from a place, from a set of networks that evolved within the African continent, but that are not limited or bound to it. We are no longer looking for a set of ethical principles but rather for ways of producing ethical action within a space. We are no longer looking for a guiding metaphysic, something like "I am because we are"; rather, we are looking at the ways in which cognition is scaffolded in a range of African communities, and the ways in which that scaffolding has been encoded in institutions, practices, and artifacts of language so that they are legible to those invested in the place.

What does not change would be any specific belief, value, or proposition within Ubuntu. Much has been written about the kind of ethical system, for instance, that Ubuntu represents. Various writers have argued for specific ideas, rooted in traditional cultural practices or texts, that should be part of Ubuntu. The details of Ubuntu are not what is at issue here. The question is what Ubuntu as a system is for and what kinds of metaphysical assumptions we bring to it prior to investigating any of these specifics. If, for instance, we begin by assuming that Ubuntu is an ethical system that can be put alongside other ethical systems elsewhere in the world, other possible frameworks have already been ceded. And so, without wanting to argue against particulars that others have raised, I want to reposition the discussion about Ubuntu, from seeing it first as a metaphysical system or an ethical system, to seeing it first cognitively.

This is more than naturalized philosophy. Some might object that holding to something like Ubuntu gives prescriptive content—it tells us how we should live, who we should listen to, what ideals look like in society. All those, though, are merely snapshots in time. This prescriptive content has no guarantee of prescribing the right thing. There is a meta-ethical problem here—while Ubuntu is presented as prescriptive in its specific standards for life, there is a larger question of what is in fact desirable, and how it is defended as desirable. We can see this in the ways in which Ubuntu has been co-opted by a wide range of political actors, to argue for any number of ends.

The rheomode, the new language, is not meant to capture a set of relations that have existed from time immemorial, but rather a process of creation that exists now. The past matters, of course, because it is the frame in which present creation can happen. The damage done by colonialism comes from the replacement of that frame with another, developed elsewhere, one in which new questions cannot be asked and new concepts cannot be created. Bohm is clear that the rheomode begins with "inquiry into the appropriateness of the question" (1980: 36), that is, asking whether the questions we have asked in the past open us up to new areas of inquiry, or whether they now stand as a barrier to that opening.

Bohm makes clear that the rheomode is a form of questioning (36). Attending to questions leads to finding new modes of language. It is impractical to create whole new languages for each question, but it is possible, he thinks, to produce new modes of language. His description of this process borders on the musical:

> Thus, we already have, for example, different moods of the verb, such as the indicative, the subjunctive, the imperative, and we develop skill in the use of language so that each of these moods functions, when it is required, without the need for conscious choice. Similarly, we will now consider a mode in which movement is to be taken as primary in our thinking and in which this notion will be incorporated into the language structure by allowing the verb rather than the noun to play a primary role. As one develops such a mode and works with it for a while, one may obtain the necessary skill in using it, so that it will also come to function whenever it is required, without the need for conscious choice. (38–9)

There is a strong sense of play in what Bohm imagines will happen with the rheomode. It is as if an accomplished musician, perhaps a jazz musician, is playing with others and reacting to the moods and movement of the other instruments, contributing something new that then is picked up by the others (and it is no accident that Ramose picks up on the musicality of this in his description of Ubuntu as well [1999: 58–60]). It is a skill that is developed to the point that one can do it "without the need for conscious choice." This form of questioning, in other words, is not simply a deliberate choice, at least not in its fullest form, but becomes action and reaction, an impulse based on the habits of the past, with the exploration possible when someone is willing to take a risk and try something new.

Bohm thinks that the rheomode will be concerned "mainly with questions having to do with the broad and deep implications of our overall world views which now tend to be raised largely in the study of philosophy, psychology, art, science and mathematics, but especially in the study of thought and language themselves" (1980: 39). These questions can be addressed using existing language, but he thinks that that leads to fragmentation. We might suppose that he is searching for a kind of holism of thought here, but that is not the only possible conclusion. He is in fact looking for a new space that questioning can open up. This becomes clear in his discussion of the idea of relevance. He argues that relevance in some sense comes before the question of truth, but in a deeper sense "the seeing of relevance or irrelevance is evidently an aspect of the perception of truth in its overall meaning" (42). Relevance is not a technique but more like an art requiring creative perception and the development of skill.

This sense of relevance as related to questioning requires a connection between the knower and the context of the known, that is, the context of the question. Too strict a sense of what might be relevant closes down any creative thought; too loose a sense turns questioning into aimless meandering. A teacher of mathematics or music or philosophy might require students to answer a question in a very restricted manner (i.e., limiting irrelevancies to a minimum) in order to train them in the practices of a method or discipline, but expertise in an area should mean that those internalized methods can be seen for what they are—shorthands to produce particular results but not guides for all actions. Musicians making music with too limited a sense of relevance produce formulaic music. They simply reinscribe a genre. But a musician who respects the tradition while experimenting with it can produce surprising, innovative, and in some cases transcendental experiences. Such a musician can create new musical forms by finding relevant sounds where others failed to perceive them or ruled them out of order. This does not mean that anything goes. It means that this stretching and adaptation of language can open new doors of inquiry when new questions that fit the givenness of the world in new ways are asked.

Bohm's specific method of doing this involves looking for the root form of verbs. He does so in a manner that might not satisfy a linguist looking to establish an etymology, but which is directed at suggesting creative connections. His example also serves as a further development of the concept of relevance in the rheomode. He starts with the Latin verb "videre," meaning "to see" (46–53). Seeing includes a wide range of cognitive activity, so he proposes a new verb, "to vidate," that refers to any act of perception of whether something fits or does not fit the givenness of the world. "Re-vidate" is a folding, a re-perception, that leads to a determination as to whether something fits. If it does not, it is "irre-vidate." So, to "re-vidate" means to continue to perceive content, and "irre-vidate" means to be caught up in illusion or delusion. "Vidation" refers to a totality of acts of perception and is related to "levation," which is the lifting of something to attention. Videre is also related to "divide" or "to see as separate." This leads us to the verb "di-vidate," or "the spontaneous act of seeing things as separate, in any form whatsoever, including the act of seeing whether or not the perception fits 'what is,' and even that of seeing how the attention-calling function of this word has a form of inherent division in it" (47). As with vidation, this folds on itself as "re-dividate," the continuing state of seeing a certain content in the form of separation or division (48).

This might just seem like wordplay. In a sense it is, but the emphasis should be on "play." This is not just pointless activity; it is an attempt to reframe our understanding so that new questions can be asked. It would be a mistake to see new questions as being made available only through disciplined scientific or academic work. Some questions build on past questions, but it is also important to see when and where the past questions have run their course and a new direction is needed.

Bohm's reason for working through the rheomode is to arrive at what he calls the "implicate order." He describes it this way:

> We proposed that a new notion of order is involved here, which we called the *implicate order* (from a Latin root meaning "to enfold" or "to fold inward"). In terms of the implicate order one may say that everything is enfolded into everything. This contrasts with the *explicate order* now dominant in physics in which things are *unfolded* in the sense that each thing lies only in its own particular region of space (and time) and outside the regions belonging to other things. (Bohm 1980: 225; original emphases)

His goal is to find a way to rethink physics, but the principle of reasoning is one that Ramose finds more broadly applicable. The move of finding a logic between wholes and parts is one we can find in many Western philosophers through time (Hegel comes to mind, but there are many others). This approach, though, has more in common with Deleuze and in fact uses a similar term to one that is central to Deleuze: the fold.

The concept of the rheomode has not had widespread use. Even Bohm does not make use of it in the seminar (*Thought as a System*, 1994) he conducted about the same kind of material as in his *Wholeness and the Implicate Order* (1994). But the logic of the rheomode is embedded within Bohm's own thought, and it becomes central to Ramose's reimagining of Ubuntu.

The Implication of the Rheomode for African Life

Ramose spends most of his book looking at various cultural practices such as religion, politics, and law "through Ubuntu," in other words, using the tools developed through Bohm and others. Engaging these activities through Ubuntu preserves the wholeness of Ubuntu and recognizes that each area of human activity is a ceaseless flow and a creative potentiality. It is tempting to only read the early chapters and from them assume that Ramose's position on Ubuntu is clear. It is important, though, to look at the rest of the chapters, since they fill in how one might think through Ubuntu without just turning it into a theory of being.

Thinking about life "through" Ubuntu does not mean applying Ubuntu to different areas of life. It would be like saying that one is applying evolution to the emergence of life. There are, to be sure, general principles, but even those principles are generalizations based on past phenomena, and while they are useful in looking into the future, they do not tell us much about which specific species will emerge over time, or how they will mutate. The principles are neither, in other words, predictive mechanisms nor specific guarantees. They tell us how creation might happen, not how it will. The same is true for any other complex system, such as the weather, consciousness, markets, and so forth. Models are invariably partial, and every action has unintended consequences and makes available new potentialities. It is not complete randomness—there are patterns of activity that frame future action.

There is another sense in which Ramose's description of Ubuntu's mode of questioning is significant. One of the common criticisms of Ubuntu is that it is not scalable. While it might be a system that works for small-scale communities in which people know each other, it falls apart (or put more precisely, it is too easy to take advantage of) when a community is large enough that members cannot know either other individuals or even their family connections. So, a community the size of a state becomes difficult to manage because the structures within it that depend on trust and on people working with a view to the "we" are overwhelmed by prospects of short-term gain and the relative anonymity of the one harmed.

But "through Ubuntu" suggests that the question of scalability misses the point. Scalability assumes that there is an analogy between the individual decision-maker and the collective decision-maker in a society, as well as the one with moral standing in each of those cases. The failure, then, is assumed to be a moral failure (as well as a political one, of course, but it starts with a moral one), which is that the balance shifts toward self-interest when a group gets too large.

The issue might, though, be seen as a cognitive one. Ubuntu might be what we could call "machine learning." There could, in other words, be a discontinuity, rather than a continuity, in the nature of cognition at a large scale. To use an example, humans have made models of complex systems for a long time—weather systems, economies, and so on. In most of these cases, machine learning algorithms have taken over from human cognition, because the human ability to collect, remember, and process large datasets has its limits. Those algorithms do not necessarily work like human cognition does, and that is a good thing. They are able to recognize patterns and predict relations in ways that humans could not do. Sometimes they make mistakes, at least from the point of view of the health of the overall complex system (see, e.g., Narkunas's example of the algorithm in the New York Stock Exchange that caused the "flash crash" in 2010 [2018: 1]). We only understand the errors of cognition after the fact.

The point is that, at the limit of human cognition, we have models of handing over cognitive processes to machines, which then do labor that we cannot do, or do things in a manner alien to our Western individualist humanist impulse, based in reflective reason and deliberation and governed by moral and intellectual virtues.

Ubuntu at a large scale might be seen as machine learning. This does not mean that it is a mystical alien cognitive process that we have no knowledge of or artificial intelligence. We can of course understand reasoning—after the fact, just as the flash crash and the products of evolution and the direction of a hurricane all become explainable after the fact. But we are required to act into the future. If we were to simply rely on our own intuition and experience to make decisions, it would be difficult to move into the future. Individualism has its limits, and this is clear not just in Africa but everywhere. There are just different mechanisms for scaffolding decisions in different places.

Ubuntu might be seen as a way of scaffolding decisions by harnessing community experience, elders, ancestors, tales and proverbs, and a range of other algorithmic features of culture. Simply seeing Ubuntu as a machine or a set of algorithms is to look at it at an abstract level. What matters is what those algorithms actually are. The violence of colonialism in Africa was that it supplanted existing algorithms, that is, existing modes of externalizing cognitive activity into a group process that has a history and patterns of thought and introduced machines that did not have their roots within African knowledge processes. This does not mean that African processes are somehow static and have no relation to any others but rather that the relationship between individual decision-making and machine algorithms in culture had been disrupted. People still made decisions, but those decisions did not have the machine tools of cognition to use that they always had. They had been substituted by algorithms developed in a different cognitive ecosystem, or in some cases substituted by nothing at all, that is, the illusion that all decisions came solely from individuals and their personal insight on the nature of things.

The function of Ubuntu, then, is the relationship between individual decision-making and the collective wisdom that is processed in a manner that is impossible to produce at an individual level. Ubuntu is, in this sense, a machine, not in a reductionist mechanistic sense but in the sense of a cognitive process that operates differently from the deliberative and reflective processes of individuals or the structures that use individual deliberation as a model. To recognize Ubuntu is not to prioritize the group over the individual, nor is it to subscribe to some form of communalism or socialism. It is to recognize that any decisions in a complex system require both the deliberative and rational activity of the individual and the machinic algorithm of the network, processing outcomes in terms of value and presenting history in the form of elders and ancestors.

Ramose speaks about Ubuntu in terms of whole/parts relations, and this gets at some of its machine nature. This comes out in places like his chapter on ecology through Ubuntu. One might imagine that a communal approach like Ubuntu would have a hard time dealing with the ethical and cognitive standing of things outside of the community. Does nature have a value only because it is valuable to humans, and therefore is instrumental to our needs? Ramose makes clear that that is not how Ubuntu would approach the environment. He rather approaches ecology as a knowledge system from which we learn, and in the context of which we make adjustments, sometimes quite significant ones. It is part of our becoming.

Ubuntu, or Botho in Sotho, should not be seen as humanism, with its focus on the centrality of the individual mind and consciousness but as humanness (Ramose 1999: 154–5). The wholeness of the world is then not primarily a human-centered space but a space of emergence within the context of systems of knowledge and practice that lie beyond human intention. Botho is to exist in this complex space, which I argue here involves an autopoietic interaction between human conscious intention and knowledge and the machinic qualities of algorithmic processes that occur in the rest of reality. To privilege only the first part of these is a loss of Botho, a loss that is poorly compensated by the "somewhat disconsolate comfort and 'easy life' brought about by technological advancement" (158). In other words, the result is to rely only on the idea that reflective reason can dominate the rest of the world through technology, and that technology is an extension of our individual will in a manner that enhances but does not intrinsically change us.

Seeing Ubuntu as something other than humanism does not mean that it is antihumanist. It is closer to ahumanist (as discussed in the earlier chapter on Sylvia Wynter). Ahumanism does not deny that we intervene in the world, but it does deny that we control the world or that control is the goal of human flourishing. We are as much subject to the complex interactions and transversal lines of causation as we are initiators of them. Every action has unanticipated consequences. Ubuntu is less about deciding on right action than it is a way of navigating the complex of forces in the world using the collected wisdom of a place. This wisdom cannot be distilled in pithy statements—such statements are just artifacts of strategies of coping with unanticipated consequence. This is why we see John Mbiti give a version of temporal experience that does not look far into the future—not because Africans do not plan for the future, but because what is more important is the wisdom of elders, tradition, and ancestors in knowing how to deal with things when they do not turn out as planned. Ahumanism, then, is a kind of humility, at the same time as being a recognition of the richness of the past when applied to the future.

Ubuntu as Enactivism: Cognition in Place and Shared Cognition

What are the implications of thinking Ubuntu in the terms that Ramose sets out for us? For one, he suggests a different kind of theorizing from what we see in the colonial project. That project was about control, about the ability to predict particular kinds of outcomes. Those outcomes generally were intended to be beneficial to the colonialists, but even when the rhetoric was about benefit to Africans (e.g., the missionary enterprise), there was still a logic of the control of outcomes.

Ubuntu understood as Ramose suggests is not about control at all. Control assumes the ability to represent a future world in our minds, and then work toward it. But this version of Ubuntu is not about representation at all, of either a future or a present. It is, rather, about the cognitive tools needed to respond to a world that is in fact unknowable, at least as a future reality. The tools in question are not simply guesses, mystifications, or mythologies, as colonial logic supposes they must be. They are about the production of the new and the ability to deal with the new.

There are other differences in how Ubuntu would proceed:

- For one thing, Ubuntu would not function as an alternate social theory to Western theories, which purport to explain or describe African society.
- Ubuntu would not be a set of first principles rooted in an African collective unconscious.
- Ubuntu would not purport to control the future. It would, rather, be a series of virtualizations, that is, reactions between actors of all sorts (human and otherwise) within a space.
- Ubuntu would tell us nothing specific about state formations, although we could imagine several different kinds of state formations coming out of its logic.
- Ubuntu would likewise tell us little about ethical systems, although again we could imagine several kinds of ethical systems. There are no principles to live by, nothing resembling the categorical imperative or the principle of utility. There are, to be sure, regularities that can be seen in past successful action and limited attempts to predict how we should act in the future, but none of these provides anything like a modernist ethical system that remains invariant over a long period of time. Ramose's commitment to the rheomode is a commitment to experimentation in language and thought. "I am because we are" would reflect a regularized set of virtualizations of African practice. In other words, this statement of collectivization would reflect successful practice in an African context over time, but neither would it be an exclusively African virtualization (i.e., other cultures may also see themselves in this kind of collectivization), nor would it direct behavior at a fine-grained level (i.e., there might be times when such collectivization has not worked or might not be the best policy), nor would it necessarily suggest any particular ethic when faced with complex future phenomena.

Usually, Ubuntu is seen as a reversal of a Western idea of individuality. The West prioritizes individuals and makes groups secondary, whereas Ubuntu prioritizes groups and makes individuals secondary. But this misunderstands how Ubuntu works. Ubuntu, if Ramose is right, is the recognition of becoming that steps back from the illusion of individuality that comes from too brief a view. If we had life spans in the thousands or even millions of years, we would see individuals not as discrete phenomena passing us by, one by one, but as moments of the becoming of human groups. It is not the groups that are becoming in some Hegelian sense of Geist coming to self-knowledge but rather the currents that flow through history and are momentarily solidified in each individual.

Individuals, and not just human individuals but all individuals, are those moments. This is why Ubuntu is not simply a reversal of a Western notion of individualism, placing groups first and individuals as derivative of them. Both what we normally think of as individuals and things such as ethnic groups, families, and many others function as individuals in the sense that they react to conditions using the resources and the history and experience available to them.

Another way of understanding this is through what amounts to a misunderstanding of the classic phrase "I am because we are." Western readers too easily read this as a tension between the individual and the collective—and then think of the collective as a kind of individual at a higher level. It might even take on a name—spirit, ancestor—and the assumption is that the statement observes that in Africa the individual's will is subordinated to the will of this other individual, the collective, which expresses its will in various ways. This, though, does not allow for the autopoietic, creative nature of individuals coming together and reaching a tipping point, so that the collective action does not resemble individual action, nor could have been predicted by it. Ramose's "humanness" suggests a complex formulation, an organization that happens only in large groups and that cannot be willed or caused by things such as democratic action, bureaucratic structures, or shared belief. It is not, in other words, about a master plan or about getting every individual on the same page, any more than the collective actions of a colony of ants is about either a single ant having a grand plan of action or individual ants understanding anything at all about their part in anything and acting toward a greater end. The "we are" of "I am because we are" is an indication of African society existing at a tipping point, as complexity theory defines it, that is, at a point of self-organization that can be maintained but that also can be destroyed (and this is the tragedy of colonialism, the destruction of the inherent complexity of African systems).

Ubuntu understood in these terms is a space of thought, not a mode of thought. In other words, it would not necessitate or predict any particular philosophical or political structure. It would rather be a space of creative thought, rooted in material, cultural, and intellectual currents in Africa. It is, as Ramose says, a "philosophy," but that does not mean that it is a set of foundational beliefs about the world, which derive from some aspect of African culture or civilization. Ramose uses the term "philosophy" to refer to a way of coming to knowledge that has its basis in the family resemblance of African cultures to each other. He does use the term "foundation" for Ubuntu (e.g., Ramose 1999: 49), but Ubuntu does not embody a set of abstract propositions meant to ground practice and theory development. It is, rather, "the foundation and the edifice" of African philosophy. As becomes clear throughout the book, he means by this the development of thought and practice by setting the stage for new exploration.

One of the damaging aspects to colonialism is that a focus on the physical and intellectual violence that colonialism wrought on Africa tends to produce a backlash against any change or evolution at all. This was overt in earlier anthropological accounts of knowledge within African communities. It was contained in traditional folkways and practices and tended to be fairly static. Such accounts led Robin Horton (1967a, b) to think of African societies as "closed systems" and led earlier anthropologists to look for stable structures and functions underlying the societies. It led philosophers looking for African philosophy to settle on a stabilizing account later called "ethnophilosophy" by Paulin Hountondji, in an effort to resist the external changes imposed by colonialism.

Colonialism was and is indeed violent and deeply problematic, but not because it brought about change. Change already existed within African cultures, as it does within all cultures. It was violent because it supplanted systems and patterns of action and reaction borne in African soil with systems developed elsewhere and insisted that the new ones were superior to the old ones. It was because the new systems purported to control a complex and chaotic world rather than react to it and enable new forms of life to emerge from old.

This does not look to philosophers much like a philosophy or to social theorists like a social theory, but that is the point. Those categories have been used to try to represent and capture a set of patterns and reactions that have their origin and sustenance in an African place, but they are at best partial accounts of what Ubuntu names. Ubuntu is future-oriented, which is why Ramose emphasizes the idea of becoming. Can any specific future be willed into existence or brought into being? No. But that is not the point of Ubuntu. We cannot predict the course of biological evolution in close detail (or, usually, in broad strokes either); we cannot predict economic markets; we cannot predict precisely the course of weather anomalies; we cannot predict the results of our engagement in any large-scale complex system in anything but the short term. This does not mean that we know nothing—of course there are past patterns that are relevant to the future. But the insight of Ramose's Ubuntu is that Africa has always had a set of strategies to deal with complex reality as it is encountered. These strategies change over time while drawing on the past. They are known by being embodied and embedded within African culture, not by abstracting from it.

Temporality and Literature

Ramose's work on Ubuntu stands at the fulcrum of this book. The previous three chapters have focused on temporality and have tied concepts such as vitalism, Sasa and Zamani, and historicity to questions around how African philosophy can be a nonrepresentational philosophy of creativity rather than a representational philosophy of culture. The two chapters that follow take up the question of literature or, more specifically, what it means for philosophy to have a literature.

The approach we see to Ubuntu in Ramose ties these two concerns together. Ramose's Ubuntu assumes a temporality oriented toward creativity rather than representation. As we have seen in this chapter, he gives a picture of harnessing the resources of the rhythms of thought and practice developed over years of individual and cultural experience and turned into myths and signs able to generate newly productive autopoietic states, to make available vibrant life in uncertain conditions. These rhythms and signs create a space of thought and action, and in doing so they create a literature robust enough for philosophy to flourish. This literature is explicated by Sophie Olúwọlé's argument for what an adequate literature of philosophy might look like and Euphrase Kezilahabi's theory of Quassia, and it is put to the test by Achille Mbembe's concern for self-writing in a space of violence.

The concepts that have undergirded the approach within this book also pivot on this chapter. In the early chapters, I established the idea of the creation of a space of thought. This came out of questions (which we have seen Ramose address directly) that lead to new problematics. Ramose exemplifies the production of a new problematic by helping the reader to rethink Ubuntu in cognitive terms (and as I have argued, in enactivist terms), but past that, his sketch of Ubuntu also opens the door to see African philosophy itself as a space of new problematics. In other words, it is not about finding some foundational ethical, political, or metaphysical principles that are then applied to experience.

It is the experience that comes first, along with the recognition that new thought emerges out of the encounters with the world that bring together the rhythms of the past with the improvisation of the present.

This is the space of dialogue—not the kind of dialogue that searches for agreement or rapprochement, but rather dialogue that recognizes that a problematic is as much a rhetorical space as it is a conceptual one. And this is the space of the event, the moment in which any individual comes into being through the combination of deliberate action and transversal elements of space. Deliberate action assumes a cause-and-effect set of relations—we act in order to produce desired effects. And yet, we act in a world of shifting circumstances and of meanings that do not remain under our control at all times.

African philosophy as event is the orientation toward the production of the new in a manner that respects the old. It is, I believe, what Ramose is arguing for in his vision of Ubuntu. In a sense, then, this fulcrum chapter is another way of imagining the ahumanism that Sylvia Wynter argues for and the Négritude that Suzanne Césaire describes. If Wynter and Césaire are the two frames of this section, Ramose stands at the center, looking in the same direction, imagining a space of thought both adequate to and generative of African life.

6

A Literary Tradition of Thought: Sophie Olúwọlé, Euphrase Kezilahabi, and a Literature of Philosophy

What Is a Literature?

Sophie Olúwọlé's essay "The Africanness of a Philosophy" (1989) is understood as part of a dialogue over the nature of African philosophy. She addresses other writers who have had this as their central question. In her case, though, there is something more going on, and it is contained in her idea of a "literary tradition of thought." While she develops this in a specific manner that seems to fit as an alternative to other answers to the question "Is there an African philosophy, and if so, what is its nature?," the literary tradition of thought offers something more interesting than simply another alternative answer.

In *Philosophy in an African Place* (2009), I argued that the search for a set of intellectual practices that were truly African and truly philosophical was a futile task and was the response to a question not posed by Africans but by a skeptical West. The question, then, is what we can make of the efforts among some African thinkers to define the practice of African philosophy? Do we simply say that they are misguided? I am more interested in seeing what is contained in such attempts apart from answering back to a Western question. "The Africanness of a Philosophy" is a good place to start with such an inquiry.

The impulse to identify true Africanness and true philosophicality is not, of course, limited to answering a Western challenge, even if its ultimate roots are there. One might want to ask these questions to identify a specific object of inquiry. One might want to define the borders of inquiry, that is, be able to have a bright line between what counts and what does not count as African philosophy. One might want to develop the disciplinarity of African philosophy to allow it to have a legitimate interdisciplinary status in relation to other areas, such as the rest of philosophy, African studies, postcolonial studies, race studies, and so forth.

Any of these might be legitimate pursuits, but they all assume that there is a kind of pre-thinking of African philosophy that must be done before the project itself can start. And, at an abstract level, that might make sense. After all, it seems reasonable that we would need to define the terms of an inquiry before it can begin and before it can have its place among other kinds of inquiry.

The problem, though, is that predefining the space of thought for a philosophy tends to also fix it and undermine the potential for change. Usually when we think about essentializing something, we think about the process of identifying some necessary and sufficient condition for the existence of that thing, some "inner" aspect to it that makes it what it is, different from all other things. And that sense of essentialism has rightly been questioned as a philosophical strategy. When it comes to an area like African philosophy, there is also a kind of essentialism possible, which can define and therefore limit the nature of the space of thought available to that area. The argument in *Philosophy in an African Place* was that a phenomenology of place that does not first start from the question of prerequisites to a space of thought, but instead works from the activated and scaffolded concepts that have currency in a place, is more likely to reflect African concerns and patterns of thought. It is in other words an enactive approach, which recognizes that doing African philosophy is significantly what establishes the nature of African philosophy.

Olúwọlé could be read as advocating that we find abstract preconditions for this space of thought. She could be read as canvassing several possibilities, finding them wanting, and then offering her own, which is that African philosophy needs a literature that is not reducible to the stylized literature of existing work in the area, but which casts a broader net and takes in other literary forms as representing African existence. I am more interested, though, in the nature of "a literature." This way of characterizing African philosophy can be seen not as defining a priori what counts as African philosophy but as setting a space for it.

The question of the nature of the text is central as well. What is a text, and what is textualizable? What is a text in Africa? It is tempting to think of a literature as simply a collection of texts, as an archive. I am more interested in thinking of it as enacted textuality. A literature is not just an archive, or rather, it is an archive whose narrative and structure are written by its use. That means that the texts are used and performed, given significance or not, recovered and rewritten, commented upon and reimagined. A literature is the performance of texts, and each text that is added becomes part of that literature to a greater or lesser degree. It is possible to forget texts but for their influence to still be felt in and through other texts and other performances.

Each new text is a kind of action as well as a statement of thought. It does not spring from nothing. It comes out of the literature. It is a new engagement with the literature, a new potentiality made actual. As with most of culture, we exist both within and above a literature. We engage in it as well as reflect on it.

As with texts, there is a history of uses of the concept of a literature. Some are narrower and some broader. A literature might refer to literal written books. More broadly, it can refer to other writing, and more broadly still it might refer to other forms of verbal communication, or any meaningful image or sound. If we allow that a literature is a set of performances, we end up with fuzzy borders for the kinds of performances we might include.

We can neither plan a literature nor predict it. This is not because our texts have no impact or agency but because the effect of performing a new text is unpredictable. We might think that we can make a "viral video," for instance, but all we can make is a video. The viral part is out of our control. A literature is a complex space. For philosophy to be grounded in a literature means that its primary activity, the creation of concepts adequate to a place and the scaffolding of those concepts with arguments, institutions, and so forth, must look to something that is essentially unpredictable.

Others have considered the question of the relationship between African literature and philosophy. Oruka, when he expanded his "trends" from four to six, added "literary philosophy" as another trend. He intended to designate literary writers who had written work that was taken by some to be philosophical, or which was intended as philosophical. Usually this work was nonfiction, although it did not have to be.

M. S. C. Okolo (2007) has also considered African literature as political philosophy. Unlike Olúwọlé, she considers literature as its own domain, separate from philosophy, and is interested in asking about the relationship between the two. In particular, she wants to have a "philosophical reading of literature" that can help to create an "intellectual framework within which the African experience can be conceptualized, interpreted and reorganized" (2). She chooses Achebe's *Anthills of the Savannah* (2013) and Ngugi wa Thiong'o's *Petals of Blood* (2018) as her primary examples to analyze. The goal is to analyze work that reflects on the political situation in Africa.

What is a literature? For something to be a literature means for it to be a narrative about forms of expression. We sometimes talk about there being a literature about specific questions or problems—the literature on diabetes, for instance, or the literature on racism. We also think of a literature as a kind of narrative about place and identity. So, a Kenyan literature or a British literature are bodies of work either from a place, or about a place, or by people recognized as authoritative or insightful on a place. There are gradations within a literature—not everything written in Nigeria might be considered part of "Nigerian literature," but some things will be thought to be more representative of the place, or more aspirational for new authors, or more insightful about life in that place, in both its positive and negative manifestations.

A literature is intertwined with life. As Sylvia Wynter puts it, "What men dreamt and wrote, and what they lived coexisted side by side. Literature realized itself in life, and life surprised itself as literature, in what a famous critic has called, '*the literaturization of life*'" (1969a: 4; original emphasis). There is, in other words, a mutual implication between the production of life and the production of literature. It is not just that literature represents reality but that both life and literature lead each other in surprising directions. They are transversal to each other, not just reflective of each other. Wynter likely has in mind a specific work of literature when she writes this, as opposed to *a* literature, but the transversality has even more significance in the space created by a literature.

A literature has legislative force. Once we recognize that a literature exists, university courses are taught on it and handbooks are written about it. We also have arguments over the formation of the literature. The literature on psychological testing, for instance, was shown to be oriented toward educated white men as test subjects, which therefore skewed results. The literature was biased. Feminist literature had a robust tradition, but it took women of color, queer and trans folk, and others to point out the blind spots in white liberal feminism.

We think of literatures as expanding when gaps like this are pointed out, but if literatures are more like a narrative than a database of approved sources and references, more is going on than expansion. Cognitively, of course, expansion has its limits. We do not easily simply add to the references we have available to us. So, while addition does happen, narratives also change. The story that a literature once told about how a field formed and what the events were in that formation change to recognize new formations.

Narrative is an aid to cognition, perhaps even an essential part to cognition. We do not operate like databases, with metatags for information that we can simply search for. We make use of devices that do that, but we do not operate that way ourselves. Narrative comes with many things that databases do not. They come with affect—we face narratives with a feeling about them, and about the information they have, as well as a mood about them that colors new information. A narrative not only tells us what is in and what is out but also what new information is likely to qualify as relevant and what is not. A narrative might classify and assign significance to various entries, as happens in a database, but it does so differently, by association, by potentially multiple narrators, by hint and allegation as much as outright statements of value.

A literature is not simply a body of work in an area, but it comes sorted and prioritized by a variety of factors. There are gatekeepers who have a hand in determining what will be included in a literature, through such means as editing collections of papers or books. A literature is not, though, constructed only by its gatekeepers. It is constructed also by its users. Some important figure in a field might insist that a particular contribution is seminal, but if no one teaches that work in classes or refers to it in research, its significance will diminish. A literature is, in other words, a dialogue along several lines—between users and gatekeepers and between users themselves. And, as we saw earlier in the discussion about dialogue, a literature is not built in a linear or progressively dialectical manner but is susceptible to all the blind alleys and ersatz exchanges that any dialogue faces.

Narratives come with internal ontologies. In other words, the structure of the narrative matters and is part of the narrative itself, and that structure is not something different from the "data" (i.e., the events and artifacts we are narrativizing). In a database, we impose an ontology on data. We might think that we are extracting the ontology from the data, but it is worth remembering that we could always have another ontology that includes the data.

A literature, then, is more like a narrative than a database, but it would be a mistake to simply identify it with a narrative. A literature can contain multiple narratives. The argument of this book has been that African philosophy has had a narrative, composed of particular events, which is retold in introductory classes, texts, and other places, so that anyone claiming to be familiar with African philosophy must know this narrative. This book is directed not at upending that narrative but putting another narrative alongside it to create a space of thought rather than a mode of thought. When we think of a literature as coextensive with a particular narrative, we end up with a narrowing of thought in the service of that narrative. But it is possible to have components of a literature that do not easily fit into one narrative.

A literature also resembles an archive in some ways, although we might still see differences here as well. A great deal of work has been done on the archive, by Derrida, Foucault, and many others. Archives are narratives, and they have authoritative power. They are constituted by specific interests—state archives determine what is to be kept by what official and unofficial narratives a state wants to support. They may support multiple paths through them, but at least with classic archives there is an authoritative sense to them. Derrida traces the archive etymologically back through the Greek word "arkhe," which refers to both commencement and commandment (1995: 1–5). The archive determines what can be said. It governs and structures memory and enables political and social power to exert itself. The place of the archive is the place of the archons or those who command based on the archive.

A literature differs from an archive in this sense. It is less formal and more open to discussion. It is like a canon, although a canon might be seen as a subset of a literature, something that identifies the events of the literature (or in some cases, the summation of the events, as in retrospective pieces that collect and interpret events). There is a legislative aspect to it, but it is also determined by use and not just by an archon. It structures memory, but the boundaries are potentially more porous. Where the archive tends toward a mode of thought, the literature tends toward a space of thought.

A literature, then, bears similarities to several things—narrative, archive, canon—but also differs from these things. There is one more element that needs to be noted—there can be minor literatures. Deleuze and Guattari (1986) spell this out most clearly in their work on Kafka. A minor literature is not a literature in a minor (i.e., nondominant) language. It is a literature in a dominant language that actualizes potentialities in that language that break it free from its despotic structure, that is, from its tendency to operationalize language in the service of power for a state structure. Minor literature has several characteristics. First, it is a deterritorialization of the space of functioning of a major language. Second, in minor literatures everything is political. Third, everything takes on a collective value. "Literature is the people's concern" (16–18).

It is within the potentiality of a literature, then, to have a minor literature, whether or not an archon might want this to be the case, or whether or not there is a narrative that has authority. Whereas a literature has the tendency to organize and assemble its metaphorical and narrative universe, a minor literature finds the potentialities that the literature affords but does not explore. One might, as someone like Paulin Hountondji seems to want to do, use a literature to constrain activity in a field to "discipline" African philosophy into a particular kind of dialectical form. Other literatures might afford philosophy but are not themselves philosophy. Philosophy's formal requirements result in specific kinds of discourse and dialogue, in particular a representational discourse in which propositions are foregrounded, questions are seen as moments to a well-defined and well-defended proposition, and individuals own these propositions as properties of themselves.

Minor literatures have used these elements in many cultures to construct a different kind of philosophical discourse. In this chapter, we will see Sophie Olúwọlé and Euphrase Kezilahabi work out what it means for philosophy to be based on a literature. Both find that a literature opens up the creativity of African culture.

Sophie Olúwọlé and the Search for a Literature of Philosophy

Sophie Olúwọlé, in "The Africanness of a Philosophy," enters into what was the rite of passage for African philosophers in times past—she wrote on the question of the nature and existence of African philosophy. Unlike many others, though, she does not look at it as an object with a set of properties. Her concern is to answer Paulin Hountondji (1996) and others who defined the terms of the question in the wake of the ethnophilosophy of philosophers such as Tempels and Kagame. If not ethnophilosophy, then what, they asked?

The answers during this period (and this is my reconstruction of the debate) typically started from the assumption that an adequate answer had to have two characteristics—it had to identify a property in some philosophical belief or methodology that was both truly African and truly philosophical. Ethnophilosophy failed on the second of these, although it might pass on the first (the jury is out on that—Tempels's version of ethnophilosophy was mediated through his Catholic theology, but we can imagine a version of traditional African knowledge production that was not mediated in that manner). What we came to call "universalism" tended to see philosophical method as the same everywhere, and the "African" part of "African philosophy" was a unique contribution to a conversation stretching back into prehistory. There was, of course, acknowledgment that colonialism and other brutalities had affected the ability of Africans to be heard in this conversation, or even to formulate their own thoughts that were not just attempts to move past the corrosive and distracting features of colonialism, but the goal ultimately was to engage in the same activity that everyone else in the world called philosophy. Particularists, on the other hand, did not see philosophy as a methodologically universal activity, even if there were family resemblances between the production of concepts in different places around the world. The corrosive and debilitating effects of colonialism were still present, of course, but the effect was not just to muffle Africans' voices in the perennial conversation but to destroy and distort unique thought systems. Despite this onslaught, though, these systems were preserved in a wide variety of ways, and so the goal was to recover, archive, and celebrate these uniquely African ways of knowing. The universal conversation did not matter, or at least did not come first; African knowledge was for Africans and needed to be recovered to reconstitute African forms of life.

What is interesting about Olúwọlé's article is that it does not neatly fall into this pattern. She does not choose a side, at least not as defined in these terms. Instead, she reasks the question. She surveys existing attempts at the time the essay was written, an exercise that might be seen as positioning her own eventual answer to the question in terms of the failures of answers that came before. What seems closer to the text, though, is that she is repositioning a new question against the questions asked by the previous writers. This is evident in that she starts by asking about a literary tradition, which is not an obvious starting point for a philosopher to take. She is not asking whether there are discursive texts of the sort we see in other traditions, or if there is a textual tradition of dialogue, disputation, and argumentation. She is also not asking about the concepts within the literature, which is where most of her predecessors focus their attention.

It is important to recognize the kinds of questions Olúwọlé is identifying with other writers. She is not interested in asking a question that depends on "definitions couched in a metalanguage" (1989: 102). Since there is no culturally neutral place from which to engage in such a process (and hence no universal answer to the question), the only other option is a particularist one—"allow each culture to present what it understands and practices as philosophy." This seems like it might then move toward something like generalization (if not universality) through cross-cultural dialogue. But that has not happened, mainly because of the rootedness of people within their own spaces and cultures. The students of cultures we have seen are "missionaries, traders, and colonial government functionaries" (102–3), hardly a reliable group for real dialogue.

Her goal here seems to be to ask about what makes a piece of African literature truly African. One must understand her use of the term "literature" to mean not just fiction or poetry but any writing. Rooting the question of the Africanness of philosophy in the Africanness of literature is a new way of asking the question about the nature of African philosophy. It is not obvious that African philosophy should be dependent on the literature that communicates it. In Africa particularly, where oral discourse has a prominent place, the texts in which it is contained seem more complex, more varied, and less determinative of philosophy than, say, a highly constrained and codified form of writing such as a medieval European monastic disputation, a treatise from Enlightenment Europe, or even a modern analytic philosophy monograph. As we shall see shortly, a text is not the same as a literature, though, and Olúwọlé clearly means something more in her use of "literature" than a specific formation of textuality.

Her survey of writers who have tried to define how philosophy might be African does not focus on the question of a literature in most cases. Placide Tempels, on her account, works out a metaphysic that lies unrecognized behind social norms and principles (103). Alexis Kagame locates Africanity in "the language rather than the social life of the Bantu" (104). Leopold Sedar Senghor locates the Africanity of a philosophy in its mode of understanding, the African being "sensibility" and the West having "rationality" (104). J. O. Sodipo summarizes five variants of Négritude, she says, and argues that their main message is that Africanness lies in the "mystical or magical nature of its metaphysics and the participative characteristics of its epistemology." The error of all these approaches comes from a poor understanding of the goal of Western philosophy. Sodipo thinks that it is "the religious goal of African philosophy that demands the use of emotionally coated terms as units of analysis. The aim of African philosophy is to give emotional or aesthetic satisfaction. This is why its philosophy cannot coincide with that of the West which aims at scientific objectivity" (105). Paulin Hountondji makes an argument from geography—what makes African philosophy African is the origin of the author. And finally, P. O. Bodunrin disagrees with Hountondji, arguing that (following Kwasi Wiredu) "for a set of ideas to be a genuine possession of a people, they need not have originated them, they need only appropriate them, make use of them and if the spirit so moves them, thrive on them" (106).

In all these cases, Olúwọlé depicts those searching for a uniquely African character to African philosophy as asking about a property, either of the philosophy itself or of the context of the production of the philosophy or the vehicle of its dissemination. As she summarizes:

> Our search is for some canons of reference which distinguish African philosophy from philosophies from other parts of the world. Candidates so far proposed include,
>
> 1. some metaphysical or epistemological features common to all African philosophies;

2. the geographical origin of an author as well as the audience for which his work is created;
3. the appropriation and dependence on a set of ideas (which originated in or were borrowed from Africa); and, finally,
4. the goal of each philosophy classifiable as African. (106)

She says "our search," but in fact the list she produces here is the search of the authors she has discussed. Her goal over the next few pages is to show the limitations of each of these strategies for ensuring the Africanity of African philosophy. Even though these have not proven to be adequate guarantees of Africanity in the hands of these authors, she is not ready to simply abandon them entirely. She does want to find something common to African philosophies. Geography does matter, as do ideas. The goal of philosophy also matters, although she demurs on Hountondji and Sodipo's insistence that that goal be something like scientific objectivity.

So, her search employs elements of these answers, but it asks a different question. We will not find a unified sense of Africanity by identifying a single element or even a group of them.

> The Africanness of a philosophy must therefore transcend those features that define the specificity of various theories of metaphysics or epistemology. Particular philosophies may be influenced by the traditional goal of African literary endeavours. But just as rationalism, empiricism, etc., do not define the goal of Western philosophy in general, no single metaphysical or epistemological position defines the goal of African philosophy. (109)

Her new question is a different one:

> I am proposing that we go back to studying African traditional thoughts which bear on problems of human existence. The purpose is not just an exercise in the documentation of different ideas and beliefs native to Africa. The aim is to unveil an existing literary tradition as an objective which is common to every rational endeavor of African thinkers. This is the only way in which we can come up with a cogent analysis of a tradition that genuinely constitutes an African literary goal. (111)

Olúwọlé keeps coming back to a search for a "literary tradition" in which African philosophy exists. For her, this is the space of thought that will undergird any claim to uniqueness or identity. What does she mean by this literary tradition? And what might it mean, even beyond her uses of the term? She talks about African and Western literary traditions of thought (113) and hopes to find a feature of an African literary tradition that can bind it together and form the basis for the claim of African philosophy to be a unique area of philosophical thought. She argues that Bodunrin and others deny such a tradition exists.

But she does not stop with the literary tradition. She argues that searching for African philosophy in literary pieces is not adequate—what is needed is "the characterization of an African scheme of thought in general" (114). In other words, African philosophy has relied on a particularly literary form that has been called "African philosophy," and we have mistaken the space of thought for a particular mode of thought, that is, a particular rhetorical form. She wants a "total revolution in the basic orientation of efforts to define adequately what constitutes the Africanness of a specific group of philosophies." In other words, she wants to ask a different question about Africanity, one that relies on a literary tradition. She frames this new question in a manner different from that which has been seen in any of the authors she discussed to this point:

> Our task is to state what African thinkers traditionally wish to accomplish through thought.
>
> The general answer is that man as a thinker everywhere in the world seeks an understanding of nature and the events of experience. This does not necessarily imply that every group of people in the world must identify the same goal. In other words, while one particular group may wish to understand nature as it physically functions, another may seek an understanding of how such natural functions and human actions relate to and affect human existence. (116)

Asking "what African thinkers traditionally wish to accomplish" is to ask about a creative strategy, a space of thought that can accomplish new things. This is the right question, but her answer raises more questions. She says that all thinkers everywhere "seek an understanding of nature and the events of experience." Is understanding the goal of philosophy? Is this not the goal of other forms of thought? She goes on to say that the "African literary goal [is] that of humanism" (117), specifically African humanism.

> African humanism, as Wiredu himself puts it, is not just an endeavor, but a literary orientation to improve the conditions of man. He notes that intuition and emotion play prominent roles here. This is for him largely responsible for the African unanalytic and unscientific attitude of mind. His recommendation is that our children be initiated earlier in life into the discipline of formal logic and into the methodology of rational thought—to create minds capable of logical analysis and fully aware of the nature and value of exact measurement. (117)

Wiredu's point is to move toward an explanatory mode, as Olúwọlé depicts him. Logic and reasoning are what will get Africans to that goal. But Olúwọlé does not want to completely go down that path, because she thinks that there is more to life than the explanation of natural events. African humanism, of the kind that Wiredu wants, must have more going for it than explanatory mechanisms. "Mathematics does not postulate the effects of human sensations and emotions as determinants of human existence. Scientific analysis does not feed emotions into its computer" (117). What she looks for is something quite different from this mechanistic vision.

> The Africanness of a philosophy lies in the fact that traditional African thoughts generally appear as various forms of wisdom in which different aspects of human experience are synthesized into *formulae* meant to guide human conduct, and these must be sentiment conscious. (118; original emphasis)

Olúwọlé gives us a common sense of African philosophy, which is that wisdom is involved and that this wisdom "guides human conduct." What does she mean by "sentiment conscious?" Presumably that the formulae must be aware of the nature of their application, that is, that they take emotion and the realities of an African lifeworld into account. I take sentiment to be more than just emotion, but to also include affect, that is, ways of facing the world, as well as what we might think of as sympathy and empathy, that is, feeling with, not just feeling about (about this, more in a moment). She is, in other words, not just describing a philosophy that deals with the way that African society is but the ways in which it could be, the ways in which it faces complex reality both individually and collectively and makes something recognizably African as a response. It is a creative endeavor, not just an analytic one.

A literary tradition of thought must precede a philosophical one. She identifies it as humanism, but by that we must not think of anything like Renaissance humanism. Instead, we have something closer to the ahumanism we saw in Sylvia Wynter's recovery of the humanist project. For Olúwọlé, this undergirds any kind of philosophy, African or otherwise. Her argument for a literary tradition is in direct contrast to Hountondji's statement that philosophy must be based on science.

> Humanism identifies the goal which such a group wishes to attain through thought. It sets their patterns and defines their style, methodology, and terms of expression. It is objective, rational, and positive but not purely descriptive. It is neither fictitious, mysterious, nor necessarily religious. It is a legitimate choice of a literary mission. It forges a specific literary tradition which does not

coincide with the scientific option. But contrary to many critics, it is neither inferior nor primitive, nor unique to Africans alone. Indeed, many would see it as the apex of human thought, the inevitable end of rational endeavors to understand man and nature as they relate to each other. This is what Senghor and others identify as a participative and sympathetic mode of thought. I call it synthetic and interpretative. (119–20)

Her portrayal of a literature is worth attending to more carefully. A literature that is adequate to an African philosophy is not necessarily defined by its formal structure. In other words, it need not be dialectical or argumentative in the classical Western tradition (although it is worth noting that even the "Western" tradition, whatever we think that encompasses, does not entirely consist in that formal structure either). The alternative to this formal structure is not necessarily religious or folk-cultural writing. In other words, we do not see the contrast that many make within something like Négritude between rational Western discourse and emotional African. The literature she has in mind is "objective, rational and positive but not purely descriptive."

But she does mention emotion, or at least, feeling:

A humanistic goal of thought is sensitive to human feeling not because it proceeds from a mind-set unique to Africans. As noted above, it once briefly existed as the style of the Greeks. Its Africanness lies solely in the fact that it was distinctively the vogue that predominated the literary endeavors of Africans as it never did in the history of Western thought. It is this common goal rather than the communalism of beliefs or the identity of ideas in all literary pieces from Africa that makes them particularly African. Literary works as oral traditions, proverbs, folklore and other tales all bear its trade marks, even though these do not express identical beliefs about every aspect of human life and experience. (120)

Often, "feeling" is understood along the lines of Négritude's approach to emotion, as a contrast to Western discursive rationality. But it is not clear that Olúwọlé should be read in these terms. Her feeling is more like "feeling about" and "feeling with" rather than the metaphysical faculty of feeling that is opposed to reason. Something closer to "affect" seems more appropriate, or perhaps "intuition." It is not that there is a nonrational element that typifies African approaches to thinking but that there is a way of interpreting the world that requires facing it in a particular manner. It is a "mind-set unique to Africans," but it once also existed among the Greeks, she says.

One reason for thinking that feeling is closer to "feeling about" is the way she describes the geographical implications. She agrees with Hountondji that there are geographical implications in determining the nature of African philosophy but disagrees that there is a clear dividing line between those born in Africa and those who are not. "But contrary to his conclusion, this does not mean that Africa must be the origin of all authors who write within that cultural style. Rather it stresses the convention of classifying philosophies according to the cultural regions within which specific literary traditions of philosophies occur" (120–1). In other words, literary traditions function not as demarcations on what is within the bounds of African philosophy and what is not, but rather as something that grows from a culture, can travel and move, can be held by those not actually from a particular place, and as such is an attitude or affect about the world that enables the philosopher to understand in a particular way.

This will no doubt be inadequate for someone like Paulin Hountondji, who wants something objectively useful in drawing a line. Olúwọlé is uninterested in that project. Her goal is rather to explicate a lifeworld in which thinking can occur. She is interested in a space of thought, not a mode of thought.

She returns at the end of her essay to humanism, which as I have said echoes elements of Wynter's version of ahumanism. Her concern is to examine thought in a place, among a people. She calls this "interpretation," but it is not clear that she is referring to anything hermeneutic, at least not primarily. One of her major targets in this paper is Hountondji, and so she is concerned to show that African philosophy does not have to be based on a scientific literature. But interpretation does not have to be understood as "anti-science," or "pro-ethnophilosophy," or anything like that. The door that Olúwọlé opens is one to a place-based philosophy, which takes seriously forms of experience, thinking, and conceptual creation that take place in cultures. A literature is not, in other words, a precondition for calling something a philosophy but the foundation for creating new concepts adequate to experience rooted in a place.

Euphrase Kezilahabi and the Philosophical Function of Literature

Euphrase Kezilahabi was best known as a Swahili novelist and poet, but he also made a case for rethinking the connection between African philosophy and literature (Kezilahabi 1985; see also Lanfranchi 2012). His focus in his unpublished dissertation was on providing a philosophical account of literature, which is adequate to an African context. He argued that existing ways of critiquing African literature were limited by the fact that they rely on Western modes of reading, which necessarily diminish and misunderstand African literature.

On the face of it, Kezilahabi's project seems quite different from Olúwọlé's, from the point of view of African philosophy. Whereas Olúwọlé is trying to explicate the space in which African philosophy might operate, Kezilahabi seems to be searching for a philosophical theory adequate to account for, and able to support a reading of, African literature. Whereas for Olúwọlé African philosophy must have a literature, for Kezilahabi African literature must have a philosophy.

I think, though, that these two projects are not as dissimilar as it might seem. Neither is really trying to explain or account for either philosophy or literature. Neither is involved in a project of demarcation, that is, an attempt to give criteria to distinguish African philosophy or literature from non-African. Rather than reading Kezilahabi as just searching for a theory of literature, we might read him as outlining the philosophical function of literature. And in that way, we can see him much closer to Olúwọlé's project.

The place to start in this dissertation, for our purposes, is the second half. The first half consists of a review of elements of African philosophy, culminating with a theory of time. By chapter 4, Kezilahabi is ready to make a fundamental distinction in readers of African literature, between "techno-critics" and "onto-critics" (1985: 190–233). Since this is such a central distinction, and since the dissertation is not published and only available in dissertation archives, it is worth quoting him at some length:

> We have therefore to distinguish two groups of critics or analysts of African culture and literature: a techno-critic and an onto-critic. The external critic of African culture and literature is here called a techno-critic and the internal critic an onto-critic. The words techne and ontos being Greek words, the former meaning "art" and the latter "being." The need for the distinction arises due to the basic differences between understanding and knowing. Briefly we may define understanding as the ability to project oneself upon a possibility by way of the present without an intermediary, and knowing as the ability to be acquainted with ideas, facts and concepts through actual experience or given data.
>
> A techno-critic seeks to know what the onto-critic understands. He is occupied with African literature. The onto-critic does not simply take African literature as

an occupation, he lives it and participates in its creation. His duty is to uncover, create and project. A techno-critic is engaged in the technology of reading in which he is a passive reader and a consumer and is hardly an ontological creator of the work he is reading or analyzing. By the manipulation of mechanistic terminologies, theories, paradigms and other passive modalities the techno-critic engages himself in putting together pieces of information and data and thereby generate new theories or expand previous ones. The techno-critic has had a tendency to look for the "beautiful" in art and literature and thereby reducing them to objects of aesthetic appreciation. There has also been a tendency to have theory interrogate data whereas it is data that should interrogate theory. There is a lot hidden in theory. Generally, a techno-critic may be called a mythological interpreter or critic that claims to reach the depth of every articulated word or behavior through techne-.

An onto-critic extends the domain of understanding beyond objectification and identifies language with Being. The onto-critic is engaged in the liberation of words from conventions, and seeks to displace and decenter logocentrism and signification by making relations empty of meaning and by dismantling the resemblance of language to the world. Because the economic and political situations in Africa are fundamental to our future destiny, the onto-critic has to retain the idea of literature as a form of consciousness. The ontocritic therefore rejects theories of uniqueness to literature and the reduction of it to a moral endeavor. To an onto-critic, therefore, literature is not a reorganization of impulses but an ontological understanding that is projective. It is the way we stand to the technologization of the Word and the way we stand to language and thinking that ultimately determine the difference between a technocritic and an onto-critic. (216–18)

It might be tempting to read Kezilahabi's distinction as one between the emic and the etic, that is, the anthropological distinction between interpretation from the inside and the outside. This temptation is all the stronger because Kezilahabi refers to these as two different kinds of critics. If, though, we think of these as people who have a place in building a literature, then the distinction includes not only critics of works already produced but those producing the works. Kezilahabi here is referring to different kinds of functions in creating a literature, and in opening the door for new works. It is an epistemological distinction—the technocritic knows, whereas the ontocritic understands—and this is also a moral distinction, in that knowing is inferior to understanding. His distinction is clearly also a political one—ontocritics are truer to African culture and far preferable but have been supplanted by technocritics, as colonialism has turned African critics into evolués.

Kezilahabi's distinction, while somewhat reductionist, gets at a real issue, which is the question of how a literature is created and what kind of narrative should be constructed. The problem with technocritics is that they often resort to mediocre structuralist analysis and stylistic analysis (218). It is a form of knowing that does not have the full resources available that understanding does, and so it can at best approximate a representation of a literature. It is a kind of analysis that asks about the beautiful in art and literature, a move that reduces the creative moment to an object of aesthetic appreciation and nothing more (217).

The real violence done by technocriticism is that it reduces African life to "paradigms or models of knowledge and the rhetoric of images and tropes" and this is a misrepresentation (220). The technocritical, Kezilahabi argues, treats African life like a dataset, which can be held as personal property of a researcher and which authorizes a narrative about Africans that is universalized. Actual Africans are marginalized and the "knowledge" about them takes center stage.

Kezilahabi envisions instead an understanding of Africa based on the "language of Being" (221). An African literature will not be a database but "an event lived." "The African onto-critic will not be a slave to structures and lose sight of the fundamental social fact that he is still 'colonized'" (222).

Kezilahabi's analysis is insightful, even if his binary analysis seems reductive. He is, in my terms, arguing for a philosophy-in-place, an attention to the vitality and virtuality of life as it is lived by Africans in their places. Representations of African life, whether they come in quasi-scientific form or as what he calls technocriticism, are at best approximations and at worst diversions from thinking about African life as such.

Leveraging Heidegger as a philosophical lens for this project has its benefits but also its limitations. There is always the question of how we understand authenticity, which is a concept Kezilahabi does not explicitly use but which is implied by his analysis and is important as well for Heidegger. Does authenticity take on a new regulative power? Once colonial influences on analysis are removed, whether brought by colonialists or through the misguided analysis of evolués, is what is left authentic African existence? What are the politics of creating this narrative? Is there one form of life, the remainder left over after knowledge has ceded its central place in favor of understanding, and if there is not one form of life, how do the lines of power work when creating the narrative of this literature?

Kezilahabi's desire is to open African literature up, so that it brings out "something new that projects possibilities and potentialities" (222). Some of what he looks for is simply creativity within literature itself. He is looking for "projective metaphors," ones that are not exhausted by a fixed meaning, but which yield new senses and new insights. Okot p'Bitek's pumpkin from *Song of Lawino* (1984) is an example for him of a metaphor grounded in African temporality and open to new senses. It "stretches from an unspecified past to an infinite future" and "cannot be reduced to knowledge for it is the ontological aspects of it that are being high-lighted" (Kezilahabi 1985: 223).

Kezilahabi analyzes the creative space of African writing as "Quassia" (or "Q"; 236–61). This is a "generic name given by Linnaeus to a tree of Surinam in honour of the Negro Quassi or Coissi who employed the intensely bitter bark of the tree (Quassia amara) as a remedy for fever" (Kezilahabi 1985: 238; from *Encyclopedia Britannica* 11th ed.). Kezilahabi is not only interested in this trope because of the reference to an African in its name (he suspects that it might have been a West African, and the name was actually "Kwasi") but because the bark from this tree has "'hallucinatory' potency and recuperatory powers which lead to a disposition to courage we have used the word to designate essence (African). Quassia is the center of orientation, and through it African writers hope to regenerate the present generation" (238).

Quassia gives rise, both medically and culturally, to the "tonicum," a term Kezilahabi uses to designate "a physical, moral and psychological experience which is undergone by an individual or social group. The individual or social group yields and surrenders to the call of Being and Becoming, and undergoes an experience with the silent language of the cosmos" (238, 237). This is more than just a purgation or purification—it is a recuperative tonic that "gives new meaning to life and Being" (237).

Kezilahabi divides Quassia into types, which he labels as Q1 and Q2. The first is "one in which an existential rapture, possession and excitement of a moment in depth merges us in the world so that we become one with it as a 'nobody.' The leap to primordial reality is made while we are in this state." Q2 is "one in which life affirms itself through a correct understanding of the human condition. This type of Q manifests itself in traditional rituals and class consciousness" (239). Q1 is further subdivided into Q1a and Q1b. The first subdivision is a long-range rhythm—seasonal, monthly, and daily activity. The second is a short-range rhythm, found in momentary experience such as dance, music, and other celebration.

Q1a's rhythms are much longer, of course, and so rarely experienced as rapture, but the farmer's experience of waiting for rain "is enjoyment of the highest kind because it touches the innermost nexus of his existence. Again between planting season and harvest, the farmer is in 'constant excitement' as he watches his plants grow" (240). Farmers and others who respond to this rhythm are responding to the tune of the cosmos. Kezilahabi sees them as intuitively reading the signs of nature. "Nature ceases to be an instrument of business or a victim of exploitation for egocentric man. In Q1a the basic phenomena of understanding are *listening* and *intuition*" (241; original emphases).

Q1b is evident in "African dance, music, possession and in any kind of celebration. This short-range rhythm is the one that is most apparent and is usually regarded as an 'African way of life' by tourists" (241). Kezilahabi saw this rhythm as having been "vulgarized" by Négritude poetry in that it purported to use Q1b rhythm as a qualitative differentiator between Africans and others. In fact, this rhythm is closely connected with the "phenomenon of passage" as the self makes a journey to primordial reality. A performer will use his whole body in dance, or everything he has in other kinds of performance, to answer the call of Being. "As he responds to this call he leaps to a world unadulterated by rational thinking. In his temporary amalgamation with the world he is *free* and *loyal to none other than his own self*" (242; original emphases). Q1b is more than a performance, though—it is a shared experience, between performers and audiences, rooted in culture and taking the form of "phenomena of passage."

Q2 is a more generalized rhythm. It is

> that in which life affirms itself through a correct understanding of the human condition. Through it the self keeps on defining itself, and is constantly in search for its ownmost Being. It has already been argued that man's substance in African culture is not a synthesis of body and soul but rather existence itself. In African culture "to live is to be known" and a person ceases to exist if there are no people to name their children after him. (242)

This understanding happens in rituals and rites of passage. These rites are "existential realities of Being and Becoming in which man responds and yields himself to the call of Being and society rallies behind the neophytes in a gathering of the fourfold world into 'the simple onefold of their intimate belonging together'" (243–4). This Heideggerian language is deliberate—Kezilahabi's sense of Being owes much to Heidegger, although as we will see, he does not entirely follow his hermeneutic ontology.

The rituals and rites of passage in Q2 are connected to both Q1a and Q1b. Both the longer rhythms of communal life and the event-based rhythms in songs and dances prepare one for the passages of Q2. All Quassia are one, in the end. African literature, whether oral or written, exhibits these rhythms and must be understood in these terms, Kezilahabi argues. These artistic forms are not just imitations of nature but rather "a listening to the pains of life and a gathering of the fourfold world as man endures, suffers and undergoes an experience with the silent language of the cosmos" (244).

Quassia then is a principle of both purgation and creation. Kezilahabi uses it to give an account of African literature that does not rely on Western literary critical or analytic language, or for that matter anthropology or other modes of accounting for African intellectual life. He is less interested in explanations of African life than he is in identifying the patterns and rhythms of creation, the spaces that allow people to leverage their individual and collective pasts to encounter an uncertain future. Literature has an "existential imperative" (247), which means that its significance is not in its meaning, but in what it makes possible as a space of action and of thought.

Kezilahabi spends a significant amount of time applying Quassia to specific works of African literature. In each case, he shows how the narrative and metaphorical structure is a tonicum, a purgation and creation in which characters find their way through their challenges by attending to the rhythms and the rites and are able to create themselves and their communities. These are images of creation but not representations of it, that is, they are not meant as moral guidebooks to life in Africa. There are no principles of action here, abstract values meant to be applied to specific situations.

Kezilahabi's focus is on Being. And yet, his description of the various forms of Q are of emergence—something closer to Becoming. He resists forms of totalization that might be read into African existence, either determinism or what he calls the "spiral of rites of passage" (279), which is a kind of predictable progress through life animated by forms of repetition with difference.

He spends most of his time, though, on a third form of totalization. Following Joseph Fell, he names this the "spiral of anyone" (1979: 332–59; Kezilahabi 1985: 280). This is

> the spiral in which the African telos is caught up in the existential realities of Western man. This is the spiral of materialistic and technological advances of Western man in the search of delusive "progress" within the context of linear historical time. It is a race in which the African has been imperceptibly incorporated through historical circumstances and now finds it difficult to get out of. (Kezilahabi 1985: 282)

Kezilahabi's version of Fell's diagram is meant to leverage the latter's account of Sartre's depiction of the tension in which the intentional self moves between

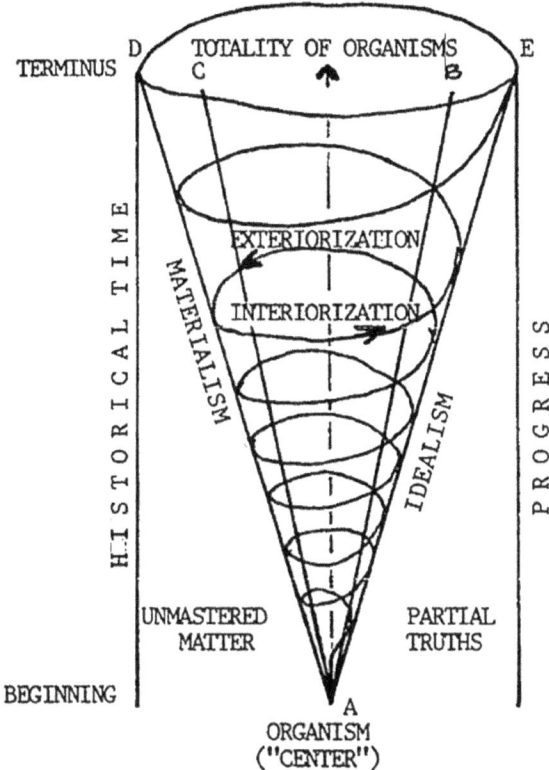

Figure 6.1 Euphrase Kezilahabi's altered "The Spiral of 'Anyone'" diagram from Joseph P. Fell's *Heidegger and Sartre: An Essay on Being and Place*. Image from E. Kezilahabi (1985: 281).

interiority and exteriority. It is a spiral that, in Fell's translation from the first book of *The Family Idiot*, is the creation of the person:

> This ceaselessly detotalized and retotalizing totalization is *personalization*. The *person*, in fact, is neither altogether undergone nor altogether constructed. Moreover he *is not* at all or, to put it differently, he is at each instant only the *surpassed* result of the ensemble of totalizing processes by which we continually try to assimilate the unassimilable. (Sartre, in Fell 1979: 347–8; original emphasis)

Fell observes that

> my diagram, "The Spiral of 'Anyone'" attempts at one and the same time (a) to picture the spiral as Sartre explicitly describes it; (b) to elaborate imaginatively upon what Sartre explicitly says about it; (c) to treat it in its ideal or truly

progressive form. Going beyond Sartre's own indications, it depicts the spiral as progressively *expanding*, in order to convey the sense of totalizing that at the same time progressively masters more of the material context and progressively incorporates and reconciles more partial truths, up to the ideal point, at the top, where the truth is "one" and is embodied in and reflected by a unified and mastered material environment, which supports it. (349)

The point here is less about Fell's interpretation of Sartre (it seems more Hegelian than later interpreters might be comfortable with, for one thing) and more about what Kezilahabi sees in this account. Kezilahabi adds to Fell's diagram by inserting more vertical projections through the spiral. Whereas Fell has one vertical line through the middle of the diagram, indicating an overall direction of movement toward the totality of organisms, along with lines along the left (materialism) and right (idealism) indicating the range of motion of intentional action by the emerging person, Kezilahabi has two more lines in his version of the diagram, one on the left of the center line labeled AC and one on the right labeled AB.

The spiral, for Kezilahabi, is Quassia. The additional off-center lines indicate misunderstandings of Quassia. Négritudinists, for instance, follow the "AB" line, because their attempt to recover African being ended up being close to reductive idealism (Kezilahabi 1985: 282–3). Ngugi wa Thiong'o's *Petals of Blood* (wa Thiong'o 2018) and Ousmane Sembene's *Les Bouts de bois de Dieu* (Sembene 1971) follow the AC line, that is, they hew toward a materialist account. Some writers contribute on both sides of the spiral. These should not entirely be seen as mistaken or failed literary attempts at Q though—the point of a spiral is that there will always be a dialectical move, privileging one side or the other, as Q is worked out in the world. But to ignore that Q is the organizing center to the spiral means that

> Africans will cease to exist as a distinct people for the Q will be taken over and will be replaced by the essence of the then dominant culture, for hegemony saturates the consciousness of the people under its sway and even constitutes the substance of that society. Left without a center, the transmuted Q would be in danger of disintegration. (284)

Kezilahabi's account, if read superficially, can look like another metaphysic of African existence. What is important to recognize is the enactivist sensibility of Q and of his appropriation of Sartre's/Fell's spiral. The point is to see in literature the accounts of those who have successfully or unsuccessfully walked the path of

Q, not for the purpose of producing generalizable insight on authentic African existence but to see models of creative living.

Those who have analyzed Kezilahabi's approach to philosophy within literature have had difficulty drawing out a distinct set of positions (Coughlin 2016: 202; Lanfranchi 2012: 74). To some extent, this difficulty might be less about Kezilahabi and more about the expectation of what a philosophy ought to look like or accomplish. If the assumption is that a philosophy represents some aspect of cultural life, as is often the case when it comes to African philosophy, then it is true that Kezilahabi is an ambiguous philosopher. Superficially, it looks like he proposes a metaphysical account of the true African spirit, which he speaks of as Quassia, and discusses the ways in which most work fails to realize that authenticity because of external influences. And yet, as one looks at how he handles his literary critique of specific writers, it seems less that he is assuming an elusive metaphysical ideal and more that he is constructing a literature that can serve as the basis and model for action in an uncertain future.

We can see this if we return to the early chapters of Kezilahabi's dissertation. The work seems to split into two halves that are quite different from each other. In the first half, he offers a critique of African philosophy as it was done at the writing of the thesis and argues for a theory of time. The second half, as we have seen, is his development of Quassia and its application to literary texts. The first half sets up the second, in the sense that it forestalls the metaphysical or essentialist interpretations of African philosophy and also in the sense that it introduces time to the discussion.

We have already seen in the earlier chapter on Mbiti that Kezilahabi outlines a range of approaches to time. This range tends to underscore the argument in that chapter, which was that Mbiti is not arguing for a cultural philosophy of time but sketching out something more like a phenomenology of time, with elements of pragmatics and cognitive practice included in it. In other words, Mbiti (and Kezilahabi agrees with this) is not arguing for anything like a set of beliefs explicitly or implicitly held by Africans. The focus is on the kind of life that is possible when we realize that the future is uncertain and is created through the rhythms of life, but those rhythms do not guarantee any particular results since transversal elements can create new conditions of life. Quassia is the process of creating life through actions that are both precedented within the rhythms of life and unprecedented within the shifting space of action.

Kezilahabi does not link temporality and literature in the manner that we might see in Ricoeur, as narrative. The characters he analyzes in the work of others, and his own work, are not attempts to show the narrative choices that individuals make within a chaotic universe. Time here is more primordial, more about creative rhythms in which humans are caught up and created anew as much as they are agents.

The Aesthetics of a Literature and Philosophy

Olúwọlé proposes that African philosophy needs a literature; Kezilahabi suggests that literature is itself the enactment of a philosophy. A literature is not just an archive or a repository, nor is it the arbiter of the legitimacy of philosophy in Africa. A literature must be something else than this, or at least, it must be more than this.

When we think of a literature we often think of an archive, a record of what has been said and thought, or a corpus, the body of work for an individual. If philosophy is a grand conference, the literature is the proceedings. And yet, given what we have said to this point, that seems too limiting to describe a literature, and we can see those limits because African philosophy does not fit easily into this story. An archive of the sort that previous African philosophers looked for was oriented toward the past. Its motivating imperative (at least in the case of African philosophy) is to serve as an arbiter between authentic and inauthentic African philosophy. A corpus, too, strives for completeness within a domain, usually that of published works by an author, and the scholarly questions tend to be around fidelity to an originally published text. Where there are multiple editions or questions about what the author's intentions were, the problem is solved by simply including everything. This is why, for instance, a corpus of Walt Whitman's work would have to include all the various editions of *Leaves of Grass* that he edited and changed throughout his life.

A literature is not like that. A literature is meant to produce more literature, not simply as replication but as evolution and emergence. It is not simply a chronicle but a living space of creation and thought. A literature is something more than a foundation on which to build a philosophy. We can see how this works if we look at the example of how something like race works. Arun Saldanha clarifies this:

> Racism is what race leads to under certain conditions. When racism is established, the productive dimension of race is domesticated but not obliterated. The task of schizoanalysis is to retrieve the mobility, indeterminancy, subversion in race. Good literature is defined by its capacity to overcome the ubiquitous postcolonial obsessions with the past and *invent a people* that no existing group can claim,

a bastard people, inferior, dominated, always in becoming, always incomplete. *Bastard* no longer designates a familial state, but the process or drift of the races. I am a beast, a Negro of an inferior race for all eternity. This is the *becoming* of the writer. (Deleuze 1997: 4). (2013: 16; original emphases)

Race here is one central vector of creation and a possible outcome of its creation is racism. But it is not a true invention, it is not a literature. It is a capture of potentiality in the service of a desire for or belief in a particular kind of outcome. Racism inevitably narrows and curtails the creative potential of race, and so alongside all the other reasons for opposing it (the damage to individuals, the erasure of history, the inequitable power structures, and many others), it also undermines the central insights of enactivism, which are that the future is uncertain, we do not and cannot control it, we can just prepare ourselves to ask new questions and pursue the flourishing of life in new spaces. No literature is built through racism; we cannot "invent a people that no existing group can claim."

But this does not mean that a literature cannot be constructed that simulates this process. Under National Socialism in Germany in the 1930s, there was a literature (both in print and in film) that valorized the Volk, the peasant, and made the moral argument that German greatness was rooted in that soil. Neo-Nazi groups have a literature of a sort—music, symbolism, narrative, as well as actual writing. Are these not as much a literature as anything Olúwọlé or Kezilahabi would argue for? Have these not grounded philosophies, defined coherent groups, created a new people?

Of course, at some level they have created these, but it is worth noting that it is generally little more than an echo of a previously invented people. The rhetorical tropes, drivers of a literature, give evidence of this. Whereas concepts are invented for the use of bastard people to articulate their experience at the edges of the molar structures of politics and society, these concepts can run their course and be captured, commodified, and turned into memes by those who want to argue for the continuance of those molar structures. Terms such as "discrimination," "marginalization," "self-determination," and "justice" can be taken over and applied to whites or other dominant groups that are eager to position themselves as aggrieved minorities. Terms such as "identity politics" render all identities equal on a level, ahistorical field. It is a rhetoric that creates not a literature but a simulacrum of a literature. There is no vitality, no creativity in this literature since it does not come from the exploration of a new problematic or an inarticulable sense of becoming but exists as a defense of an existing molar structure.

A literature is the potentiality of a new problematic, and the moment of the actualization of that potentiality is the event. The event does not just reflect a people, it creates a people, and it creates individuals as well. A literature is the foundation of philosophy, but one need not be literally literate to inhabit a literature. Literatures have genres, but they also bend the borders of genres. As we have seen in Olúwọlé, philosophy needs a literature not for demarcation between its activities and those of others, but in order to have a space of vitality. And as we have seen in Kezilahabi, it is possible to misunderstand a literature, misuse it, try to essentialize it, and those activities inevitably forestall the creative and disruptive potentiality. The literature exists in its performance, in the event of acting within its space of thought.

We are, though, faced with a reality in the event of literature within Africa—the history of slavery, colonialism, and apartheid. These are fundamental disruptions to the creative existence of a literature. In the next chapter, we will see how Achille Mbembe helps to think through action within an exhausted and conflicted space of thought.

7

How Do We Speak of Our Place? Achille Mbembe's World

Writing of any sort is a challenge, writing the self calls into question the very act of writing itself. Are we characters in a story? Are we Nietzschean *ubermenschen*, writing our story in such a way that we could exercise our will and return to it over and over, and the writing would be the same? And, what happens when the story that is told about us is overwhelming, stretches back centuries, and places us as minor or inconsequential characters in our own story? What if that longstanding story does not confer agency but turns us into the reviled other in someone else's story, at worst drained of all humanity and at best a stock character in a fiction of someone else's telling? How does one self-write in those conditions? Does it, in fact, require opacity (Glissant 1997: 111–20) to protect the diversity of the kinds of stories and communities that have previously been marginalized, and if so, how is it possible to deal with the fact that self-writing for many has been suppressed and ignored for so long?

Achille Mbembe has been facing this question, in a variety of ways, for over two decades. While his engagement with life in Africa has been vast and varied, there are threads that run through them. One of these is a concern for the challenge of reconstituting or reinventing life in African space. We see this as a central concern in *On the Postcolony* (2001) and in essays such as "At the Edge of the World" (2000) "African Modes of Self-Writing" (2002) and many others, up to his most recent work. This chapter will use "African Modes of Self-Writing" as a programmatic statement of the challenges facing writing the self with the history and social reality that Africa presents. The problem will be analyzed as one of place, and Mbembe's response, evident in many writings but especially *Critique of Black Reason* (2017), is a way of understanding the world. This too is a question about place.

In what follows, I will take a detour that will hopefully clarify what Mbembe is trying to do in "African Modes of Self-Writing" and other subsequent work. The argument, in brief, will be as follows. Mbembe identifies three foundations that, I argue, are essentially ruptures in place. These are slavery, colonization, and apartheid. We can see in other related ruptures, such as torture and solitary confinement, other kinds of ruptures of place. I will analyze torture in particular as instructive for the kinds of place rupture that also exist in the areas he identifies. This will include some tentative responses to torture as a rupture of place.

Once we understand more about how that rupture works, we can move to other responses to it. Mbembe identifies some responses he regards as inadequate. These are Afro-radicalism and nativism. Both exist as attempts to respond to the ruptures in place, and both attempts are a form of self-writing. Mbembe rightly points out the inadequacies of both. There are other forms of response, which are also attempts to write place. These include variations on cosmopolitanism, such as Afro-politanism, and utopian or dystopian formulations, such as Afro-futurism and Afro-pessimism. While these might offer some reconstitution of place, they do not in themselves address the initial ruptures of place that we find in Mbembe's three areas and my addition of torture.

Mbembe points to a hopeful and creative writing of place, and that possibility will be explored in the final part of the chapter. At least one of his early respondents, Souleymane Bachir Diagne, picks up on this, and later writers (including Leonhard Praeg and Mbembe himself) develop this. I frame this version of place, following Mbembe in *Critique of Black Reason* (2017), as "The World," and in particular, using Rosi Braidotti and Praeg, follow up his claim that "there is only one world."

As we saw with Olúwọlé and Kezilahabi, the necessity of textuality raises the question of what a literature of philosophy might look like. That literature is a creative space, an event of thought that enables the vitality of philosophy in a place. Philosophy is enacted, that is, it is lived as it is thought, and it is written in formal dialectics as well as leaving its traces in the habits and rhythms of life. But this image of creation must not be understood benignly, as a march toward a flourishing life that has no barriers. This is true anywhere, but especially so in Africa, where the spaces of thought have so often been compromised or worse by forces from outside of the continent. Mbembe's "African Modes of Self-Writing" and other works take on this reality and point toward the creativity that remains in this exhausted space.

Place and Its Discontents

Achille Mbembe argues that Marxism and nationalism give rise to two narratives on African identity: nativism and Afro-radicalism (2002a: 240; 2002b: 629). These he calls "faked philosophies" because they are dogmas rather than methods of interrogation. They are both forms of historicism (Mbembe 2002a: 240). Both of these currents of thought rely on three historical "events"—slavery, colonialism, and apartheid. These might be events in the sense I mean, in that they establish a problematic. They set the terms of an inquiry. That problematic comes from what these three share, which is historical degradation:

> Finally, there is the idea of historical degradation: slavery, colonization, and apartheid are supposed to have plunged the African subject not only into humiliation, debasement, and nameless suffering but also into a zone of nonbeing and social death characterized by the denial of dignity, heavy psychic damage, and the torment of exile. These three fundamental elements of slavery, colonization, and apartheid are said to serve as a unifying center of Africans' desire to know themselves, to recapture their destiny (*sovereignty*), and to belong to themselves in the world (*autonomy*). (241–2; original emphases)

These share historical degradation but are not simply historical. They set the possibilities for sense-making long after their time and far from actual sites of violence.

So, the problematic is set based on these negations, and the desire to overcome them. Mbembe suggests that Africa might have followed the Jewish model of reflection on suffering, contingency, and finitude, but that would have meant using theology, literature, film, music, and other things. These things, he argues, have rarely been done, and the preferred route has been to opt for one of the two narratives.

Mbembe's goal is to show how the two narratives come out of similar, intersecting practices, which opens the way for "self-styling." His alternative is to reinterpret subjectivity as time (242).

The two narratives have several characteristics:

1. They have a mechanistic and reified vision of history.
2. This leads to the idea that Africa is not responsible in any way for the catastrophes that have happened there (243). Since the causes are external, this undermines the idea of free will, it tends to emphasize violence as a privileged avenue for self-determination, it fetishizes state power, it

disqualifies the model of liberal democracy as relevant, and it supports a populist and authoritarian dream of a mass society.
3. There is a desire to destroy tradition and invest primary significance in the working class.
4. There is a polemical relationship to the world, based on three rituals. The first contradicts Western definitions of Africa by pointing out bad faith and falsehoods. The second denounces what the West has done in Africa based on these definitions. The third suggests that once the West has been debunked, Africans can finally narrate their own fables.

All this, which seems to be an "apotheosis of voluntarism," actually displays a lack of philosophical depth and also a cult of victimization. Mbembe argues:

1. that such nationalist and Marxist narratives of the African self and the world have been superficial;
2. that as a consequence of this superficiality, the formulations of self-government and autonomy they engender are founded, at best, on a thin philosophical base; and
3. that their privileging of victimhood over subjecthood is derived, ultimately, from a distinctively nativist understanding of history—one of history as sorcery. (245)

"African Modes of Self-Writing" can be understood as a set of tensions and contradictions over how Africans can engage their own place. The ways that Mbembe regards as illegitimate, Afro-radicalism and nativism, are both ways to misunderstand (one's) place. Afro-radicalism misunderstands place by idealizing it, and nativism misunderstands place by treating it like an essence to which only some people have a right. It is worth noting that both of these concepts are multiples, containing within them variations. So, for instance, Afro-radicalism has the variants of Afro-centrism and Black consciousness, while nativism has "milder" versions like nationalism, as well as more extreme forms of racially based separation and entitlement. All these, to one extent or other, are implicated by an imagination of place that seeks to restore ownership and, by doing so, restore the ability to inscribe the self. The ways of restoring or creating place will differ, but they all depend on the connection between subjectivity and place.

The "three historical events" that these share as foundations, slavery, colonization, and apartheid, are themselves ruptures to place. Slavery consists of a person or people being taken from their place, colonization consists of a place being taken from a person or people, and apartheid consists of both of these being written into law and practice, that is, the alienation from place being normalized within a legal, political, and educational system, as it had already been within an economic system. It is worth noting that there are other variations of assault on the self, and invariably these can also be understood as an assault on the place of the self. So, for instance, incarceration in general and solitary confinement in particular are deliberate uses of place to punish and "correct." Torture, likewise, can also be understood as the deliberate compromising of a person's embodied place. It will be useful to think of all these as ruptures of place, and consider the version that is most immediate to the lived body, which is torture, in order to understand how that rupture works for all these.

Torture as the Exhaustion of Dwelling

Most discussions of torture start from issues such as:

- What are the moral reasons for the prohibition or toleration of torture? Is there a "ticking time-bomb" scenario that justifies torture?
- Is torture properly an action of a state, government, or political entity against individuals, as opposed to anyone against anyone?
- How should the victims of torture be treated?
- How might we identify the causes, perpetrators, at-risk groups, social correlates of torture?
- How do we define torture, that is, how do we distinguish it from other acts or effects, or distinguish literal from metaphorical uses?
- What is the status of testimony to instances of overt or covert torture?
- Is it even possible to represent torture, or is it a phenomenon beyond representation?
- How can we define international laws or standards of human rights so as to prohibit torture?

These questions focus for the most part on the ethical, political, and social questions around torture (see, for instance, Wiśnewski and Emerick 2009). Another set of questions might be tied to mental health and could be understood using models such as psychosocial, neurobiological, and economic ones (Gerrity, Keane, and Tuma 2001). Neither of these groups of questions, important as they are, address the lived experience of torture as it pertains to meaning or the resistance of meaning. Questioning experience in that register has often started from the existential threat to subjectivity and human dignity that torture brings about. Torture is an assault on the self, on the existential conditions for selfhood (see, for instance, Graessner et al. 2001). Elisabeth Weber moves past this existential account by following Derrida to think through how torture represents a fundamental rupture to the possibility of living together (Weber 2012; Derrida 2012). It is the "*achieved* destruction of compassion" and is a kind of self-betrayal since it forces "the victim to betray what could be called *rachamin*, compassion, for oneself" (Weber 2012: 252; original emphases). Yochai Ataria and Shaun Gallagher approach torture as a question of embodied experience (Ataria 2016; Ataria and Gallagher 2015).

If, as hermeneutical thinkers such as Heidegger, Edward Casey, Jeffrey Malpas, and others have argued, being human in the world is to dwell in it or in-habit it, I want to suggest that torture is an assault on and an exhaustion of dwelling and the ability to in-habit. It is an assault on the conditions of habitation in the world, as well as an assault on our bodily existence in the world and our ability to live together. Moreover, it raises the issue of whether there is a breaking point to in-habitation, whether it is ever possible to be physically present in the world but not of the world. If this approach has merit, it might suggest some ways of rehabilitating victims of torture in addition to existing forms of therapy.

It might be objected from the outset that I want to conflate torture with other assaults on the human person such as genocide, exile, the Holocaust, and so forth. I will argue that in all these cases torture in the sense that I will describe it here underlies those other conditions and separates all these things from other kinds of assault on the person that might happen within a state apparatus or moral structure. The point of torture, even state-sponsored torture, is to separate a person from their dwelling in the world, from their ability to dwell. Other kinds of crime occur within a meaningful order that allows dwelling to continue, and thus allows things such as retribution and rehabilitation to occur. Torture is, to use Agamben's phrase, a state of exception. I will not take up all the ethical issues that surround that concept here. My intention is to consider the state of exception in quite literal terms—as a state in which the self has been removed from its dwelling in the world.

It must be emphasized that this is no small claim. To dwell in the world has been seen as a fundamental condition of being human. Heidegger, Casey, Malpas, and many others are surely correct in identifying our place as our being-in-the-world, something central to our humanity (Casey 1993; Malpas 2006). We do not exist as Cartesian beings first, and then incidentally find ourselves in a place. We do not use place as if it were a tool, and it is not simply a set of spatial coordinates. We are emplaced, first as bodies in the world and then as actors in meaningful space. And, furthermore, for most phenomenologists, dwelling may be covered over, abstracted, or forgotten, but it is never completely severed. Even technologically advanced society, for Heidegger, suffused as it is by standing-reserve and the reduction of dwelling to instrumentality, still affords some memory of dwelling that we can access, and that enables sociality, meaning, and so forth. So, to regard torture as a severing of one's ability to dwell is to depict it as a fundamental and, perhaps, irrevocable assault on the human.

The starting point will be with some accounts of torture, which yield a striking amount of material for the discussion of place, or rather the systematic destruction of place for a person or for a people. Jean Améry's incisive *At the Mind's Limits: Contemplations by a Survivor on Auschwitz and Its Realities* (1980) provides the central phenomenological analysis, supplemented by the work of others. In torture the assault on the self succeeds because of a systematic assault on place, draining it of significance, connection, and points of reference. All that is left is the most abstract sense of place, that is, spatial location.

This radical de-platialization is not the same as Deleuze and Guattari's deterritorialization. There is no sense of being pushed or pulled in a direction, nothing new to afford a reconstruction of the self. It is not heterotopic in Foucault's sense, for it is neither a heterotopia of crisis nor of deviance, even though both crisis and deviance are used as justifications for engaging in torture. This is not simply the attenuation of Lefebvre's production of space under capitalism, even though the torture victim might be seen as the ultimate disposable object. In other words, many of the ways that we have of framing platiality and spatiality in recent literature do not easily fit the experience of torture. They do not do justice to the radical rupture that torture represents.

When thinking about torture (if it can be thought at all, and not just named), distinctions are important. Torture is a rich word, used in a vast array of circumstances ranging from the quotidian to the exceptional, from the personal to the political. We might say that the traffic is torture today, but clearly that sort of use is at best metaphorical, intended only to express minor frustration or displeasure. "Torture," like "terror," "slavery," and other terms, slips away, becoming tamed by its multitude of metaphorical uses. "Third period English was torture," we hear a student say, when what he really means is that he was mildly bored. Without wishing to co-opt the example, many Holocaust survivors would insist on the use of the term "Holocaust" only for the mass extermination of the Jews and others during the Second World War. Any other use would diminish the uniqueness and severity of the event. Similarly, we might wish that "torture" had so exclusive a designation, but that is not the case.

There are, though, other questions about what the concept of "torture" encompasses that are less about the metaphoric uses and more about the conditions in question. Pain, even extreme or fatal pain, is not necessarily torture. Religious ascetics such as Julian of Norwich might wish to experience the pain of Christ's crucifixion and death, which in the stories was surely described with similar terms to torture, but even if Julian experienced the same pain to the same degree, the fact that she wished for it and that it had a purpose (purgative, contemplative, transcendental, mystical) seems to rule out her experience as being torture. Furthermore, trauma is not torture. Torture might be traumatic, but so might other things. Trauma is felt pain, and that pain can come from many sources, both intentional and not. Torture is always intentional, and as I will argue, intentional in a specific way—it undermines dwelling.

Solitary confinement has a somewhat different provenance but is likewise a rupture of place. Its range of uses is more limited, in particular to the exercise of state power. We do not speak of kidnapping or hostage taking as solitary confinement, as these do not have the force of law behind them, even if the victims are kept by themselves during their captivity. This distinction is important, because as I will argue in the case of both torture and solitary confinement, there is an aspect of dwelling that these two actions attempt to obliterate. That obliteration occurs in the context of the specific meaning, or withdrawal of meaning, of the acts in question. As with torture, a religious ascetic could easily decide to live a solitary life (indeed, anchorites did this in the Middle Ages, as did the desert fathers earlier), and that would not be solitary confinement. Members of a religious order could be under instructions to remain in their cells for the vast majority of the day (at least as much as the current guidelines might be for solitary confinement in a penal system), and even under the "compulsion" of the abbot or the mother superior, that would not be considered solitary confinement.

Solitary confinement's debt to place is different—it is about (lack of) movement. There are other ways to speak of forcible location in a place or removal from a place that are not solitary confinement (e.g., exile, banishment, a child's "time-out," kidnapping). We might say that solitary confinement is forcible removal from all but one place by a state authority for an extended period, except that this still does not address the meaningfulness of the experience. It is generally not a removal to a desert island or some other confinement far from any human contact. It is confinement in proximity to human activity, which can be sensed in various ways, but which serves only to disorient and erode one's sense of place. A person is not merely put in a cell but put in a cell while hearing the screams of others, or while hearing footsteps, or while being cut off from any indication of the passage of time, or while being deprived of sleep. Solitary confinement, then, is not merely a restriction of place but a corrosion of the potentiality for dwelling.

One danger of writing in these areas, and in making distinctions in particular, is that it can seem as if one is attempting to adjudicate the severity and extent of pain or suffering that occurs in particular circumstances. So, it needs to be made clear right from the beginning that attempting to isolate specific kinds of torture, or work with a specific definition, does not imply that the pain felt by others subjected to other circumstances is not as severe, as real, and its causes are as reprehensible as anything discussed here. We will bracket questions of morality for the moment; obviously issues of morality are central, but the issue at hand is to ask about what might ground any claims to morality in the cases of torture and solitary confinement. The argument will be that there is a phenomenology of dwelling at work here, and in particular a form of placelessness, which provides a way of thinking through these experiences and suggests both the basis for an ethical condemnation of torture as well as an ethical response to it.

This approach does not supplant existing ways of understanding torture and solitary confinement but rather adds a nuance to them. Currently, the effect of torture is often described as "unbearable helplessness." This is understood to be connected to a loss or weakening of identity, a loss of self-esteem, a sense of guilt, and so forth. In other words, the focus has largely been on issues of identity as understood in a classic psychological manner. Sanford Levinson speaks of a phenomenology of torture that leads to the view that the victim is a totally "rightless individual," making him or her even more threatened than in the state of slavery itself (2007: 164). He recognizes, following Elaine Scarry, that torture is tied to pain, but as we have already discussed, there is no necessary or sufficient relationship between torture and pain. Much pain is not torture, and it is possible to have torture without (at least physical) pain. And so, for Levinson the key is the loss of all possible rights. He is surely correct about this, but this does not go far enough. It is not simply the loss of rights but the loss of dwelling, tied to the ways in which the body is allowed or restricted from engaging in the world. Embodiment has not been the focus, despite the fact that torture depends on a threat to the body (and I am including the body as central even in what we might call "psychological torture"). Past the question of embodiment, though, is the place of the body and the ways in which its ability to be emplaced have been compromised or destroyed.

The body is our first place, and it is that connection that leads me to add the issue of dwelling to the description of torture. The place to start is with the experience of torture, and there is no better place than with Jean Améry.

The Mind's Limit and the Body's Loss of Place

Jean Améry, in his book *At the Mind's Limits*, gives an account of the limits of the intellectual in Auschwitz. Written originally in 1966, his account is rooted in the common existential depiction of life in concentration camps—that it was dehumanizing. There is no doubt that he, and others such as Primo Levi who have written about the camps, is correct. These accounts, though, depend on a platial understanding of human existence. People were dehumanized, but this was done by de-platializing them.

Améry's phenomenological memoir is one of the best treatments of the assault on self, meaning, and place in the wake of the Holocaust. It has been taken by some as a strong argument in favor of resentment and not forgiving after extreme torture (Brudholm 2008). While it may be that, what is missed in such accounts is the basis for the ethical stance (and to be fair, Brudholm was focusing mainly on one essay in *At the Mind's Limit*, which had been published earlier). Améry did not refuse to forgive just because some acts are so heinous that they are unforgiveable. He did not and could not forgive because the basis for ethics itself had been destroyed. Ethics is, in part at least, *ethos*, to the extent that values and virtues arise from our ability to dwell in a world, interconnected and always already meaningful (Janz 2009b).

Some of Améry's account focuses on the trauma to the self that is tied to the body. He frames this as a loss of trust in the world:

> Yet I am certain that with the very first blow that descends on him he loses something we will perhaps temporarily call "trust in the world." Trust in the world includes all sorts of things: the irrational and logically unjustifiable belief in absolute causality perhaps, or the likewise blind belief in the validity of the inductive inference. But more important as an element of trust in the world, and in our context what is solely relevant, is the certainty that by reason of written or unwritten social contracts the other person will spare me-more precisely stated, that he will respect my physical—and with it also my metaphysical—being. The boundaries of my body are also the boundaries of my self. My skin surface

shields me against the external world. If I am to have trust, I must feel on it only what I want to feel. (Améry 1980: 28)

This loss of trust in the world is a breach in the social contract, but he also describes it in much more basic and empirical ways—loss of belief in causality and inductive inference. And the loss of trust in the social contract is a loss of trust in the platiality of the body. The body is no longer an unassailable barrier. Whereas once a breach of the body-barrier was regulated by law, and could be rectified within a legal structure, now there is no law. It is Agamben's permanent state of exception. More than that, though, it is a normalization of a physical breach. The place that one occupies in the world is no longer something a person has exclusive claim on.

> The other person, opposite whom I exist physically in the world and with whom I can exist only as long as he does not touch my skin surface as border, forces his own corporeality on me with the first blow. He is on me and thereby destroys me. (28)

So, it is rape, but more than that, it is a rape that has no hope of rectification or even recognition within an ethical or state structure. All rapes are crimes of power; torture is the rape of one's place in the world.

Améry ends his wrenching description of torture by making it explicitly platial: "Whoever has succumbed to torture can no longer feel at home in the world" (40). And this observation leads him directly to his next chapter "How Much Home Does a Person Need?," which the reader might think is no longer about torture but about exile. Améry is very clear that the line between these two is a direct one. The removal of one's dwelling in the world at a fundamental level as happens with torture gives exile a particular character. One might be exiled for a variety of reasons—in this case, it is not merely a political act but an existential one. Jews effectively lost their home in the world, not just their home in Germany. Améry is very clear, eloquent, and damning on what that meant.

> We, however, had not lost our country, but had to realize that it had never been ours. For us, whatever was linked with this land and its people was an existential misunderstanding. What we believed to have been our first love was, as they said there, racial disgrace. What we thought had constituted our nature—was it ever anything else but mimicry? Given some intellectual honesty, it was quite impossible for us, who during the war lived under the occupation by the hostile homeland, to think of our country as oppressed by a foreign power. (50)

And homesickness comes along with the loss of home. It is not merely an emotion of loss, not just "self-pity, but rather self-destruction" (51). There were "no more songs, no effusive evocation of lost landscapes, no moist eye that at the same time winked, asking for complicity." The loss of home meant "dismantling our past piece by piece, which could not be done without self-contempt and hatred for the lost self." Home was not simply lost, but it had become hostile. It was not that they were taken from their homes but that their homes were taken from them.

> The combination of hatred for our homeland and self-hatred hurt, and the pain intensified most unbearably when, during the strenuous task of self-destruction, now and then traditional homesickness also welled up and claimed its place. What we urgently wished, and were socially bound, to hate, suddenly stood before us and demanded our longing. A totally impossible, neurotic condition for which there is no psychoanalytic remedy. (51)

What we see as a response is not far from what Fanon saw as the response to the occupation of Algeria by the French—a violent uprising that had an existentially purgative and purifying effect: "The only therapy could have been history in practice. I mean the German revolution and with it the homeland's strongly expressed desire for our return. But the revolution did not take place, and our return was nothing but an embarrassment for our homeland, when finally the National Socialist power was crushed from without" (Améry 1980: 51).

Even as torture itself undermines and poisons the possibility of dwelling in the world, the conditions have to be set for that to take hold. Dwelling had already been taken from the Jews—the physical torture of the camps was the last step. This is a more expansive definition of torture than the usual discussion of inflicting pain on someone for some political or other purpose, and perhaps we need other words to distinguish the noble resistance or death that someone might undergo in the service of country or an ideal, or the pain that an innocent victim of crime might feel, from the systematic poisoning of dwelling that occurred in the Holocaust, and also in other examples of systematic state-sponsored torture. Instead of starting with the first of these as the paradigm of torture, I would like to use the second as the paradigm.

The phenomenology, in other words, must be hermeneutic, that is, it must be embedded in the context of meaning or the assault on meaning (which I take to be the assault on dwelling) that torture represents. We might empirically describe both the physical and psychological results of torture, and we might further provide a descriptive phenomenological account of the experience of torture, but until the assault on the structure of meaning is involved, we cannot account for things like the Musselmänner of the camps.

Musselmänner and Torture

The image of the Musselman in the camps has been widely discussed, first by survivors and then by theorists such as Giorgio Agamben (1999). Ataria and Gallagher (2015) have unpacked the implications of the image in terms of the loss of bodily agency. Agamben takes it as the image of what he calls "bare life." The figure, so abject as to be disgusting to both torturers and other prisoners, is the true witness. He is the one who stands outside of humanity but who is nevertheless not dead. He is a "dead man on leave," as Améry describes being a Jew in the wake of the Holocaust.

> The denial of human dignity sounded the death threat. Daily, for years on end, we could read and hear that we were lazy, evil, ugly, capable only of misdeed, clever only to the extent that we pulled one over on others. We were incapable of founding a state, but also by no means suited to assimilate with our host nations. By their very presence, our bodies—hairy, fat, and bowlegged—befouled public swimming pools, yes, even park benches. Our hideous faces, depraved and spoilt by protruding ears and hanging noses, were disgusting to our fellow men, fellow citizens of yesterday. We were not worthy of love and thus also not of life. Our sole right, our sole duty was to disappear from the face of the earth. (1980: 86)

An assault on dignity, certainly, but also a permanent condition of bare life. The torture renders him sui generis, the only one of his kind in the world by virtue of the fact that he has no place in the world. There is no class of those who may be called "alien"—all aliens who become alien by virtue of torture are their own species.

> I must accept being foreign as an essential element of my personality, insist upon it as if upon an inalienable possession. Still and each day anew I find myself alone. I was unable to force yesterday's murderers and tomorrow's potential aggressors to recognize the moral truth of their crimes, because the world, in its totality, did not help me to do it. Thus I am alone, as I was when they tortured me. (96)

In other words, the fact of torture continues, and so the loss of home continues. Agamben describes the Musselman in these terms:

> No one felt compassion for the Muslim, and no one felt sympathy for him either. The other inmates, who continually feared for their lives, did not even judge him worthy of being looked at. For the prisoners who collaborated, the Muslims were a source of anger and worry; for the SS, they were merely useless garbage. Every group thought only about eliminating them, each in its own way. (1999: 43)

Agamben's use of the image of the Musselman has come under criticism (Justin Clemens summarizes these [2012: 93–7]), but the image is useful in this case because of what Clemens goes on to argue about Agamben's purpose. It is to establish the "threshold between the human and the inhuman" (Agamben 1999: 55). This threshold has been understood as an existential threat to subjectivity, and it certainly is that, but more importantly it is a threat to the possibility of being in place. As Clemens puts it, "The potential for speech (to speak or not) had therefore been expropriated from the *Musselmänner*; it would be impossible for a *Muselmann* to say 'I am a *Muselmann*'" (2012: 96). This loss of the possibility of self-identity is the loss of the possibility of a project and the loss of place. There is no longer a reliable world that can show the results of the project of subjectivity back to the victim. There is no mode of self-writing possible.

Achille Mbembe gives another account of the person subject to torture, this time a torture that is the result of a kind of domination of place that produces a hallucinatory space, one with no bearings in materiality and no possibility of authenticity.

> For the dominated subject, subjection can be transformed into a sort of magical song, at the point where nightmare, trance, hilarity, and madness meet.
>
> In this process of mutual brutalization, the hallucinated subject only sees, hears, and believes power at the price of an original arbitrariness that those dominating and those dominated must constantly reiterate. It is only in this way that power can get inside its subjects. This indwelling manifests itself in several ways: everyday suffering, laughter dragged from the bottom of the chest and which "surprises beyond any warning," mortification of the flesh, the torment and torture and beatings that drive the native to loose great inhuman cries, the trembling that overtakes the native faced with soldiery, the shaking and raw expressions of horror and terror when, for example, pummelled with blows, he faints, falls down, and, eyes bulging, slobbers—or, again, when he is made to sing both literally and figuratively, for days and nights, without a break, to the

point of making him laugh and dance despite himself, thus causing him to blot out his own sufferings, incapable of responsibility for what he says and does, put at the disposal of power, in a sort of duplicity and servile repetition.

The hallucinated subject can then become the beast of burden of the "thing" and his demon become his "jester." The autocrat sits on his subject's back, harnesses him, and rides him. And makes him shit. (Mbembe 2001: 167)

Agamben and Mbembe in their different ways give us an image of a being outside of place, for whom dwelling is no longer possible. For Agamben, it is the rejection of everyone, including those who might seem to be natural allies (other prisoners). It is the loss of the potential for constructing subjectivity because of the loss of the place that can sustain it. For Mbembe, it is the long-term hallucination, which is not a place of refuge or a safe fantasy but rather a hall of mirrors, a place of unending torture. It is the adoption and ingestion of placelessness as a continuing state of being.

Torture in this sense is not, in other words, merely a specific act, a point in time, but a compression of time that writes itself on all future times and places. It is a haunting, to use Derrida's term. We may use the term "torture" for the specific act designed to bring about a specific purpose (finding out how to defuse the ticking time-bomb, an example so often used in discussions about torture), but the argument here is that there is another more fundamental sense of torture that has placelessness at its core. The terrorist being tortured in order to find out where the ticking bomb is certainly feels extreme pain, but that person could (and presumably usually does) also take comfort in his or her service to country, or higher purpose, or moral clarity. That person is not the Musselmann, for there is no threat of placelessness here. The issues are unquestionably moral ones but not platial ones. But another kind of torture, the kind meant to reduce a population to insignificance, to dominate and subjugate—this is the threat to place that we find in so many accounts and testimonies of survivors. So, if this kind of torture has as its central feature placelessness, is there a way of reconstituting or repairing that place? Is it indeed, as the victim experiences, gone forever, rendering the world as permanently alien to them?

Cosmopolitanism, Afro-politanism, Afro-pessimism

The question of dwelling and its exhaustion or assault in the form of torture and solitary confinement must be added to Mbembe's list of ruptures of place, which are slavery, colonialism, and apartheid. These are, I would argue, on a related continuum, not of severity but of variations on and modalities of rupture. They are the reason why self-writing becomes an issue at all. Place is cognitive and affective. Place allows us to face (up to) something. It is tied to our embodiment in the world—our first place is our body. We leverage our material and physical space as symbolic and as information space. Just as a memory palace helped ancient orators remember their speeches, our places become part of bodily patterns and eventually they exist as unreflective space.

All of this is placed in jeopardy by slavery, colonialism, and apartheid. These are all ruptures of place, at the most basic level and all the way up to the most abstract level. Bodies are controlled, owned, and disciplined; social patterns are bent toward production or restraint; politics loses any connection to or memory of the habitation within a place, whether that is understood materially or in other ways, such as culturally or ethnically. Mbembe's question about self-writing, then, is not simply a question about subjectivity or self-narration; it is a question about how one might constitute a self in the face of a systematically compromised set of places.

The possible responses to these fractured versions of place are themselves a kind of abandonment of place. One is to draw on cosmopolitanism to produce an African version: Afro-politanism. The other is to posit a utopian (or, in this case, anti-utopian) stance, Afro-pessimism. One might see these as a kind of transcendence from the pain of the place, or a recognition that the fragmentation and damage are too great, and so the alternative to Afro-radicalism and nativism is not just the reassertion of a liberal democratic version of place, which itself would be an illusion, but instead a diminishment of place, an emphasis on networks in the case of Afro-politanism or an ironic suspicion and exhaustion of place that animates Afro-pessimism.

One might, as I say, see these as abandonments of the discourse of place, except for the fact that Mbembe himself does not take that route in other writing. The whole of *On the Postcolony*, for instance, is about how living can go forward when the possibility of the reconstitution of place is remote. He ends that book hopefully, sharing a vision with Nietzsche of "learning to live as free men."

The recovery or reconstruction of place, or the ability to live in a place that is forever fractured, has been a concern of Mbembe's ever since *On the Postcolony*. Places are fraught with ambiguity and false promise, though, when it comes to self-writing:

> The *différend* concerning origins is supposed to be the starting point for becoming conscious of identity. At the same time, however, every such identity

is expected to be translated into territorial terms. Indeed, to this way of thinking, there is no identity without territoriality—the vivid consciousness of *place* and mastery of it, whether by birth, by conquest, or by settlement. Territoriality in its clearest manifestation is to be found in the cult of locality—or, in other words, home, the small space and inherited estate where direct, proximate relationships are reinforced by membership in a common genealogy. This is the same matrix, real or supposed, that serves as the foundation for the civic space; in fact, funerals and burials are one of the chief ways of ritualizing membership in the civic space, as enacted within the boundaries of home. It can thus be seen that from a combination of ideological categories (membership and origins) and spatial categories (territory and locality) emerges citizenship, which might be defined as the ability to enjoy a home, the ability to exclude foreigners from this enjoyment, the right to protection and to access to a range of collective goods and resources situated in the space thus delimited. (2002a: 266)

In other words, if we expect a naive or superficial version of place to make up for the systematic damage done by slavery, colonialism, and apartheid, we will be disappointed, or, perhaps more to the point, grasping a false hope. Mbembe defines home here not in the embodied sense developed in this chapter but in a more common sense—the conservative and traditional ground of relation, ritual, and politics. If home is that, then it will not save us. If that is what it means to dwell, it will not restore what was lost. But that is an image of dwelling, a politically charged version of place meant to stand against the threats of the world. Homey-ness is not what was lost in slavery, colonialism, and apartheid, much less in torture and solitary confinement. That version of home, in fact, could easily be the site of these things.

So, it is not this that has been ruptured or exhausted. And it is not this that is the site of becoming. It is only an enticing narrative, no different from narratives provided by Afro-radicalism or nativism (and indeed, nativism often uses exactly these narratives to define entitlements to home place). What we need is something more than this. Mbembe suggests that in the epilogue to *Critique of Black Reason*, and we see it further in Leonhard Praeg and Rosi Braidotti. It is the one world.

Diagne, Praeg, Braidotti, Mbembe, and Becoming-World

We see, at the end of *Critique of Black Reason*, a declaration: "There is only one world" (Mbembe 2017: 179). Mbembe returns us to place again, in a sense, but is this the dream of cosmopolitanism, after all, coming back to us? Not in its classic form, surely. Not as a unitary, liberal project, one that can produce pious abstractions about universal rights and opportunity for all in a capitalist utopia.

No, it is not that. It is place, not its abstraction or retreat, or some network that stands in for place. The world is a project, a way of thinking: "Thinking through what must come will of necessity be a thinking through of life, of the reserves of life, of what must escape sacrifice. It will of necessity be *a thinking in circulation, a thinking of crossings, a world-thinking*" (179; original emphasis). It is "composed of a totality of a thousand parts. Of everyone. Of all worlds" (180). It is a project.

The world-project, the result of thinking, is difficult to imagine in the face of Afro-radicalism and nativism, as sketched out in "African Modes of Self-Writing." "What must escape sacrifice" sounds hopeful, but vague, even metaphorical. Humanity as a whole "delegates itself in the world" and receives confirmation from the world, just as a seed that is planted dies, is reborn, and grows to produce fruit. The systems of exchange in the world, not limited to humans but between all parts of the world, are like silt to each other—Glissant's "castoff of matter: a substance made up of seemingly dead elements, things apparently lost, debris stolen from the source, water laden" (Mbembe 2017: 181). Life, in these conditions, is an "imperishable form, one that could not decay" (182), and because there is both change and permanence, we find ways of existing by creating borders, building walls, and making hierarchies.

The idea of life finding a way becomes tangible when Mbembe advocates reparations and restitution to those whose humanity was stolen by being "subjected to the processes of abstraction and objectification" (182). The foundation of this position is that, first, each person is a unique repository of intrinsic humanity, and a lack of recognition damages this; and second, a history of slavery, colonialism, and all forms of marginalization have left "cuts and scars" that prevent the realization of community (183).

So, if the world is one, but community cannot be realized for both historical and structural reasons (and, we might add with Fanon, psychological and existential reasons as well), something must be done to put the world back in order and make universal community possible again. And it is *universal* community—no matter how we might imagine that communities are their own little local entities, their own places, they still are embedded in and depend on the networks of the world. These universal communities are "by definition posed in terms of how we inhabit the Open, how we care for the Open—which is completely different from an approach that would aim first to enclose, to stay within the enclosure of what we call our own kin" (183). Mbembe calls this "unkinning," which he says is the opposite of difference, in that difference is usually "the result of the construction of desire." Desire is often seen as linked to power, but Mbembe argues that "desire is not necessarily a desire for power." And since this is the case, it is possible to have, and indeed yearn for, difference, while at the same time have a desire, reminiscent of Heidegger, "to be protected, spared, preserved from danger." He ends the book with this dream:

> But as we can see within certain strains of modern Black criticism, the proclamation of difference is only one facet of a larger project—the project of a world that is coming, a world before us, one whose destination is universal, a world freed from the burden of race, from resentment, and from the desire for vengeance that all racism calls into being. (183)

There is a sense in which *Critique of Black Reason* stands as a fulfillment of the promise of "African Modes of Self-Writing" (and, in another way, a fulfillment of the promise of *On the Postcolony* as well). If we think about the fundamental problem in the earlier essay as one of place, that is, the violation of place in the great affronts of slavery, colonialism, and apartheid, and the misshapen places that arise from Afro-radicalism and nativism, we do not see a satisfactory response to the question of how place might be constituted, especially given the argument of *On the Postcolony* that Africans might be faced with the continuation of personal and structural violence indefinitely, and the problem becomes whether we can "first learn to enjoy as complete men" (Mbembe 2001: 242), even if that enjoyment means existing "in uncertainty, chance, irreality, even absurdity."

The problem with Afro-radicalism and nativism as a response to the exhaustion of dwelling that we see in slavery, colonialism, and apartheid (and its related conditions of torture and solitary confinement) is that these cannot engender a new problematic by asking new questions about these conditions. It is not that neither of these ever raise questions related to these things, but that the question is a new one, establishing a new ground and range of other questions. Why are these questions new now? Because some problematics have run their course. What does it mean for these to run their course? They do not yield any more useful concepts. They do not ask any more interesting questions. They do not describe peoples' experience adequately. They use concepts that do not create anything. Mbembe sees two major problematics (he calls them "thematics") as exhausted: anti-imperialism and race (Mbembe 2002a: 264).

It seems strange to think of these as exhausted, particularly because both are so central to a great deal of critical postcolonial discourse. The initial respondents to this article, in *Public Culture*, were divided about how to take this. Some (e.g.,

Gilroy, Dirlik) see these as remaining central to understanding the alienation of the self. Others (e.g., Dirlik, Verges) see explanatory power, and the potential for resistance, still existing in the examination of world capitalism, including cosmopolitanism.

The general reaction to "African Modes of Self-Writing" was clearly not what Mbembe hoped for. In his reply to the responses, "On the Power of the False" (2002b), he seems frustrated that the respondents did not more directly address the positive side of his case. He returns to the idea that there needs to be something else that takes us forward, since the existing discourses have not enabled the construction of a creative version of Africa since it is committed to a narrative of victimhood:

> How to explain this fixation on the past and this frenetic claim to the status of victim? One reason is that as a dominant trope of nativist and Afro-radical discourses, the past is imagined as not only the home of the truth of the self but also the site of its falsification through the violence committed by the Other. To summon the future, one must first unlock the past, or more precisely, break the chains that link that past to a demonic lie: the supposed existence of a hole at the very heart of the African being. A horrific thought, the hole invokes the contested humanity of the African on the one hand and the apparent meaninglessness of his or her life, labor, and language on the other. (2002b: 635)

The "hole at the very heart of the African being" is the question at stake here. It is Mbembe's diagnosis and his fundamental disagreement with some of his commentators. Thinking must be thinking about the world, not against the world. And it requires the restoration of "a separation on an intellectual level between *the desire to know and to think* and the *urge to act*" (636; original emphases). This means a form of thinking that does not have, as its first mission, the justification of some action, however laudable. It means, I believe, the possibility of following thinking where it will lead, in creative and unexpected ways.

Not all commentators, though, focused on Mbembe's seeming abandonment of the tools of resistance. Souleymane Bachir Diagne was instead interested in authenticity. He argued that Mbembe's understanding of authenticity is that meaning does not come from the past (the figure of tradition, or repetition). It is not, in other words, the projection of tradition on the present and future. The focus is on the future. There is a different philosophy of time, one that allows multiple possibilities. Diagne sees something like a Bergsonian version of time in what Mbembe is proposing. He connects this with the Deleuzean notion of the rhizome (Diagne 2002: 622).

> Mbembe's contention—and this is an important point—is to reply that writing back is not self-writing. This sort of practice of writing back fails in its purpose—misses its mark of authenticity—because it is not affirmation but resentment, to use Mbembe's Nietzschean categories. (622)

The goal, Diagne argues, and the reason Mbembe challenges the partisans and practitioners of Africanity, is "to reformulate Africanity as an open question—for the sake of creativity" (623). This is separating out the desire to know and think from the urge to act.

Mbembe responds indirectly to the model that Diagne suggests. In his response to the responses ("On the Power of the False"), he addresses the idea of multiplicity and proliferations.

> What relationship is there between language and what is called truth? What coefficient of truth can be granted to the sign that is Africa, which I said, right at the start, was above all a geographical accident? The examples quoted above indicate that there will always be a part of the sign that escapes the prison of our discourse. How, then, do we enrich the discourse so that this accidental sign can be represented as closely as possible? This requires developing a technique of reading (*lecture*) and writing (*écriture*) that would also be *an aesthetic of opening and encounter*. (Mbembe 2002b: 640; original emphases)

We also see a similar response to Mbembe in Leonhard Praeg's *A Report on Ubuntu* (2014). Praeg uses Deleuze and Guattari's concept of "conceptual personae" to work out both an idea of what self-writing might look like and a sense of what the potentiality of Ubuntu is (97–119). Conceptual personae are inventions that enable one to investigate a problematic, that is, a space of thought established by questioning.

> The conceptual persona functions something like the detective in crime fiction. He is the everyman who must orientate himself within the image of thought. So, for example, Deleuze shows how the "rational" man of scholastic thought is replaced by the Cartesian "idiot," who is later replaced by the Russian "idiot." This "underground man" has what Deleuze calls in a characteristically wry statement, the "necessary modesty" not to manage to know what everybody knows. He is like a character in a Russian novel, paralysed and stupefied by the coordinates of problems that do not correspond to representational presuppositions. (Marks 2010: 285)

It is an exploratory figure, one who makes sense of a space in a way that is fundamentally different from others. He is the one who asks a new question and follows the path where the question takes him (see Lambert [2017] for a fuller account). Praeg makes clear the political nature of the conceptual personae—each one might be sympathetic or not, and each one moves easily between the question of how we know the world and how we act in the world. Every philosophical tradition is full of these figures—they are responsible for the problematics discussed earlier. In some cases they are tired figures, held on to because they are familiar or because they enable some people to hold on to power. In other cases, they are new and fresh, allowing us to ask new questions and explore new ways of being.

Praeg analyzes some conceptual personae, which he names as "the Prophet (with a subdivision into the Revolutionary and the Saviour), the Archivist, the Conformist, the Cosmopolitan and the Text Worker or Construction Worker" (Praeg 2014: 100). His purpose in outlining these is to address some spaces that talk of Ubuntu has opened up. Even though Mbembe's purpose in "Self-Writing" was not to consider Ubuntu directly, Praeg has used the opening that Mbembe provides in that essay to consider openings to thought. Significantly, Praeg leverages the concept of conceptual personae to think through the kinds of responses we see to the very conditions that Mbembe outlines, and casts these as affectual, that is, as ways of facing the ruptured place. He groups all his responses under the general heading of Ubuntu, as forms of Ubuntu at different times and places. His message is hopeful—Ubuntu is not a singular thing but a multiple and as such might hold the potential for addressing ruptured place. It is also pessimistic—these various conceptual personae have, to this point at least, still left us with ruptured place.

Rosi Braidotti rethinks cosmopolitanism as "becoming-world," understood as follows:

> I want to emphasize the relevance for contemporary cosmopolitanism of the ethics of accountability that takes "Life" as its main referent while avoiding the twin pitfalls of biological essentialism on the one hand and unreflexive anthropocentrism on the other. In order to implement this meta-methodological shift of perspective, classical cosmopolitanism needs to become-world, in the sense of developing a radical relational model of interaction. This is based on the awareness and the acknowledgment of a structural interconnection among subjects that are complex and material singularities in process. The notion of cosmopolitanism, in other words, needs to acquire increased respect for complexity, so as to evolve in the direction of Deleuze and Guattari's "chaosmosis," that is to say being-one-with the vital processes of transformation alongside and with a multiplicity of human and non-human others. (2013: 8)

Mbembe's promise of one world is close to Braidotti's becoming-world, in the sense of its material foundation, its emergent nature, and its ability to recognize that, while the stains of racism, slavery, colonialism, and apartheid never go away, they become the basis for moving into something new. That "something new" is not the hopeful liberal story of individual triumph over insurmountable odds through some sort of internal character or resilience. Becoming-world does not make the wounds all better; it does not make it worth all the pain in the end. Neither Mbembe nor Braidotti are dreaming of that happy ending.

Braidotti starts from a place that looks familiar to theorists of cosmopolitanism—the idea of global flows of capital and labor and networks of exchange and migration. She points out, as many have, that this constitutes biopower, the control of bodies and populations through capital that achieves its ends by being both centralized and distributed. It turns life itself into a site for financial investment and profit.

What is apparent in the material exchanges as cosmopolitanism describes them is that there are generative as well as destructive forces. The combination of these forces of destruction, control, and creation lead to Achille Mbembe's "necropolitics," a state that is not controlled by law and morality but in fact enabled by it. Braidotti makes clear that this state is a fundamentally racialized process in which she draws on Arendt and Agamben to show that the abstraction of humanity is in fact applied differently to different people. The result, the underside of cosmopolitanism understood in these terms, is the vulnerability of "bare life," that is, a variation on Agamben's Musselman, which we met when thinking about torture.

But Braidotti's becoming-world is not about this version of cosmopolitanism. The divisions and differences made possible by the biopower—colonialism, fascism, racism, genocide, and sexism—are a necessary conclusion of the circulation of capital and labor in a postcolonial world. The move to becoming-world requires a move away from this.

> One can venture the conclusion that the main implication for the practice of a new cosmopolitical sense of planetary interconnection is that the political, scientific and juridical laws need to be retuned according to a view of the subject as a complex singularity, an affective assemblage and a relational vitalist entity. This could also be described as a metamethodological shift from classical cosmopolitanism to what I described as "a nomadic ethics of sustainable transformations" and Ronald Bogue, quoting Deleuze, has aptly defined as: "chaosmopolitanism." (Braidotti 2013: 15)

Her shift away from classical cosmopolitanism means taking seriously the politics of location, as developed by feminist scholars, which she expresses as a "cartographic method of accounting for multiple differences within any subject position" (16). A cartography is a "theoretically based and politically informed reading of the present," which

> accounts for one's locations in terms both of space (geo-political or ecological dimension) and time (historical and genealogical dimension). It also provides alternative figurations or schemes of representation for these locations, in terms of power as restrictive (potestas) but also empowering or affirmative (potentia). I consider this cartographic gesture to be the first methodological move towards a vision of cosmopolitanism attuned to the complexity of our era and to the diversity of locations and power relations that structures the global mobility. (16)

Understood in these terms, the world is seen not in terms of identities but in terms of what we are capable of becoming. For Braidotti, this brings together a significant number of anti-colonial theorists, race theorists, and others, such as bell hooks, Vandana Shiva, Ernesto Laclau, Paul Gilroy, and others. While their approaches and concerns differ, they share an ethics of neo-humanism that strategizes ways to reengage marginalized and oppressed peoples. This ethics is motivated by showing a form of community and interaction made possible by shared oppression. "Our co-presence, that is to say the simultaneity of our being in the world together sets the tune for the ethics of our interaction" (19).

Being in the world together takes many forms, but all involve a reconsideration of the place that race, gender, class, ability, and so forth play in relation to classic cosmopolitanism. More than this, though, there is a process of defamiliarization, in which the "ethical, knowing subject evolves from the normative vision of the self he or she had become accustomed to" (20). The willingness to engage community makes possible this kind of defamiliarization, since a community committed to facing the implications of racism, sexism, and so forth bring forth a potentiality of the self that can create new anomalies and new possibilities of life.

Braidotti also argues for a decentering of anthropocentrism, that is, a recognition that if we are going to pay attention to life, we need to do so in all its forms and not assume that intelligent human life is the pinnacle of life, the "that for which" everything else exists. Contemporary science in a wide range of areas has demonstrated just how embedded humans are within the networks that span the world. Becoming-world does not mean that we are simply expanding the ethical circle to include nonhumans (Janz 2018c), as this just keeps anthropocentrism intact and uses its structure of rights and duties as an analogy for nonhumans. Becoming-world means becoming-animal/nonhuman, which is "a process of redefinition of one's sense of attachment and connection to a shared world, a territorial space" (Braidotti 2013: 23). The world changes from being a threat to us, and therefore something to be dominated, to being a space of interaction in which we leverage potentialities that are made available by our differences from each other that interact within a territory.

This vision offers some affirmative directions, in particular ones that are different from the standard cosmopolitan opportunities, which are usually framed in terms of market economies, efficiencies, and so forth. We have already seen that that logic is the remainder of slavery and colonialism and has left its mark in the sense that it retains structures of exclusion and oppression even while denying that these are still in place. Braidotti suggests that there is a new kind of political and ethical agency possible in becoming-world. She places her hope in "more visionary power or prophetic energy."

Her sense of vision and prophetic energy does not, in the end, lead to many concrete proposals, nor would we expect it to. In that sense, Mbembe's suggestion of reparations and restitution (2017: 182) has a more practical and direct application, even though there are unanswered questions there as well. Braidotti's "becoming-world" places its faith in the justifiable observation that we are all multiple, that our identity formation happens within the networks we are part of (we are, to use Deleuze and Guattari's term, bodies-without-organs, BwO), and that while the molar structures of slavery and colonialism have led to a cosmopolitanism that just perpetuates the marginalization, those very structures are themselves unstable, open to other and new formations. The forced and alienated communities produced by the assaults on place are the same communities that can invent and create. In the end, Braidotti agrees with Mbembe that it is one world, but the oneness of her world suggests strategic options that are implied in Mbembe.

Can Ruptured Dwelling of Torture Be Reconstructed?

Most therapeutic approaches to torture in mental health focus on reconstructing a fractured identity. We might suppose that the issues of rehabilitation for bodily injuries might be separate from, and handled differently from, issues of rehabilitation for the psychological and mental trauma of torture. But if, as I am suggesting, torture involves an element of forcible destruction of dwelling, the line between these two is likely to be less clear than it seems. Disciplinary competencies in treatment make it likely that physiological and psychological torture will be compartmentalized and dealt with using the tools and methods available to the professionals who are charged with addressing the torture victim's suffering. Those disciplinary methods may, though, be unable to address a rupture in dwelling, as this does not fit easily into any one discipline's area of expertise. Nevertheless, if the argument to this point is correct, this is precisely what is needed to properly respond to the experience of the survivor. It is not just about holism in treatment, and it is not about rejecting the work that is already done by these disciplines. It is about directing treatment toward a fundamental aspect of human existence that is made available in a phenomenological analysis of torture, but that is much harder to see using classic scientific method.

Of course, everyone recognizes that physical and mental torture happen together, but the discussions concerning treatment tend to focus on one or the other. So, the reports of treatment of physical symptoms tend to deal with psychological issues only inasmuch as they present barriers to physical therapy. Danneskiold-Samsøe, Bartels, and Genefke (2007), for instance, assess the treatment of some Namibian torture victims who had been detained underground, exposed to sleep deprivation, and subjected to a variety of humiliating and painful treatments. As the authors admitted, they had been exposed to both psychological and physical torture. The focus of the study, though, was on physiological treatment, and so the psychological issues were raised only to ensure that the patients could deal with the physical treatment. The researchers did not measure the psychological well-being (16), but they recognized that "physiotherapy combined with the psychotherapy may therefore be of great importance for the beneficial effect of the treatment" (16). This may be true, but it is worth noting that the physical and the psychological are regarded as separate arenas.

This tendency to focus on either physical or psychological sequelae, or to regard one as in some sense a moment on the road to the other, is echoed in much of the therapeutic literature. Many of the studies explicitly focus on one or the other (e.g., Gerrity, Keane, and Tuma 2001; Başoğlu and Şalcıoğlu 2011).

While this approach is overwhelmingly evident in the literature, there are some who try to work with both physiological and psychological effects. This does not necessarily mean that there is work on the issue of dwelling, but there is at least potential. One example is Graessner, Gurris, and Pross (2001). Originally published in Germany in 1996, this collection starts from the premise that torture is an assault on dignity and "the soul," as opposed to being just an assault on the mind or body. This may seem more poetic but less therapeutically useful, on the surface, and yet at least some of the included articles are based on case studies and therapeutic interventions. Even here, though, the tendency on the part of some contributors is to extend the psychological issues to the level of existential psychoanalysis. In other words, psychological issues of coping are seen as more than just issues of shame, self-worth, and so on but as crises for the survivor's very being. This is undoubtedly true, but it still does not investigate the question of how dwelling in the world, including bodily dwelling, might underlie these other issues. As with other professionals, the psychotherapist's methods define the nature of the problem, and that problem becomes the construction of self.

Without explicitly using place terminology, there do seem to be a few researchers who are trying to address issues of dwelling. Lisolette Grünbaum (1997), for instance, describes engaging in repetitive behavior and play with children who have survived torture. The intervention is framed in terms of psychotherapy, specifically in addressing the damage to "psychic structures for symbolic representation and metaphoric language" (439), but there seems to be more going on here than just this. Grünbaum is surely correct that torture can drive one toward inner strategies of survival (440), but if Améry is correct, there is something else happening. Améry did not retreat into an inner fantasy world. The destruction of his dwelling did not come with any compensatory or failsafe illusion. In some important sense, there was no "inner" left at all. When dwelling in the world was removed, everything was removed. At the most extreme, the Musselmänner exhibit this condition, but Améry also takes on the effects of that lack of dwelling.

Grünbaum's account of working with a child victim of torture (she uses the name "Laila" for her) focuses on the symbolic content of the therapy, and what might be deduced from that about Laila's experience, condition, and most importantly the integration of her sense of self. What is less recognized is the child's physical engagement with the world. Indeed, her repetitive actions (stirring sand in a sandbox, other kinds of compulsive play) were seen by the therapist as "compulsively keeping herself busy." Laila showed a preoccupation with feet, symbolic (as Grünbaum inferred) of the moment of final parting with her father before he was murdered.

I do not have any specific problem with Grünbaum's analysis, not least because I did not observe the therapy or the child and am not a trained therapist myself. The point is not to suggest that there is any misdiagnosis here but rather to suggest that another layer, that of dwelling, may be at work. The compulsive action may also be the remnants of meaningful action from a time when the self did or could dwell in her world. In other words, while there may be symbolism involved in the psychoanalytic sense, it is also possible that there is a continued attempt to bodily recover a sense of dwelling in a world where dwelling has been compromised. The issue may not be that there is an inner self being protected by a fantasy, but an embodied self trying to remember how to dwell in the world, but not having the connection between bodily action and place available to it anymore. Habits, including the habits of play, are meaningful even if only at a somatic level, and torture may be seen as severing the relationship between habit and the somatic. The habits struggle for meaning but cannot find it. The body does not dwell in the world anymore.

Another example is dance/movement therapy. David Harris (2007), for instance, describes work with African adolescent torture survivors, and Amber Gray (2001) describes therapy with an adult survivor of torture. The stated goal of most torture therapy is to deal with either the psychological or physical trauma. Dance/movement deals with both and does so by reinscribing the physical patterns of movement through space that may have been restricted or damaged in torture. Neither Harris nor Gray (nor, for that matter, other practitioners of dance/movement therapy) emphasize the issues of dwelling that are at stake. All emphasize the body itself. And yet, the body is neither an object nor a possession. It dwells in the world, and to the extent that torture has compromised or destroyed the ability to dwell, the effectiveness of dance/movement therapy helps to address dwelling. How does it do this? At the most basic level by reinscribing patterns of bodily habit, body memory, that torture compromises.

Torture does more than affect the body; it affects the body's ability to dwell in the world, to move through it as home. Gray's work with Rita helps to make this clear:

> Through various DMT interventions, Rita began the process of reintegrating physically, emotionally, cognitively, and spiritually, and infusing her past experience with present meaning. When we first began to work with her pain, I chose a fairly standard DMT intervention specification of sensation to one area of the body. Another common intervention is the generalization of sensation to a larger area of the body, or to the entire body (Caldwell, 1996). I chose specification so that Rita could begin to re-establish the sequential organization of her experience that was violently disrupted by torture. In her case, I feared that generalization would produce flooding, and later sessions indicated that this may have been true. As she began to recover her bodily experience and integrate it, she was more prone to hyperarousal and flooding ... Only through carefully-paced exploration of sensation, could she give her movement impulses

expression, complete the movement sequence, and restore the sequential integrity of her experience. By relating these movements to the healing images of village healer and angel (her resources), she was able to begin to connect these physical experiences to her grief, express her anger, and eventually make peace with being forced to leave her children. Ultimately, we were able to literally dance her familiar dances together in the safety of our therapeutic relationship. Her pregnancy was evidence that she had restored relative safety and returned home to her body. (2001: 40–1)

Note that this account attends to the body, both what it can do and cannot do and how any intervention may bring back elements of the torture ("flooding"). Gray, by the end, uses the metaphor of "return[ing] home to her body," but I would like to take that more literally. In an important sense, the experience of dwelling had been separated through torture from the embodiment in the world. The therapy made it possible for the body to dwell again, which meant in this case for Rita to move as she once had moved.

The point here is not to champion dance/movement therapy but to use it to illustrate torture's destruction of dwelling and the recovery of one's place through movement. The habits of place, whether expressed in dance or in other forms of previous movement in the world, can and should be a goal of torture recovery. Jean Améry remained alienated from any sense of dwelling he once had, and torture may well have that effect. Even as he struggled to dwell, though, he profoundly articulated the limits of dwelling. He was a witness.

A third example, from Sylvia Karcher (2001). Karcher, to her credit, recognizes the fundamentally embodied nature of torture, not simply in terms of physiological damage but in terms of bodily perception. She describes the survivor as having disorders in bodily experience ("Patients no longer feel at home in their body" [73]), a loss of bodily perception (can "no longer sense certain parts of their body ... they then become almost rigid or frozen, and they no longer have any feelings about the boundaries of their body"), a feeling of fragmentation in bodily experience (the trauma can "cause the survivor to feel that parts of the body are split off. Connections between the head, arms and legs, and the rest of the body are no longer perceived"), and body image disorders. This is closer to a phenomenological account of the survivor's experience and does not reduce the experience to either literal or symbolic symptoms.

Karcher's treatment plan uses basic physical and psychological therapeutic techniques, but it also incorporates bodily movement, touch, and posture ("concentrative movement therapy," or CMT). The effect of this therapy is often to put the survivor back in the place of torture. Karcher also has the survivor draw maps of diagrams of their places before torture. The therapy clearly draws on body memory of trauma and also body memory of healthy movement before trauma. As the body is our first place, there is a clear connection to dwelling in this kind of body awareness. The body awareness takes patients back to healthy movement, as much as they are willing and able to be taken there, and resists a reductionist account of the trauma. It is neither just PTSD nor just treatment of sequelae or the reintegration of the self through encounter with symbolic elements of the survivor's world. As promising as this beginning is, though, it would be even more useful to take further steps to investigate what it means to dwell in the world now for the survivor.

A fourth place to look for therapies that possibly address the issue of dwelling would be in the application of mindfulness techniques to torture victims. Barry Kerzin (2014), the personal physician of the Dalai Lama, tells the story of an old monk who had been imprisoned in a Chinese gulag for about twenty years.

> This monk was released, and met the Dalai Lama. He told His Holiness about his experience in prison. At one point he was afraid. His Holiness thought this meant afraid of losing his life. But the old monk said he was afraid he was losing his compassion for the Chinese prison guards who were systematically torturing him. For they would suffer greatly in the future for their heinous actions.

This is not so much an issue of therapy, of course, but an issue of addressing the experience of torture in the moment. Compassion amounts to a way of holding on to dwelling in the world by holding on to human connection, even if the torture perpetrator is trying to sever or undermine those connections. The monk exhibited a kind of mindfulness that was not just about controlling his own responses and preserving his own placefulness but also about preserving the placefulness of the prison guards.

Jean Améry's account of his experience during the Holocaust makes clear that the rupture in dwelling might well be complete and irrevocable. His account is one of deep homelessness and alienation from his world, from his body, and in the end, he did commit suicide. Therapists would more than likely translate his experience into something they could understand and address, but part of his point is that nothing will be sufficient. He presents the experience of torture as extending past the personal, the physical, and the psychological. The structures of dwelling have been ruptured, so that as a Jew his place in the world and his history are thrown in question. The meaning of every one of his actions becomes absurd, because the conditions for meaning have been severed. The world will not deal with its treatment of the Jews in a manner that will restore dwelling, and in fact, the world may just move on, or even continue the attitudes that lead to the loss of dwelling that they have experienced.

Under these conditions, therapy may miss the essential nature of the pain. And to be fair, most therapists recognize this. Few speak of cures. But as torture becomes framed as PTSD in our age, it is possible that the rupture of dwelling that the survivor feels is even further away from being addressed.

Self-Writing in a Ruptured and Exhausted Place

To what extent can we think of self-writing in the model of the reintegration of the self's place in the world after torture? If slavery, colonialism, and apartheid are all other versions of an assault on and rupture of place, is there a similar move suggested in these cases that responses like Afro-radicalism and nativism miss? If dwelling in the world means moving through a live problematic, and creating events that make available new problematics, is it possible to think and live in these creative spaces in the wake of other kinds of rupture of place?

The problem as Mbembe sketches it is clear—the systems of response developed since the fall of slavery, colonialism, and apartheid have not been adequate to rethink the places that were compromised or destroyed. Existing options, primarily Afro-radicalism and nativism, but also to some extent cosmopolitanism and its variants, have not really dealt with the ruptures of place, in part because those ruptures are of a piece with those caused by torture. Something else is needed. None of this means that resistance is passé or that critiques of world economies and networks are not still needed. It means that new questions are needed that can produce new problematics. The old problematics are exhausted:

> When the question was asked, during the heyday of colonialism, whether self-government was possible, it was never to engage the general question of being and time—in other words, of life—but rather to facilitate native people's struggle to take over the apparatus of the state. The power to risk one's life—that is, in Hegel's terms, the ability to put an end to the servile condition and be reborn as the subject of the world—peters out in the prose of autochthony. And in the end, it can be said that everything here comes down to that one, perverse structure: autochthony. (Mbembe 2002a: 263)

Mbembe mentions "some of the genuinely philosophical inquiries neglected by African criticism in its reflection on slavery, colonization and apartheid"

(258–9). What is noteworthy is how these inquiries pick up on the rupture of place, and the experience of torture, just as much as they pick up on his three central traumas.

1. The status of suffering in history—the various ways in which historical forces inflict psychic harm on collective bodies and the ways in which violence shapes subjectivity. It is here that a comparison with other historical experiences has been deemed appropriate. The Jewish Holocaust furnishes one such comparative experience. Indeed, the Holocaust, slavery, and apartheid all represent forms of originary suffering. They are all characterized by an expropriation of the self by unnamable forces. In each case, the forces assume various forms. But in all, the central sequence is the same: to the orgiastic intoxication summoned by the administration of mass murder corresponds, like an echo, the placing of life between two chasms, so that the subject no longer knows if he or she is dead or alive. This combination of destructive animus and the dislocation of the self constitutes the Dionysian terrain shared by these three events. Indeed, at their ultimate foundation, the three events bear witness against life itself. On the pretext that origin and race are the criteria of any kind of valuation, they indict life. Whence the question: How can life be redeemed, that is, rescued from this incessant operation of the negative? (259)
2. The work of memory, with the function of forgetting, and with the modalities of reparation. Is it possible to lump together slavery, colonization, and apartheid as a memory? That is to say, not in a sort of distinction between before and after or past and future, but in what might be termed the *genetic power* of these events—their revelation of the impossibility of a world without Others and of the weight of the peculiar responsibility incumbent upon Africans themselves in the face of tragedy (which is not the only element!) in their history. It is here that the comparison between African and Jewish experiences reveals profound differences. In contrast to the Jewish memory of the Holocaust, there is, properly speaking, no African memory of slavery; or, if there is such a memory, it is one characterized by diffraction. At best, slavery is experienced as a wound whose meaning belongs to the domain of the unconscious—in a word, witchcraft. When efforts at conscious recollection have been made, they have scarcely escaped the ambivalence that characterizes similar gestures in other historical contexts. (259)

Mbembe argues that slavery is not the same experience on both sides of the Atlantic, and that Africans on the continent have yet to deal with the fact that they were both subject to slavery but also had an active part in shaping it. As far as the former slaves in the new world are concerned, there can be a refusal to acknowledge ancestry. This is not forgetting, it is denial.

3. The question of the symbolism of exile. The metaphor of the concentration camp is used to compare the condition of slavery with the predicament of European Jewry as well as, on a more general level, relations between race and culture in modern consciousness. But there is something hasty and superficial about this comparison. (261)

Marxist and other forms of analysis have not done justice to the sheer range of experience in the diaspora and formerly enslaved peoples, as well as the range of experience among colonized peoples on the continent. At the same time, the range of experience does not mean that the only way to address these issues is through microtheory, that is, very specific theoretical approaches calibrated only to one specific form of trauma. It is more useful to think of each of these areas as new problematics, that is, new areas in which questioning might occur and in which the differences of experience can be used to produce new ways of writing the self. Bodily torture, of the sort that Jean Améry talks about, is not identical to slavery, colonialism, or apartheid—and yet, if all are forms of the rupture or exhaustion of place, we might start to ask how each of these might shed light on the others.

This is already happening—we can see the term "apartheid" used for the Palestinian experience within Israel. We might want to say that there are historical and phenomenological differences between these experiences, and there are, but the goal here is not to produce a taxonomy of suffering. It is to write the self. To bring these together in such a way that each can metaphorically illuminate the other is a way of doing that. It does not just highlight the trauma, but it also suggests a direction for becoming-world.

8

"The Poet Becomes a Prophet": Suzanne Roussi Césaire's Négritude

The textual studies that have been done in the previous six chapters together make a case for an enactivist version of African philosophy, one that already exists in these key texts (and in other places as well, but we only have limited space to explicate this). It is a nonrepresentational space of thought, one that makes possible the creation of concepts adequate to African lived experience. We saw, before those six chapters, Sylvia Wynter as laying the groundwork for understanding how this creative questioning can be more than just the dismantling of oppressive conditions of thought but can also suggest forms of life steeped in a meaningful past but at the same time looking to create a new world.

This chapter is a bookend for Chapters 2 through 7, which revisited classic works in African philosophy with a view to showing that enactivist elements have been at least a potentiality all along. The other bookend was Chapter 1 on Sylvia Wynter, and in a sense Suzanne Césaire anticipates some of what we wrote about Wynter earlier. Both look forward, both are interested in the new space of creativity. Both rethink temporality to do this and see the necessity for a literature to ground it. Both, I want to argue, give us an image of the practice of philosophy that is not dependent on essences, and which is incremental, rooted in place without being straightjacketed by it, and able to leverage the concepts and practices of thought in a place to ask new questions and move toward new problematics. Wynter sets the terms for what this might look like through her recovery of humanism through the Ceremony Found, what I am calling ahumanism in order to recognize the embeddedness and dependence of the human within other complex structures, along with the decentered nature of being human (i.e., it is not all about us). Césaire, I will argue in this chapter, gives us another look at Négritude, one that takes us away from the essentialism and exoticism excoriated by so many, and toward a creative production of a new black existence. She writes long before Wynter, of course, and it is perhaps only now, with the reconsiderations of Négritude that have happened in the past few years, that we are prepared to see her positive and creative agenda.

To understand what Césaire is doing, we have to extricate her from the narratives about Négritude over the past decades. We will also have to see how she leverages Leo Frobenius, an inspiration for her who seems problematic on first glance, and how she uses surrealism, a common point of inspiration among Négritude scholars. Césaire writes to and from her place, and her Négritude is not a universalist or ontological statement on Black existence but rather a vision of a new space of thought and experience and the conditions for its emergence. She writes not primarily to Blacks everywhere but to her fellow Martinican citizens, to those who she sees as unwilling or unable to grasp the potentialities available to them, since they are so deeply rooted in the colonial mindset. She uses what she can—poetry, jeremiad, the publication of *Tropiques*—to try to jar her people from their slumber and take the next steps.

Négritude and Essentialism

Suzanne Césaire is usually put in one or both of the categories of Négritude writer and surrealist writer. She can, for those who want to, be dismissed that way as well. Both Négritude and surrealism are easily simplistically parodied, and if we add to that Césaire's brief oeuvre (only seven essays, plus a play that has been lost), she can be ignored in favor of her more famous ex-husband and other male members of the movement.

What we will do here, then, is make a case for taking her seriously. I am not the first to do that, by any means, but what I want to do will be different from what others have done. Simply put, I see in Césaire a non-essentialist (indeed, anti-essentialist) version of Négritude, and a version of surrealism that likewise does not foreground Freudian elements but instead focuses on excavating Blackness on its own terms rather than those imposed by French political or philosophical structures.

Perhaps the best way to see the first of these, her version of Négritude, is to approach it anachronistically, through the work of Emmanuel Eze, in particular his final book, *On Reason* (2008). In that book, Eze lays out a theory of rationality that is not fundamentally indexed to race or culture, but which still has the ability to recognize collective, historical, and geographical commonalities. He catalogues various forms of reason: formal, hermeneutical, empirical, phenomenological, and finally, "ordinary." Everyone has all of these and uses them at different times for different purposes. Rationality is the capacity to mix and rank these forms of reason and know what the right one is to use at any particular time. (For more on this, see Janz 2008.)

Why is this significant for Négritude? Because Eze is covering similar ground to the Négritude debate going back as far as the 1920s, but he is coming to a different conclusion. In those debates, there were also different forms of reason, but they were essentialized, which in this case means that they were attached to races. So, discursive abstract reason was supposed to be the province of Europeans, whereas intuitive emotional reason was what Africans were supposed to have. And while one might celebrate the humanity of intuitive reason, if one wanted technology and all the other aspects of modernity, it was discursive reason that was needed. Africans, to be modern, would have to give up being African.

And so, for good reason, that model of reason was roundly criticized, even as its proponents produced great poetry. No doubt some of these proponents saw themselves as exemplifying this essentialist, racialized distinction in forms of reason, but as we see with Eze, there are other ways to think about reason and culture that do not amount to assigning forms of reason to cultural or racial groups.

Eze writes long after Césaire, of course, and so this is not a question of intellectual history but of spaces of thought. If what is differentially distributed is not forms of reason but modes of rationality, that is, ways of ordering and prioritizing forms of reason that we all have based on cultural (which includes historical) factors, then we have something much closer to cognitive strategies than epistemological ones. And as cognitive strategies, the ordering of forms of reason need not be metaphysically located. Négritude, like Mogobe Ramose's version of Ubuntu, could describe the space of thought and action available to Africans based on their history and their ways of creating in an uncertain and complex present and future. The initial impulse of Négritude was always aesthetic, but Négritude artists were asked to turn their creative impulses into metaphysical ones, that is, to say what their sense of African autopoietic existence meant in metaphysical terms. And so, given that question, the answer looked like the assertion of an essence for Africanity.

We see the same in Diagne's treatment of Senghor, often thought as the most metaphysical of the Négritude artists. Senghor's turn to metaphysics, something that Diagne suggests distinguishes him from Aimé Césaire (2011: 8), allows him to explicate a way of being embedded in artistic performance and production that, contrary to the stereotype, is not simply "intuitive" reason, which is defined as a secondary form in comparison to discursive reason, but rather shows artistic performance and production as a space of action in which knowing becomes available. What kind of knowing is this? Is it mystical or mythic? Is it poetic? Senghor did, after all, say that if he was to be remembered for anything, he would like it to be his poetry. Senghor's own sense of knowledge, though, comes much closer to the enactivism in this book than anything metaphysical (as Diagne demonstrates in the structure of his own study of Senghor in *African Art as Philosophy* [2011]):

> It will be noted that each of the titles of the book's chapters are keywords in Senghor's thought: rhythms, *co-naissance* (a way to write the French term for "knowledge" that Senghor adopts from Paul Claudel to express the notion of a knowing [*connaître*] that consists in being born to and with [*naître à et avec*] that which is known), convergence, mixture; though, rather than "exile," it is "kingdom" that is the Senghorian keyword. It is rather Sartre who speaks here to say that Négritude is exile, whereas the entire Senghorian project will be to proclaim it a kingdom. (15–16)

Diagne frames this, following Spivak, as "strategic essentialism" (15), but an enactivist frame seems to work even better. There is no necessity for any identity talk in Négritude to be understood the way Diagne does in this book. That metaphysics may well be part of the discussion is an attempt to capture and solidify moments in the expression of African existence, but as aesthetic production they are also ways of knowing that are based in rhythms, that is, repetitions and parallel structures in different instances, which draw on strategies of knowing developed and tested in a community stretching back into time (*co-naissance*) and which create anew based on true dialogue (convergence). None of this need be essentialist, strategic or otherwise, because these function in the same manner that Eze's different forms of reason function—as capacities available to everyone, but which are ordered and deployed differently based on the history, culture, geography, and incentives one has. Indeed, Diagne describes Senghor in words that could almost have been lifted straight from Eze:

> What constitutes originality, Senghor tells us, is not a specific feature that would belong solely and exclusively to one race but, rather, a certain "equilibrium," let us say a certain ratio, between various features that can be found everywhere because together they make up the human condition. Different cultures, then, will be characterized by different ratios between the same features that they combine in separate ways. (95)

Diagne focuses on a version of metaphysics; Eze focuses on a version of epistemology. Both end up in roughly the same place, with a philosophy that is not culture or race specific, but which is sensitive to place, circumstance, and history. What enactivism adds to this is a performative element, that is, the idea that we live into an uncertain and complex future, and the skills of coping with that are different from the skills of describing performances that have already happened. Enactivism places both metaphysics and epistemology in a place—not an exclusive or siloed place but one that has its own integrity. That integrity does not preclude that this kind of place also can be violated and submerged under the cognitive strategies of other places (which is exactly what happens in colonialism, slavery, apartheid—a kind of torture that takes us out of our places and takes away the cognitive tools of coping).

So, the Négritude of Senghor (at least) might not necessarily fall to essentialism, and this might by extension apply to other versions. But there is another criticism of Négritude, tied to its dependence on vitalism. Donna Jones, in *The Racial Discourses of Life Philosophy: Negritude, Vitalism, and Modernity* (2010), makes the case that vitalism in any of its forms trades on a kind of fascism and to that extent is tainted by it. The fascism comes about because of the essentializing tendencies one finds in *Lebensphilosophie*, that is, the idea that there are fundamental characters. From that starting point, it is a straight line to constructing a mythic past, positing a unique form of reason that accesses the character that is known and recognized only by those who have it themselves, and in doing all this, trapping Négritude thinkers in a way of thinking that ontologizes Black inferiority in the name of difference and uniqueness. Jones does not reject Négritude entirely, and in fact by the end of her book argues that "Negritude has been too often caricatured as simply irrationalist and culturally particularist and that a more nuanced reading of Senghor and Césaire reveal both a subtle vitalist epistemology and a complex theory of culture" (132).

Jones's approach to Négritude has been met with a range of responses, from Drabinski's (2011) review essay that is broadly supportive but nevertheless raises significant questions, to Thiam's (2014) recovery of Négritude as an African epistemology by moving away from the German and French influences, to work that only addresses Jones's argument obliquely, such as Gary Wilder's *Freedom Time* (2015) and Souleymane Bachir Diagne's *Postcolonial Bergson* (2019).

The issues Jones raises must be taken seriously. Is it the case that vitalism of any and all sorts must be rooted in *Lebensphilosophie*, which necessarily assumes fascism? Clearly, in this book I am assuming that is not the case. But why not?

Jones identifies two kinds of vitalism, "one beginning with Schopenhauer and Nietzsche and the other with Bergson" (2010: 61). This is not the only way to break down the differences among vitalists and account for its history, though. We can, for instance, see an eighteenth-century vitalism that came about from a revival of interest in Lucretius (Deutsch and Terrall 2012). Scott Lash identifies three generations of vitalists, which do not align with Jones's: "There is a generation born about 1840–45 including Nietzsche and the sociologist Gabriel Tarde; the generation born about 1860 including the philosopher Bergson and the sociologist Simmel, and the generation born about 1925–33 including Gilles Deleuze, Foucault and Antonio Negri" (2006: 324). Like Jones, Lash sees two forms of vitalism, although they differ from Jones's: "One connects Tarde to Bergson and Deleuze, and the other runs from Nietzsche through Simmel to Foucault." Franz Wuketits (1989: 8–10) divides versions of vitalism into "animist" and "naturalistic" varieties, "where the first is explicitly metaphysical and teleological in orientation, while the second posits organic natural laws that transgress the range of physical explanations. Both varieties of vitalism are described by Wuketits—who speaks from the perspective of general systems theory—as 'untenable in the light of modern biological research'" (Greco 2005: 16–17). And Benton (1974) has a separate taxonomy from any of these, focusing on nineteenth- and early-twentieth-century versions of vitalism in science.

The point in listing these various taxonomies of vitalism (and we could continue with more) is to show that vitalism as a concept follows Deleuze's observation that all concepts are multiplicities (Deleuze and Guattari 1994: 15), and that vitalism is configured in answer to a specific question or need that a researcher has. Much of the discourse around vitalism is rooted in debates over whether scientific accounts of the world, particularly reductionist, materialist, or mechanist accounts, are adequate to explain particular phenomena, especially aspects of life or life as a whole. "Explain" is the operative word here—vitalism has its roots in the attempt to provide a more adequate account of phenomena that at least some people believe are diminished or destroyed by modern scientific explanation. The spectrum of kinds of vitalism come into being in part because there are different kinds of alternatives to reductionist accounts, and in part because the work that vitalism is put to changes in different hands.

This accounts for Jones's way of framing vitalism and the relatively narrow scope she uses. It allows her to connect vitalism to Négritude (which is, after all, a clear connection in the literature, but which still needs an account), and it also allows her to limit the kinds of vitalism that will be regarded as relevant to her story. Perhaps most problematic in this regard is her treatment of Deleuze (Jones 2010: 66–72). Deleuze is reduced, mostly via his critics such as Hallward and Badiou, to a mystical, anti-intellectual vitalist. Jones's own assessment is that the problem with Deleuze "does not seem to be mysticism but mystification or actually a failure to understand the tragic obdurateness of our own social forms" (70). The problem is, ultimately, the same problem that *Lebensphilosophie* has: "Vitalism provides the metaphysics for the Deleuzean devaluation of classes for creative minorities yet to come" (71). If this is all that vitalism can bring, then its implied use by Suzanne Césaire (and others in the Négritude movement) is a mistake at best and a self-imposed limitation on Black experience at worst.

The issue, I think, lies in the question to which vitalism is an answer, particularly for Suzanne Césaire. That question affects how it accomplishes what it is meant to accomplish. If vitalism remains a metaphysical account of life, an alternative to reductionist scientific theories of biology, psychology, and culture, then it seems inevitable that vitalism will both end up positing quasi-mystical forces and tend toward fascism, as cultural and racial characters end up beyond the reach of meaningful politics or even human reason. If, however, the question is not primarily metaphysical but cognitive, the landscape looks different. If it is not that we are looking for an alternative account of human life, though, and development, one that does not lose what we might want to see as quintessentially human, but rather we are looking for a description of how we might, individually and collectively, navigate complex space and conflicted history to create oneself anew.

The difference is that this cognitive approach is anti-representational. There is no attempt to give a picture of the "true" or "real" African, the one caricatured or obscured by Western science and culture or valorized through a celebration of emotion and intuition. It is not that that project is not worth doing—it surely is. But the search for the real African stands in tension with the creation of the African-to-come, the one living in the current world and creating a new one out of it. Why is it a tension? Because the search for the real is the search for being, whereas the search for the conditions of creation is the search for becoming.

Jones's questions about Négritude's debt to vitalism stem from this metaphysical question. It connects to a particular understanding of mysticism: "The popularization of vitalism through the occult underlines a key element of vitalist discourse: the belief in inner and hidden causal factors. Occultism provided a perfect vehicle through which the contradictory vocation of a science of the 'unknown' could be practiced" (Jones 2010: 75). This is a popular way of thinking about mysticism, that it is about agency from unseen or spiritual places, but again, this requires that we ask a metaphysical instead of a cognitive question about it. Mysticism can be seen as a way of putting together phenomena in the world in a coherent manner. Sometimes this rejects scientific verification, sometimes it runs ahead of it, but it always takes a chaotic set of phenomena and gives them a narrative. This narrative does not require spiritual agency, although it often does include it. But even when it does, the point is that there is an attempt to come up with an account of an incomprehensible or contradictory world that enables action within it.

None of this means that we should take seriously any and all mystical claims, any more than we should take seriously any and all cognitive strategies for action. What it does mean is that if we shift the question about Négritude to one that asks about the existing resources within culture to take the next steps, we need not be committed to any large-scale metaphysical claims about Black essentialism, different forms of reason from the West, and so forth.

The focus of this chapter is not on Négritude in general but on Suzanne Césaire in particular. In other words, I leave it to others to work out a version of Négritude that does not fall into the problems that Jones outlines for Senghor, Aimé Césaire, and others. We have already seen Diagne do this for Senghor. In this chapter, I am interested in how Suzanne Césaire presents a creative future for Blacks in the diaspora and on the continent, one that does not pit evolutionary science against a search for and championing of fundamental character. She rarely refers directly to vitalism (she mentions "vital force" in one essay and speaks more generally of vitality in other places), although one might see elements of vitalism in her thought, especially when she discusses Leo Frobenius.

Césaire's Seven Essays in *Tropique*

Suzanne Césaire is not Senghor, or Damas, or even Aimé Césaire, but if a case can be made even for the most seemingly metaphysical of the Négritude thinkers that in fact there is something closer to enactivist thinking happening, the case for someone like Césaire should be more obvious. Our task here will be to make the connections that she tries to make to a Négritude inspired by elements of Leo Frobenius and by surrealism but rooted in her native Martinique. She too is interested in a way of knowing that draws on her place, but not one that is an essentialist rehearsing of the same patterns over and over. And, as we can see in Emmanuel Eze's analysis of reason, it is entirely possible to think of Négritude as a way of deploying rationality by ordering forms of reason based on learned and reinforced patterns from the past, to live joyfully in a world of uncertainty.

Suzanne Césaire's oeuvre is slim—only seven essays and two plays, one of them lost. Yet, in these seven essays we can see glimpses of a world of joyful creation. She wrote and edited (for we must not forget that she was an editor as well as a writer and as such had a hand in shaping *Tropiques*) when Martinique was a Vichyist French outpost, and so writing had to be done carefully. Even with that care, the chief of information services, Lieutenant de Vaisseau Bayle, wrote a letter on May 10, 1943, to object that the journal was a "revolutionary, racial, and sectarian review" (Sharpley-Whiting 2002: 125–7). The editors responded within two days: "'Racists,' 'sectarians,' 'revolutionaries,' 'ingrates and traitors to the fatherland,' 'poisoners of minds,' none of these epithets are in essence repugnant to us" (128). There is no record of the lieutenant's response, but the editors made it very clear—"expect neither pleas from us, nor recriminations, nor even debate. We do not speak the same language."

And that is exactly it—the language Suzanne Césaire and the others were speaking was a different one from the molar political structure of the white French aristocracy. It was a minoritarian literature. Perhaps ironically, the response letter was much more pointed than most of what is in *Tropiques*, particularly by Suzanne Césaire. She did not spend much time on the likes of the lieutenant or on fomenting revolt against France. Her concern, almost exclusively, was Black Martinique and its unrealized potentialities. She dreamt of the kind of energy and creativity that might be released through surrealism and railed against those who were satisfied with the status quo and lacked the intellectual curiosity and artistic daring to be better.

The seven articles that Césaire published in *Tropiques*, along with their dates, are as follows:

1. "Leo Frobenius and the Problem of Civilizations" (*Tropiques* 1, 1941)
2. "Alain and Aesthetics" (*Tropiques* 2, July 1941)
3. "André Breton, Poet" (*Tropiques* 3, October 1941)
4. "Poetic Destitution" (*Tropiques* 4, January 1942)
5. "The Malaise of a Civilization" (*Tropiques* 5, April 1942)
6. "Surrealism and Us" (*Tropiques* 8–9, October 1943)
7. "The Great Camouflage" (*Tropiques* 13–14, 1945)

Some overviews of her work already exist. T. Denean Sharpley-Whiting's overview in *Negritude Women* is very useful (2002: 80–102). The introduction by Keith Walker and the editor's notes by Daniel Maximin at the beginning of the 2009 translation of the essays also give excellent context (Césaire 2012: vii–xxxvi). And Kara Rabbitt analyzes Césaire's work in several essays (2006, 2008, 2013, 2015). It is not my goal here to try to supplant all this excellent work but rather to link Césaire to the enactivist program, not causally but as someone who saw independently that the process of coming to know is a kind of self-creation, not based in some essentialist story about unique African capabilities of reason but as an account of how one might create within uncertainty.

Surrealism is not mentioned in the first essay. André Breton's book *Mad Love* (1987) makes an appearance in the second, and throughout that essay one waits for a mention of surrealism, given the way she is discussing Alain's work. After that, though, surrealism and Breton are ever-present in her essays. One reason for this was no doubt the timing of Breton's visit to Martinique. He fled Marseilles in spring 1941 on an overcrowded ship (one fellow passenger was Claude Levi-Strauss), and upon reaching the first stop, Fort-de-France Martinique, he was taken into custody as a "dangerous agitator." He was released a few days later and spent about three weeks in Martinique. He knew Aimé and Suzanne Césaire from Paris in the early 1930s, and so they were his guides on the island. He discovered that they had just published the first issue of their new journal, *Tropiques* (see Franklin Rosemont's introduction to the English translation of Breton's *Martinique: Snake Charmer* for more on this; Breton 2008: 2–4), which led to extended discussion about the relationship between surrealism and Négritude. And the influence did not just flow in one direction—surrealism gained focus on lived experience in place, colonialism, and the Black world just as Négritude gained a way of breaking through the strictures of the French language to create something anew. Breton was fascinated with Martinique and read histories of the island while there. He stayed in touch with Aimé Césaire for years later and promoted his work in other surrealist venues (why he did not do the same for Suzanne is an open question—Rosemont says, "That Breton regarded [Césaire] with high esteem is shown by the moving prose poem he dedicated to her, in 'Trembling Pins'"; Breton 2008: 24).

Her writing on surrealism almost feels like the words come tumbling out, so excited is she to describe the potential. And yet, with a form and a direction. One cannot help but feel the excitement in her writing in, for example, her essays titled "André Breton, Poet"—about Breton, yes, but also about the potentiality within surrealism. There is autopoiesis here—the "Nameless woman Who splinters the jewel of the day into a thousand shards," a quote from Breton's *Mad Love*, is the one who shows the compositionality and the contingent interactions of reality.

It is not a reality already set, but one that is to come, not by plan or design but by catching the energy of the interactions already there and imbuing them with fire (Césaire 2012: 20–1). The oppression of colonialism must be ended, yes, but the entire focus is on what might come when freedom is really possible. "Freedom to do and to undo" (22).

In some entries, for instance "Poetic Destitution," she does not mention surrealism, but she certainly explores Martinique through its lens. Her version of surrealism has little of the Freudian undertones that many come to expect in such poetry. Instead, she almost gives you whiplash, giving us images of the lush, exotic Martinique and then telling us that what she is writing "will delight imbeciles," and then returning again to more lush imagery. And yet, in that exoticism, she signals her disdain of the "Good Blacks cast upon the water like ever so many flies" (25). There is no Henri Rousseau exoticism here, dreamscapes reaching back to the primitive imaginary and the collective unconscious.

Leo Frobenius and Paideuma

By modern standards, Leo Frobenius is an unlikely source for writers of Négritude to pick up. There is no question that Frobenius shares colonialist and racist assumptions with most other Europeans of his time, and his affectionate portrayals of Africans does not extend to regarding them as full equals in every way but rather as trainable for colonial purposes (for more on this, see Ita 1973). One might also include his problematic research methods, by modern anthropological standards, and his questionable politics (Sylvain 1996). It is certainly true that he represents a change from the attitudes of his time, steeped in Hegelian assumptions about the potential of African civilization (recall that for Hegel Africa does not even merit a mention in the progress of the dialectic toward freedom), but that respect for Africa also seems on its face to be an exoticization of African life, more akin to Rousseau than to any emancipatory thinkers at his time, such as W. E. B. Du Bois. He is a neo-Romantic.

As a model, then, Frobenius seems less than ideal, to put it mildly. He is, at the very least, proposing an essentialized view of Africans, and so it is no surprise that Négritude ends up being charged with essentialism. But it might be that Frobenius's essentialism was not what attracted writers such as Césaire to him. It might not have been fascination with the metaphysics of Black essence at all, whatever Frobenius himself might have intended. Suzanne Césaire is not asking whether Frobenius gives a reliable picture of Africans as Africans, or whether he enables an equitable picture of Africa. She instead asks what he makes available, what potentialities he points to. He is without question flawed if the question is whether he accurately represents Africa. He is, if not racist himself, an enabler of racists, someone who exoticizes the African other in much the same manner that Leni Riefenstahl does with her Nuba photographic and cinema projects (for more on this, see Sontag 1981). Africans become noble primitives, exemplary Black bodies that are closer to the ontologically pure than anyone else, and who suffer to the extent that they deviate from that purity.

And yet, Frobenius was an inspiration to many writers of Négritude, including Senghor, Aimé Césaire, and Suzanne Césaire. In some cases, we might see these writers as responding to a rare positive depiction of Africans within Western scholarship and willing to live with the essentializing implications. In the case of Suzanne Césaire, however, I want to argue that she sees something else in him. Rather than a representation of Africanity in the sense of the excavation of some pure essence of the African spirit, she sees a set of cognitive strategies for living in, recovering, and creating a world in which Black existence is at the center. This is for her the link to surrealism, which we shall see shortly, and it is a clearer and stronger link than some of the others that took up surrealism as a lens for African life. She sees not a door into the irrationalism reputed to be at the center of Africanity but instead a set of disruptive and creative strategies to get out of existing patterns of life.

Césaire's focus is on Frobenius's concept of Paideuma. Paideuma is for Frobenius (in an unfortunate phrase) "das dritte Reich," the third dimension or kingdom past organic and inorganic nature (Kramer 1985: 344). Sabine Jell-Bahlsen describes the effect of it as providing "a rationale for regarding African cultures as juvenile—a view well in line with colonial protectionism and paternalistic attitudes towards Africans" (1985: 318). Senghor, though, described Paideuma as follows:

> For every race possesses its own Paideuma, that is its own: peculiar capacity for and manner of being moved: of being "possessed." Nevertheless, the artist, whether dancer, sculptor or poet, is not content to relive the Other; he recreates it in order the better to live it and make it live. He recreates it by rhythm and thus makes of it a higher, truer reality, one that is more real than the factual reality. (1973: xi)

Claims about Paideuma, and by extension about Négritude, are usually put in metaphysical terms. That is, Paideuma is a spirit, a force outside of the self that animates the self. It is manifest in the expressive arts. What is missed, though, in this kind of analysis is that the discussion of the intuitive and creative in Négritude and in Paideuma is a high-level, generalized account of creativity. It does not ask about the mechanisms of creativity (and how could it, since to have a schematized mechanism at all would undermine the creative process?). One way to put the contrast between Négritude and European reasoning is between knowledge of the whole and knowledge of the parts. But even this is partial since the whole is not static. The whole is, rather, an understanding of the connections between things, an emphasis on those connections over the discrete entities that they connect. Paideuma is, as Senghor puts it here, a re-creation "in order the better to live it and make it live" (xi).

Césaire, in her essay on Frobenius, makes much out of his distinction between the Ethiopian and the Hamitic forms of civilization. These can seem like they are in the tradition of *Lebensphilosophie*, that is, static and essentialist modes of being at the level of civilizations, a descriptive and causal set of structures that purport to account for large-scale cultural phenomena, susceptible to fascism (as Donna Jones noted earlier when she connected vitalism and fascism). But this is not what we see in Suzanne Césaire. Frobenius's Paideuma, present in the Ethiopian form, can be understood not as an essence that governs all action but as a shock, a change of direction. Keith Walker, in his introduction to the collection of Césaire's essays, describes it as follows:

> Frobenius's most curious idea … surge-shock-seizure, which is a Manichean—bipolar—force of life and death, good and evil, potential that precipitates transmutation in the human. Such transmutations are economic, social, cultural, epistemic alterations of consciousness and worldview, alterations of, as he calls them, the *sentiment of life*. (Césaire 2012: xiii; original emphasis)

It is in other words a kind of event, a change that does not simply require civilizations to hew to a specific material form but to transmute in a wide variety of ways. The sentiment of life might in fact be seen mainly in retrospect, as one looks back on the changes that occur in a culture. Césaire in several essays critiques Martinican society as not living up to its Paideuma. But does this mean that she or anyone else knows what it should be in advance? No. She might know what it is not, but as to the question of what it might be, what potentialities it might activate, this is not at all clear.

Still, even if Paideuma can be seen as an account of change, the potentiality of essentialism remains. Césaire's first of her seven essays comes very close to presenting Paideuma as an essentializing force at times. But she also tries to resist that move, mostly by emphasizing the shock that leads to new creation. She finds language to articulate that shock in subsequent essays, for immediately after the publication of the first issue of *Tropiques*, André Breton made an unannounced stop in Martinique, and the significance of surrealism and Négritude to each other was reignited.

Surrealism, Tightrope of Our Hope

T. Denean Sharpley-Whiting says that "perhaps the most glaring omissions in Négritude's evolution have been the 'by-the-by' analyses of Paulette Nardal's body of ideas, the complete erasure of Jane Nardal, and the ceding of Suzanne Césaire to the surrealist camp" (2002: 16–17). She is correct about these omissions, but the goal here will be to get a clearer sense of Césaire's interest in surrealism and what that has to do with enactivism. *Tropiques* was sometimes seen as a journal more focused on surrealism than on Négritude, especially after the earliest issues, and a superficial look at the content would bear that out. André Breton's support and interaction cast a long shadow over the run of the journal. But what was that shadow, and was it the same for all the principals involved? I would like to argue that whatever we might see in Aimé Césaire and René Ménil, Suzanne Césaire was doing something slightly different with surrealism and, I believe, more in line with enactivism. Surrealism, as perhaps befits its fascination with the nonrational, the subconscious, and the intuitive, can be pressed into service for quite different philosophical agendas.

It might be tempting to see Césaire's interest in surrealism as starting with André Breton's visit to Martinique in 1941. In fact, surrealism had a vigorous presence in Martinique well before that. Writers such as Etienne Léro (1910–1939) declared their support of surrealism (along with Marxism) as early as 1932 in the *Légitime Défense Manifesto*, coauthored with Thélus Léro, René Ménil, Jules-Marcel Monnero, Michel Pilotin, Maurice-Sabas Quitman, Auguste Thésée, and Pierre Yoyotte (Rosemont and Kelley 2009: 38). The engagement with surrealism by Black intellectuals and writers was mixed with Marxism at that point (Michel 2000: 20), but by the time of the founding of *Tropique* in Vichyist Martinique, much of that strand was submerged or absent.

> Come on now, real poetry lies elsewhere. Far from rhymes, laments, sea breezes, parrots. Stiff and stout bamboos changing direction, we decree the death of

sappy, sentimental, folkloric literature. And to hell with hibiscus, frangipani, and bougainvillea.

Martinican poetry will be cannibal or it will not be. (27)

These oft-quoted lines from Césaire give a glimpse of this enactivist project within surrealism. Césaire rejects the romanticism, the island paradise aesthetic. There is no noble savage here, meant to counteract the negative images of Blacks in European literature but in fact just solidifying their otherness and exoticism. She excoriates the predictable Martinican literature—she calls it "Hammock literature. Literature made of sugar and vanilla. Tourist literature" (Césaire 2012: 26). One can almost see her spitting it out as she talks about it.

So then, why does she use the word "cannibal?" What a strange word to choose in this context! Is she not afraid that, with this choice, she has just brought that Romantic savage back to mind? Perhaps it is just the other side of the savage that she hopes for here, not the one wearing grass skirts and playing traditional instruments but the one waving spears. This seems like a risk.

But it is a risk only if we are not precise about what is cannibalized. It is not humans eating other humans, in reality or in metaphor. We see in her writing a clear focus on creating a new way of being for Martinicans. Where is that going to come from? Not from the colonial structures in place—they are what prevent anything new from happening, by regimenting life under foreign structures. It will have to come from Martinicans themselves. But (and this is where I think she deviates from other Négritude writers) it also does not come from excavating an "authentic" Africanity, a core metaphysical self that must be recovered and uncovered. For her, it is instead the recognition that what is new must come from what is old. There is no Romanticism here, but there is enactivism, a yearning to see in what is already there, the beginnings of a new question about Black life. The poet is at the forefront of this questioning because it cannot be put in discursive, logical terms. Not yet. It must be felt. That feeling is not some alternate rationality endemic to Africans the way that discursive rationality is supposedly endemic to Europeans. The feeling that the poet trades in is the feeling that happens when a space of thought has become constricted, worn out, uninteresting. A new space of thought and experience is needed. Poetry is, for her, the event that makes this possible. Surrealism is the birthing chamber, the *chora*, the space in which something new can be intuited and moved toward, without already having been cognized and conceptualized. Césaire describes the space of freedom in her essay on surrealist André Breton:

> And from that point when time is abolished, when the past, the present, the future are merged, when we live this unique state which permits us to recapture plenitude and that sense of the moment which thrills us so in young children so similar, as they are, to cats, dogs, calves, butterflies, flowers, and sand—can we not reasonably speak of freedom? (Césaire 2012: 22)

We see several things in this hope she expresses. She collapses temporality, not to abolish it but to see the past, present, and future implicate each other. There is no linear temporal development, in other words, that necessitates the future. And in this release from necessity, we have the possibility of chance, a key feature in surrealism. "Objective chance" was theorized by Breton and others early in the development of surrealism. We might think of chance as an intervention in the otherwise causal structure of reality (that would be a rationalist incorporation of chance alongside necessity), but surrealists did not think of it that way. Chance neither abolishes necessity nor stands alongside it as a flaw in its logic. It is the possibility of encounter, of change, of a new question. Breton describes objective chance like this:

> Every life contains these homogenous patterns of facts, whose surface is cracked or cloudy. Each person has only to stare at them fixedly in order to read his own future. Let him enter the whirlwind; let him retrace the events which have seemed to him fleeting and obscure among all others, which have torn him apart. There—if his questioning is worth it—all the logical principles, having been routed, will bring him the strength of that *objective chance* which makes a mockery of what would have seemed most probable. Everything humans might want to know is written upon this grid in phosphorescent letters, in letters of *desire*. (Breton 1987: 87; original emphases)

What he describes here is emergence. It is the intervention of a transversal element within "patterns of facts," and Breton is arguing (as is Césaire) that the causal logic of these systems is not set because chance makes it possible for changes in those systems, interventions in their logic. For both Césaire and Breton, freedom is possible. For Césaire, it points to plenitude, richness. It points to the hope of children, and at the same time the natural and instinctive reactiveness of animals.

Surrealism's use to Négritude, for Césaire, is not simply in the overturning of a dominant and oppressive system put in place by colonialism. It is not the celebration of some deep alternative black essence. It does not look back, but forward, and it does not simply fantasize about the new, but it dreams. "The poet becomes a prophet" (Césaire 2012: 23). The poet is the one who produces a literature that can sustain these dreams and their realization. But that literature is surrealist. It is cannibal.

Césaire has an account of how the system of oppression replicates itself within Martinicans. In "The Malaise of a Civilization," she describes the condition she calls "pseudomorphosis" (31), which is the condition of trying to lead a life that is not one's own. This happens because of the instinct for self-preservation. During slavery, Blacks were prohibited from engagement in society in multiple ways. They were meant to assimilate into a white world. That meant there were laws that narrowly restricted the kinds of labor they could engage in. After slaves were freed in Martinique in 1848, they became wage earners, but trained by years of restrictions, they took the safer path and submitted "to the new discipline of the hoe and the cutlass" (31). At the point when they might have explored who they were, they instead repressed it. What emerged instead was the "unaccustomed desire for competition" (32).

Césaire draws on Frobenius's distinction between the Ethiopian and the Hamitic and argues that the Hamitic desire for competitiveness overcame and subsumed the "Ethiopian desire for abandon" (Césaire 2012: 32). It resulted in a desire for imitation, or mimicry. This has become so ingrained that most sincerely believe they are living a meaningful life and do not know they are just mimicking those who have more than they do. Césaire anticipates what Wynter will see later, which is that the human must be recovered from the life that is currently lived, not by looking back for models but by using what came before as resources for the future. "It is not at all about a backwards return, a resurrection of the African past that we have learned to know and respect," Césaire says. It is instead about the "mobilization of every living strength brought together upon this earth where race is the result of the most unrecognizable intermixing; it is about becoming conscious of the incredible store of varied energies until now locked up within us" (33).

We see in this vision something very different from both the Négritude of some other writers, the mythopoetic research of Frobenius, and the playful disruption of surrealism. Césaire draws on all of these, but her focus is on her place, on Martinique. She is not, in the end, interested in theory, but practice, specifically the practice of creating the new out of what already exists. Her Négritude is explicitly not one of drawing on the past or celebrating the successes of Blacks as a race. It is, rather, a matter of leveraging the resources that have been covered over, not to recreate what is gone but to reenact the strategies of creativity contained in those ways of life.

We see how surrealism fits this in "Surrealism and Us." It is ultimately the search for freedom. We already saw this in her essay on Breton, and she reiterates it in this essay. "Surrealism is," she says, "living, intensely, magnificently, having found and perfected a method of inquiry of immeasurable efficiency" (Césaire 2012: 37). This inquiry is what is important here. It liberates humanity by "revealing it to the unconscious." This serves to illuminate the myths that people take for granted, such as the antinomies between whites and Blacks, Europeans and Africans, civilized and savage (38). In other words, the answers to the existing questions will be shown to have run their course. New forms of interrogation are needed.

Césaire's Négritude as a New Space of Thought and Action in Martinique

There is a tension between the model of Paideuma and the version of surrealism that we see in Césaire, and perhaps her most insightful contribution is the way she balances that tension. On the one hand, we have Paideuma, which can tend toward *Lebensphilosophie*, toward a description of philosophical types or styles, and toward essentialism. If there is an Ethiopian style and a Hamitic style, as Frobenius claims, these can start to look like sets of restrictions rather than potentialities. Césaire takes pains to not present it in those terms, but the possibility remains.

Surrealism, on the other hand, emphasizes imagination. Franklin Rosemont points out that Breton said, "The imaginary is what tends to become real" (Breton 2008: 36). And this sounds preferable to the essentialism implied in Paideuma. However, there is a potential dark side to foregrounding imagination. Many thinkers other than the surrealists were interested in how imagination could overtake and control reality, produce a new reality. One such person in the United States was Neville Goddard (he commonly went by "Neville"), who espoused a radical faith in imagination, along with an uncompromising individualism. Believing was what was necessary to personal and societal success. If the world is not to your liking, you conduct yourself as if your imagination is already real. We can see a similar move in the "health and wealth" gospel in some evangelical and fundamentalist Christian churches.

In other words, imagination sounds great, but it can turn out to be very bad, and it can ignore things like science and evidence in favor of its preferred vision of the world. It can argue from desired effect to cause and concoct wild accounts of both why things are the way they are and what is keeping the imagined reality from coming into being (think Deep States, Illuminati, and so forth). It can lead to the idea that all one has to do is believe, and reality will follow. It can support brutality and suppression against those who do not share the vision.

We see this in fascist philosophers like Julius Evola, who believe that only under fascism can the imagination truly be free, and we need to put a social order in place that can allow us to follow an imagination that responds to the mystical and magical rather than the material. And we might see the moment the United States was in from 2016 to 2020 as the apotheosis of imagination, that is, a president's imagination that things are as he wants them to be, and thus anything that does not line up with that either does not exist or happens because of some conspiracy theory. This is a compelling story to millions who otherwise see little hope in their own imaginations, but what they imagine is simply heightened racism, fascism, fear, and anger.

Imagination by itself, in other words, can just as well lead to hierarchy and unfettered individualism as it could to Black consciousness. In Césaire, though, it does not. Is that because she simply ignores that possibility and revels in the creative potential of imagination for Black existence? Or does she recognize that imagination by itself, within complex space, can be captured by these ideas and result in something that would, in the long run, trap Blacks every bit as much as colonialist ideology did?

I believe she does recognize this potential, as well as the potential of Paideuma to be essentialist. As we look at her seven essays, we do not see an essentialism that reaches into African past to direct the future, either through principles of thought or through something like a *Lebensphilosophie*. Neither, though, do we see a version of imagination that comes with an undercurrent of Gnosticism, or which is easily susceptible to capture. Nor does she take the route that some advocates of imagination have and posit Paideuma as a mystical substrate that reins in and directs imagination. The question of freedom is central and given the situation in Martinique in the early 1940s, completely understandable.

Césaire does not give us a theory or a plan, much less answers. She opens a space of thought and action. Many questions are left unanswered—what exactly does freedom mean? Is it expressed at an individual level, or can it be collective? Is that what the point of Paideuma is, to both have a shock to the system but also to have an avenue for collective freedom? What does surrealism look like outside of Vichy France and its colonies, when there was a repudiation of everything that had happened since the French Revolution?

For those looking for a Négritude step-by-step guide to Black liberation, this falls short. But it was never intended as such. Living into an uncertain future means that freedom is always simultaneously a reaction to given circumstances and the asking of new questions that allow new concepts to be formed. There is nothing comfortable or settled about the Négritude that Césaire shows us, no revolutionary plan. For many, this might suggest that its uses are limited. But recognizing that Négritude is aesthetic before it is theoretical means that it is meant to prepare a mental space for what is to come. We may have to feel before we think, and that does not denigrate the importance of thinking, but it recognizes that thinking comes in multiple forms, each appropriate to different circumstances. She asks us to do what Emmanuel Eze, years later, will recognize as the capacity of rationality to order and deploy modes of reason in a manner other than the way that Martinicans had come to do, burdened by colonialism and its imperatives. This, I believe, is what Suzanne Césaire is trying to tell us.

Conclusion: Future Events?

This book has explicitly been about African philosophy but implicitly about philosophy itself. The goal has been to broaden (African) philosophy's scope from being a discipline focused on the defense of propositions about things, to a discipline that also creates concepts that are adequate to its place(s). One might use the analogy of William Whewell's distinction in the philosophy of science—between the context of discovery and the context of justification. Philosophy, including African philosophy, has seen its remit as the context of justification. It is a normative space, one in which the question of what we ought to believe is paramount. It is a representational space, which strives to give the best picture of the world. It is a mode of thought, that is, a set of interlinked justified claims that assemble into a coherent structure that can support belief, and that can be claimed by an individual.

And this activity is necessary, but it is not sufficient. It is not all that philosophy is or should be. The context of discovery is just as important to philosophy. This refers not just to the discovery of concepts (or, as I have put it, to the creation of concepts) but also to the discovery of questions that can lead to spaces of thought. In striving to establish a space of thought, thinkers are not simply trying to find the answer to a problem of existence but also to articulate a question that will allow a way of understanding existence, and which will also enable people to act within that space.

Unpacking Enactivist African Philosophy

This book has been an exercise in imagining a shift in how African philosophy is done, from the dominant mode that exists. This shift is not an invention on my part but something that I believe can be found in a series of significant works already well known by African philosophers. The point is not that these works have been misread but rather that they have been read with a particular set of assumptions in mind about how one can and should do philosophy in general. That set of assumptions did not lead to problematic or deficient philosophy per se, but the lack of recognition that there were assumptions in play led to a solidification of how to do philosophy. While this solidification was not unique to African philosophy (one can see it everywhere), it is apparent in African philosophy because of the relatively recent imperative to define and defend the practice of African philosophy in the world of philosophy more generally.

One way to read this book is to focus on individual chapters or writers. Many readers coming to this set of studies may well only be interested in a particular author or issue. The real value of the book comes, though, as the parts come together to make a single argument. There is an arc to the book, one bookended by Sylvia Wynter and Suzanne Césaire and worked out in the texts of the figures chosen for inclusion here. That arc is one that moves historically by the publication of the texts. More importantly, it is one that moves intellectually, from concepts related to temporality and historicity to the idea of a literature, and the implications that has for African philosophy. The arc is meant to show that, through all these figures, we can identify a set of concerns that do not focus on representing African thought as much as they are concerned with how philosophy revitalizes itself, creates its space of thought through questioning what it means to be human, and African, in a place.

In Sylvia Wynter, we see someone who is trying to recover humanism as what I come to call "ahumanism," an open-ended creative experience that recognizes the meaning embedded within cultural spaces and uses them and their encounters with each other positively to think through what becoming-human might mean. She gives us the tools to not simply and superficially reject the Renaissance in favor of some other way of thinking but rather to live into an uncertain future without trying to capture or control it.

Placide Tempels is often seen, for better or worse, as the inception of a new space of thought in African philosophy. The focus in my story has not been to relitigate questions of ethnophilosophy, but rather to look in a place that philosophers have almost never looked—at the Jamaa movement that directly arose from Tempels's book and his leadership. We see a version of temporality, specifically embedded in vitalism, that has nothing to do with mystical or metaphysical forces that flow through everything, and everything to do with how to live well into an uncertain future. Jamaa was the recognition that Tempels's Bantu philosophy was not just a representation of what was supposed to be an African version of philosophy, but rather it was the ability to live in love (which is the real vitalism, the real connecting force) and use the successful patterns of thought, action, and social structure from the past and improvise on them so that the present is rich and creative.

The space of thought in John Mbiti's *African Religions and Philosophy* (1969) opens up as we do a mundane, relatively rare thing: read the whole book. Most philosophers look at Mbiti for a theory of time and find that contained in a single chapter of his book. If we look at the whole book, though, we can see that he has something much more like a theory of temporality than a theory of time. And that theory of temporality is meant to articulate what it looks like to live in the world as African, at the nexus of thought and practice. What commentators often see in him, which is a representation of African experience as having little concern for the future, can instead be seen as the enactivist sense that our knowledge into and about the future is based on past individual and shared cognitive practices extrapolated into the future, practices that have a mixed success rate because the future always comes with intervening factors. Along with this we see an approach to memory, one that encodes significance in narratives, ancestors, traditions, and so forth, and that as coded practice then can be interpretively used in an incremental fashion as becoming-African and becoming-human happens. It stands as an alternative to more hubristic approaches to memory and the future, which supposed that the future is a blank slate ready to be dominated by our will and the tools we bring to bear on it.

The turn that Odera Oruka takes in the final major work of his life, on Oginga Odinga, gives another sense of the potentialities of sage philosophy. In that work, Oruka largely abandons the motivating question from his earlier writings on sage philosophy, which was posed by Paulin Hountondji—is there philosophy in traditional Africa, and if so, what does it look like? Hountondji was largely skeptical that there was, and Oruka took up the challenge to demonstrate that there was, in fact, philosophy and that it did not run afoul of Hountondji's criteria—that it be held and articulated by individuals and not just contained as general cultural wisdom and that it be critical. By the time we reach the final book on Odinga, Oruka is asking very different kinds of questions, ones that elicit memories of specific circumstances, tactical decisions, and impressions of people and not just abstract descriptions of philosophical concepts. I proposed that Oruka was in fact adding a new category to his list of sage philosophy types: there was now the pragmatic sage, alongside the folk and philosophical sages. The pragmatic sage was one for whom historicity mattered, for whom process and emplaced wisdom mattered. More than that, the Odinga book demonstrates what an actual dialogue might look like (as opposed to an interview) and suggests the possibility that philosophy might be created in the liminal space between figures, in a second-person mode.

Mogobe Ramose shows us a version of Ubuntu very different from the commonly circulated ones. I argue that he articulates a fully enactivist version of African philosophy, one that does not attempt to represent received wisdom as much as it attempts to recognize the wisdom encoded in multiple forms that stands available for becoming-African. Ramose also explicitly introduces a component that is crucial for this enactivism to work—questioning. He is interested in the disruption of existing modes of explanation and action in favor of new and fresh questions that establish new spaces of thought and action. Ramose uses David Bohm's term, rheomode, for this shift in thought that comes about through a shift in questions. Ubuntu is not simply the binary opposite of Western individualism, as is often thought—that simply takes the Western question of action as given and posits its shadow. Ubuntu is a space of thought rather than a set of foundational beliefs and practices.

From Ubuntu we moved to the question of the nature of the space of thought, which I called a "literature." Sophie Olúwọlé had a seminal essay at a time when many were trying to define African philosophy, in which she argued that philosophy did require a literature (as Hountondji had said) but that the literature was not modeled on an African equivalent of Western science as Hountondji suggested. She returns to traditional thought but not as a guarantee of the Africanness of thought. It is rather the literary tradition, the canon, and the vocabulary and store of concepts that make African philosophy possible but do not bind it to simply replicate what came before. It is an open space, one that suggests an affect toward thought that allows creativity to happen.

We saw in the same chapter that Euphrase Kezilahabi approached a similar question from a different angle. His concern was with how philosophy already existed within African literature, and what kind of credible analytic approach one might use to see that literature from that place rather than from a foreign place. Kezilahabi leverages an approach to time, one that has some similarity to what we saw in Mbiti but which is also more sophisticated, to understand how literature written by and for Africans can be understood as models for creative living. A literature properly understood is the basis for a new problematic, a new way of questioning one's existence.

That questioning of existence must face the possibility that questions can not only go wrong but also hijacked and turned against themselves. A space of thought is a risky space. In the chapter on Achille Mbembe's work, particularly his "African Modes of Self-Writing" (2002), we see another aspect of literature—that which is created in the face of systematic forces that undermine the very possibility of such a narrative. Put in enactivist terms, if knowledge is embodied, it is possible for the body to be so broken and violated that there is a deep, even permanent rupture. Mbembe considers this, as he works through the effects of these assaults on the possibility of creating new questions within the literature of African philosophy. Slavery, colonialism, and apartheid leave people and cultures alienated from their place. I argued that this is perhaps best represented by how we can consider torture to be a violation of the ability to live in a place. There is no easy way forward, no magical new cognitive move that can be invoked to make it all go away. There are ways forward, though, which is what Mbembe says, in this essay and other places since then.

We end with Suzanne Césaire. By this point, we have seen that doing philosophy in Africa can start from questions of cognition rather than epistemology or metaphysics and can face forward into an uncertain future rather than just back into a violated, but also glorious, past. Her version of Négritude does not search for an African essence; rather, she leverages all the concepts and tools we have outlined in this book, adds surrealism and Paideuma as disruptive/creative elements, and writes about her place, Martinique, and what it might be.

The arc of the book moves from questions of temporality to questions of literature, but throughout all the studies, the conviction is that philosophy must live facing forward.

Enactivism as Philosophy

Those coming to this study with a background in cognitive science in general or enactivism in particular might have hoped for more specifics drawn from the robust literature of enactivism that might relate to Africa directly. However, my purpose has been different. It has been to treat enactivism as a way of doing philosophy rather than providing an alternate explanation for cognitive phenomena. It has picked up on elements of enactivist explanations, such as its anti-representationalism and its commitment to the 4E model that decenters cognition from the brain and invests significance in the material, technological, and social world of the knower. This enactivist approach resists the paradigm of philosophy that sees the task of philosophy as solely analytic, based in the defense of propositions and claims in order to populate a well-ordered mental world. My purpose has been to move African philosophy from what I believe it often falls into, which is what I earlier termed a mode of thought, that is, a way of thinking that has its preferred (or required) methods, which relies on abstracting from the world rather than living in it, and which sees living into the future as the attempt to control uncertainty through a set of concepts that are first worked out abstractly and applied to the world thereafter.

Enactivism returns us to the beginning of philosophy, the question of what is necessary to philosophize at all. The concepts that are the lifeblood of philosophy are not simply there to be found but are virtualities that arise from our engagement with our places, and which also arise from our places engaging with other places, both horizontally (i.e., other geographical and cultural places) and vertically (i.e., other focal lengths of place). What we do not get, then, with enactivism is hermetically sealed philosophical practices, with an internal identity, but rather virtualities that may or may not bear resemblance to other situations of philosophical cognition elsewhere. Every concept produced in this manner is a multiple—it does not have a single definition and hard boundaries. Rather, it exists inasmuch as it is scaffolded with other concepts in a coherent lifeworld that people in a place can navigate successfully, at every level from the mundane and material to the profound and abstract.

The enactivist understanding of philosophy does not begin from the conviction that there is a single substrate underlying the blooming, buzzing confusion of the world, which it is our job to find. There is no realm of the forms, either in another world or embedded in this one. An enactivist understanding of philosophy treats the world as a flow, as complex space that is not simply random, but which has elements of organization, some of which persist over time but are no less autopoietic virtualizations for that persistence. We are not helpless in this complex and chaotic space. We too are agents of organization, both in our practices and in our thought, but it is important to recognize that we do not solely think first and then deploy our thinking into the world as action. That does happen, of course, but so does the reverse—in our acting, we come to think. Concepts emerge that could not have emerged except for the phenomena in the world.

The mission in this book has been to work out a philosophy that starts from these premises. Or rather, the mission has been to show that this philosophy has been there all along, embedded within the writings of significant thinkers, and we have often missed these hints because of how philosophy has been conceived. We have, in effect, asked the wrong questions about the task of philosophy, and in so doing limited it and limited what is possible within African space.

So What?

What implications does any of this have for the doing of philosophy in Africa? At one level, enactivist African philosophy does not make the case that anything done in African philosophy to this point by anyone else has been wrong or should not have been done. The argument is, rather, that the philosophy was incomplete, and as such it led to the illusion that the only way to do African philosophy was as the search for variations on essentialist roots or grounding. In that scenario, the only question to answer was still the question I argued against in my first book: Is there an African philosophy? That question is as inadequate now as it was then, but the attempt here has been to paint a fuller picture of African philosophy, one drawn from the philosophers themselves, that does not depend on the representational forms of thought that typified African philosophy throughout most of its modern existence.

If what I have argued here is correct, we might ask what has been gained. If there really is a way of thinking of African philosophy that has the characteristics of enactivism, what should that mean for how philosophy can be done? There are some answers to that.

First, one thing it need not mean is that the project of representing African lived experience should stop. What is being represented, though, must be recognized as virtual—brought into being through the intersection of existing forces and cognitive strategies that are held by Africans. It could change, and more importantly, acting into the future is different from simply abstracting from past experience, finding rules or laws, and then applying them. As we saw with Oginga Odinga, his practical sagacity was flexible, able to meet a shifting and changing landscape. There were many ways of being African, indeed many ways of being Luo for him, and these were not constrained by some structure of what it meant to be African or Luo. It was invented in his actions, and the actions of others, and shown anew in each encounter, which others could then learn from.

Second, so the projects of engaging African lived experience do not stop. But how can they continue without being reduced to essentializing activity? By asking better questions. The focus really must be on the question, not the claim or the belief or the proposition. Questioning opens a space of thought. There will always be those who want to capture the results of questioning, harness it for predictability and control. For the philosopher, this is the death of philosophy. Turning philosophy into a set of precepts or beliefs that can be operationalized by a government or by other power structures may be desirable for controlling people or maximizing profits, but philosophy must always disrupt the questions that become too comfortable, especially to those with power. Power seeks its own maintenance and expansion, and this will always eventually either solidify a structure to the detriment of those living in it or overthrow a structure to install one that is more amenable to its own goals, also to the detriment of those living in it.

This is where we must learn from Mbembe and recognize the damage that has been done by the imposition of structures in the interests of power, and the resultant violence done to the ability to question and the ability to draw upon shared wisdom to imagine a new future. Even faced with torture and its analogues, we must live. Living means asking new questions in the space in which one exists. That may end up being so violated as to seem impossible (and we have the accounts of Holocaust survivors and other genocide survivors to attest to that). But if new questions are possible and new ways of dwelling exist, they must be found.

Third, we must also think about the cognitive space in which questions can be asked. Instead of first thinking about the metaphysics or epistemology involved, ask what it takes cognitively to understand. If our intellectual, artistic, social space has an energy to it, what is that? We can always abstract out of the specificity and materiality of that space, but the first question must be about how we can engage the space itself.

This seems far from how philosophy normally proceeds. Attention to place usually comes at the end of thought rather than the beginning, as the application of principles already worked out. But this is in fact an essential part of the process even of abstract thought. We can see, if we compare philosophical traditions around the world, that while there is sometimes commonality among the kinds of concepts these traditions generate, there is also vast difference between them. There is no sense that one of those traditions "got it right," has the right collection of concepts and the right way to think about things, and the others are simply on the way to the reality discovered by that one tradition. Each tradition exists within its own complex space, and as such the virtualities of thought differ. The concepts adequate to their places differ.

This is perhaps the chief value of engaging in the study of world philosophy—the realization that different philosophical traditions do not simply have different answers to the same questions but that they are in different cognitive spaces entirely, with a different constellation of concepts that spring from their own lived experience while also directing it, and they are addressing different questions. We could try to shoehorn the concepts from those different cognitive spaces into categories that purport to contain them all (ethics, politics, theories of self, theories of art, etc.), but these invariably end up doing violence to the concepts. Even the demarcation of philosophy itself does not always fit from one cultural cognitive space of thought to another.

If we can see that different traditions of world philosophy are different cognitive spaces, it is not much of a leap to see that the cognitive space of a single philosophical tradition may also change. This is the autopoietic turn/overturn of Sylvia Wynter—the creation and engagement with a new space, not just as remediation of a colonized tradition of philosophy but as the way philosophy itself engages human life in place and allows us to cope with an uncertain future.

Fourth, all this suggests that we must identify concepts that are adequate to their places. We need to ask what concept might be necessary to understand something, if it does not already exist. Africa, like any other place, deals with its own changing future, and it needs to create its own lexicon of concepts to address that. What does an African philosophy of technology look like? What does it look like for an African theory of personhood to grapple with genetic engineering or the biology/technology interface? What does an African philosophical approach to climate change look like? All these have had some level of engagement in recent times, but what I am suggesting is that they require more than just the application of principles generated from a space of thought where these phenomena did not exist. African philosophy is perfectly capable of addressing any and all features of the modern world, certainly anything that appears in its own lived reality, but that engagement requires attention to how those questions are asked and what the cognitive conditions are in which philosophy is developed. These phenomena are like perturbations in a system, and the system itself changes in response.

Fifth, perhaps more prosaically, if all I have argued is correct, we need to reconsider how we engage intellectual content at all. If African philosophy has been about representing Africa in some sense, the governing question then becomes, is the concept or argument before us truly African and truly philosophical? The categories for what count as philosophy have been established and then we go out looking to see what in African cultures might fit.

In an enactivist account of African philosophy, philosophy is made, not discovered. It can be made anywhere, if the right questions are asked. And so, we can summarize it this way: read charitably. We saw this repeatedly in the chapters in this book. We could have, for instance, come to the conclusion that the adherents of the Jamaa movement were just under the influence of a powerful and charismatic priest, and their beliefs were simply cult-like. Or we could recognize their agency and ask what they saw in *Bantu Philosophy* (1959) that philosophers had not seen. Read charitably, their interest becomes a space of thought for that book that had not been considered, or rather, had only been considered by anthropologists and not philosophers. Their engagement was not seen as philosophical activity and so was not engaged as such.

Another example: reading the entirety of Mbiti's *African Religions and Philosophy* suggests an approach to his theory of time that does not become apparent if we only look at the fourteen pages that are usually the focus of philosophers. We might think of Mbiti as a theologian who said some philosophically interesting things, and his theological reflections are irrelevant to his philosophical ones. Or instead, we could look at him as doing philosophy even in his theological reflection and regard him as knowing what he was doing in the book as a whole.

We could continue with examples of what it looks like to read charitably or not charitably, but the only way new philosophical questions are likely to emerge is if we take seriously the experience of those living in and writing from a place.

Sixth, finally we need to understand the scholarly cognition surrounding the problem or the document in question. "Scholarly cognition" is my term for the "dark matter" of scholarly production, all the practices and local knowledge and scaffolding that goes into the decisions made about which questions are worth asking, how to support asking them, how information is disseminated and valued, and so forth. (For more on this, see Janz 2019). If philosophy has been conducted as the activity of the lone inquirer (or even lone genius), we have to ask why that is and what it would look like if it were done differently. Is there a collective engagement of philosophical thought, even one described by Ubuntu? If philosophy has been subject to gatekeepers, what would it look like to change them or change their structure? How would that relate to African modes of knowledge authorization? What kinds of knowledge are incentivized or motivated and what kinds are overlooked, and are these similar to the ways these lines are drawn in other cultural spaces of thought? How are the modes of production of philosophy changed when it becomes interdisciplinary—can philosophy be imagined in a smartphone app or in an urban design or something other than the discursive argument?

We can imagine many more questions that would get at the scholarly cognition around philosophical production. The point is that enactivist African philosophy can ask questions with these vectors of experience and many more besides.

Enactivist African philosophy opens up a creative space in philosophy. It is a creative space that can absorb and make productive cultural forms that previously had been thought as not philosophical or as having to be transformed into specific argumentative structures in order to be philosophical. None of this means that argumentation is not crucial to philosophy or that discursive long-form arguments are not important. This book is a discursive long-form argument. What it means is that philosophy can be found in many places and being able to engage the existing spaces of thought and imagine new ones opens philosophy up to exactly what we would want in African philosophy—the recognition of the uniqueness and connectedness of African place.

A Cycle of Question Cycles

Some question cycles, always returning to beginnings.

1. *Where does philosophy begin?* It begins with the question.
2. *Do all questions qualify as philosophical?* No, in fact very few do.
3. *Then what makes a question philosophical?* It asks about beginnings.

1. *Is a question philosophical when it is in a philosophical text?* There are no philosophical texts, but rather philosophical questions about texts.
2. *Is a question philosophical when a philosopher asks it?* There are no philosophers, and there are only philosophers. The person does not guarantee the question, but rather the question is the becoming of the person.
3. *Is a question philosophical because its answer is profound, insightful, complex, or long?* No.

1. *Are philosophical questions a means to an end, that end being a proposition worth defending?* No, the opposite: propositions are points on the road to questions. They "pro-pose," and as such, anticipate questions, rather than simply providing a conclusion to the process of questioning.

2. *Are philosophical questions about being?* No, they are about becoming. Being too is a point on the road.
3. *Where does this road of philosophical questioning lead?* Back to the beginning.

1. *Is there a uniquely African philosophical question?* Not in the sense of a question that has never been asked before. But there is a uniquely African becoming, and to that extent there are uniquely African questions. Much damage has been done by mistaking non-African questions for African ones, the most damaging question being "Is there an African philosophy?"
2. *Is there a uniquely African philosophical method?* No. But method is a distillation and codification of questioning, and as such it can disguise another's becoming. Method encodes, elides, and summarizes specific approaches and answers to questions but itself must be questioned. Method is the technology of becoming-African, and as such can create African concepts with force and power, like a bridge, or enframe, reduce, and tame questions, like a dam.
3. *Is there a uniquely African philosophy?* Not in the sense that some proposition, some method, or some area of study must be present in order for a philosophy to be truly African. There is no position, no belief, that someone must hold in order to be an African philosopher. But there is becoming that owes debts and duties to its places.

1. *Where do philosophical questions come from?* They come from places.
2. *What is a place?* It is the event of individual and collective human becoming, enacted in materiality, cognitive practice, and pre-reflective experience.
3. *What is the uniquely philosophical aspect of place?* The concept.

1. *Are concepts not the same as propositions?* No. They are not static. Concepts are a mode of becoming distilled for the moment. They are the digital elements in the analog space of becoming. Propositions are moments in the process of questioning, whereas concepts enable becoming. Concepts, properly understood, are events. They are the vector of the process of questioning and pro-posing.
2. *Do concepts stand alone?* No. They are part of ecosystems. Sets of concepts mutually reinforce each other; other concepts enable us to reach outside of those ecosystems to larger systems. No matter how activated a concept is, though, it can never lose its tie to place and remain a concept. A concept that has lost its tie to a place becomes a word.

3. *Are concepts contents of the mind?* No, or rather, they are not only that. They are extended and enacted. They scaffold our reality. They become manifest in spatial organization, bureaucratic convention, cultural practice, language, religious doctrine, and many other things. Concepts are engines of cultural creation, but at the same time can become ossified if they are not renewed. Their success, as often as not, is their failure.

1. *How are concepts created?* By questioning place, and in particular our place in place. By attending to those concepts that are and have been. By violence. By asking about the concepts that are commonly held to be activated and ask whether they really are.
2. *How are concepts activated?* By their scaffolding. Or to use another metaphor, by their ability to bring a place into sharp focus. Concepts are organizing entities. We might think that the philosophical impulse is to look for universal concepts, that is, entities that organize everything. This regards concepts as completed tasks, as being rather than becoming, and almost invariably represents an ossified concept.
3. *How are concepts applied?* They are not applied. Their ossified and cooled crusts are broken open. We do not apply concepts to a situation or place; rather, we ask what concepts arise from the place.

1. *Then if concepts are not applied, what do they do?* They create a problematic. They are a vector, a virtuality, an event.
2. *What is a problematic?* A line of flight. A new space for questioning. A khora.
3. *How does this happen?* It happens when concepts travel.

1. *Do concepts travel?* Yes, but not intact. And their changes are moments of potential reflexivity. They show forth a place. At best, a conversation between people from different places uses concepts that are substantially shared, but which are also the occasion for self-questioning.
2. *Are there not many places at different levels?* Yes. These are "topemes" (Janz 2009a: 13–14, 223-4), structures of place at different focal lengths. They are defined by their questions. It is why we can coherently talk about "African" philosophy when we know very well that the continent is vast, complex, and contradictory. There are questions directed at and engendered by that topemic level. There are other questions operative at other topemic levels, at the level of region, nation, ethnicity, urban area, and so forth. There are

questions that arise from women's experience, gay experience, disabled experience—these are other places, practiced place that gives rise to space. Concepts travel between places and also between topemic levels.

3. *Is the philosopher's task to map these highly complex and interrelated places?* No, or at least, not primarily. The philosopher's task is to create concepts adequate to their places and to consider the process of their activation.

1. *Is there nothing left of the universal in philosophy?* Yes, there is. Questioning is universal, just as the capacity for language is, although the particular questions we ask may not be. Concepts strive for universality inasmuch as they are modes of becoming whose success is noticed and copied. That striving, though, must always be anchored to place for its renewal, and as such concepts will inevitably speciate. Universals are earned, not presumed.

2. *Is there an ethics of concepts?* There must be. The mere creation of a concept does not guarantee its life-affirming nature. Apartheid was filled with concepts that had currency and that were activated by a profound scaffolding. It was a centripetal ecosystem, pulling all concepts to its center, resisting complex topemic engagement. Notably, it was also an ossified system, built on solidifying a social order. Concepts became propositions, and so they died. Its order, although brutal, was also fragile, and could not stand in the face of newer, more adequate concepts, many of which were born in the cramped ecology of the ossified concepts. Self-questioning had been lost. The same can be said of any brutal regime—Rwanda in 1994, Uganda in the 1970s, and of course, the entire history of colonialism.

3. *Is the success of the concept merely a recognition of its popularity?* No. Some extremely widely used (and in that sense popular) conceptual ecologies have also been some of the most ossified. Colonialism, national socialism in the mid-twentieth century, Soviet communism, and of course apartheid—these were presented as systems of being, not becoming, even though in every case the inner workings were highly dynamic and ultimately unstable. In each case, place was not so much lost as fabricated, turned into an imaginary or utopian space. If an image of place is fabricated that valorizes the *Volk*, it is not far to reach *Blut und Boden*. This is what happens when concepts lose their place—they become fantasies.

1. *What is the task of African philosophy?* To create new concepts adequate to African lived experience, which are true to African places, and to resist the ossification of existing conceptual ecologies. Some of what goes under

the label of "African Philosophy" does not meet one or more of these requirements, but the overwhelming pressure from outside of Africa is to abandon these in favor of a set of alien criteria.
2. *How can this be accomplished?* By questioning our questions. By asking whether our questions are really allowing African lived experience to show itself.
3. *How do we know if we have succeeded?* There will be virtualities or events, that is, there will be concepts that allow us to understand that experience in its uniqueness and universality. There will be new problematics.

1. *Is this pattern limited to African philosophy?* No, but I believe African philosophy is one of the best spaces in which to see this dynamic. We are continually called back to beginnings—by Socrates, Kant, Husserl, Heidegger, and so many others. The beginning that African philosophy calls us to is the beginning of place. We see more clearly here than anywhere else the place of philosophy, rather than the philosophy of place.
2. *How might African philosophy contribute to the wider project of philosophy?* Not by being a flavor of philosophy. Not by being a local variant, a regionalism, a derivative space, an identity within philosophy. Not by converging on an implicitly agreed-upon narrative. By being a place in all the richness that that provides.
3. *Is there a further problematic that opens up when we take African philosophy seriously?* There is "scholarly cognition," the cognitive process connected with scholarly production that goes beyond the established methods and procedures enshrined in disciplines. The attention of African philosophy to its own place means attention to the affordances and borders of intellectual place of all sorts. Habituation in thinking African place means learning the ability to notice the affective and felt aspects of scholarly production.

1. *Where does African philosophy begin?* It begins with the question.

References

Achebe, Chinua (2013). *Anthills of the Savannah*. London: Penguin UK.
Agamben, Giorgio (1999). *Remnants of Auschwitz: The Witness and the Archive. Homo Sacer III*. New York: Zone.
Améry, Jean (1980). *At the Mind's Limit: Contemplations by a Survivor on Auschwitz and Its Realities*. Bloomington: Indiana University Press.
Ansell-Pearson, Keith (2018). *Bergson: Thinking beyond the Human Condition*. London: Bloomsbury.
Asouzu, Innocent I. (2007). *Ibuanyidanda: New Complementary Ontology Beyond World-Immanentism, Ethnocentric Reduction and Impositions*. Zurich: Lit Verlag GmbH.
Ataria, Yochai (2016). "I Am Not My Body, This Is Not My Body." *Human Studies* 39:2, 217–29.
Ataria, Yochai, and Gallagher, Shaun (2015). "Somatic Apathy: Body Disownership in the Context of Torture." *Journal of Phenomenological Psychology* 46, 105–22.
Bachelard, Gaston (1966). *Le Rationalisme Appliqué*. Paris: Presses Universitaires de France.
Bal, Mieke (2001). *Travelling Concepts in the Humanities: A Rough Guide*. Toronto: University of Toronto Press.
Başoğlu, Metin, and Şalcıoğlu, Ebru (2011). *A Mental Healthcare Model for Mass Trauma Survivors: Control-Focused Behavioral Treatment of Earthquake, War, and Torture Trauma*. Cambridge: Cambridge University Press.
Benton, E. (1974). "Vitalism in Nineteenth-Century Scientific Thought: A Typology and Reassessment." *Studies in the History of Philosophy of Science Part A* 5:1 (May), 17–48.
Bergson, Henri (1935). *The Two Sources of Morality and Religion*. Trans. R. Ashley Audra and Cloudesley Brereton. New York: Henry Holt.
Bewaji, John A. I., and Mogobe B. Ramose (2003). "The Bewaji, Van Binsbergen and Ramose Debate on Ubuntu." *South African Journal of Philosophy* 22:4, 378–415.
Birhane, Abeba (2017). "Descartes Was Wrong: 'A Person Is a Person through Other Persons.'" *Aeon*, April 17. https://aeon.co/ideas/descartes-was-wrong-a-person-is-a-person-through-other-persons (accessed June 8, 2018).
Bohm, David (1980). *Wholeness and the Implicate Order*. London: Routledge.
Bohm, David (1994). *Thought as a System*. London: Routledge.
Braidotti, Rosi (2013). "'Becoming-World.'" In Rosi Braidotti, Patrick Hanafin, and Bolette Blaagaard (eds.), *After Cosmopolitanism*. London: Routledge, 8–27.

Braidotti, Rosi, Patrick Hanafin, and Bolette Blaagaard, eds. (2013). *After Cosmopolitanism*. London: Routledge.
Breton, Andre (1987). *Mad Love*. Lincoln: University of Nebraska Press.
Breton, Andre (2008). *Martinique: Snake Charmer*. Austin: University of Texas Press.
Brudholm, Thomas (2008). *Resentment's Virtue: Jean Améry and the Refusal to Forgive*. Philadelphia: Temple University Press.
Casey, Edward (1993). *Getting Back into Place: Toward a Renewed Understanding of the Place-World*. Bloomington: Indiana University Press.
Césaire, Suzanne (2012). *The Great Camouflage: Writings of Dissent (1941–1945)*. Ed. Daniel Maximin, trans. Keith L. Walker. Middletown, CT: Wesleyan.
Clastres, Pierre ([1962] 1987). "Exchange and Power: Philosophy of the Indian Chieftainship." In *Society against the State: Essays in Political Anthropology*. New York: Zone, 27–48.
Clemens, Justin (2012). "Oath, Torture, Testimony: Language, Law and Life in the Work of Giorgio Agamben." *Res Publica: Revista de Filosofia Politica* 28, 77–99.
Coughlin, David (2016). "Dancing in Their Own Style? Philosophy in Euphrase Kezilahabi's Nagona/Mzingile and the Uses of Postcolonial Discourse in Its Analysis." *Journal of African Cultural Studies* 28:2, 196–208.
Crahay, Franz (1965). "Conceptual Take-Off Conditions for a Bantu Philosophy." *Diogenes* 13:52, 55–78.
Danneskiold-Samsøe, Bente, Else Marie Bartels, and Inge Genefke (2007). "Treatment of Torture Victims—a Longitudinal Clinical Study." *Torture* 17:1, 11–17.
De Craemer, Willy (1977). *The Jamaa and the Church: A Bantu Catholic Movement in Zaïre*. Oxford: Clarendon.
Deacon, Moya (2002). "The Status of Father Tempels and Ethnophilosophy in the Discourse of African Philosophy." In P. H. Coetzee and A. P. J. Roux (eds.), *The African Philosophy Reader*, 2nd ed. London: Routledge, 97–111.
Deleuze, Gilles (1992). "Postscript on the Societies of Control." *October* 59 (Winter), 3–7.
Deleuze, Gilles (1997). *Essays Critical and Clinical*. London: Verso.
Deleuze, Gilles, and Felix Guattari (1986). *Kafka: Toward a Minor Literature*. Minneapolis: University of Minnesota Press.
Deleuze, Gilles, and Felix Guattari (1987). *A Thousand Plateaus*. Trans. Brian Massumi. Minneapolis: University of Minnesota Press.
Deleuze, Gilles, and Felix Guattari (1994). *What Is Philosophy?* New York: Columbia University Press.
Derrida, Jacques (1995). *Archive Fever: A Freudian Impression*. Chicago: University of Chicago Press.
Derrida, Jacques (2012). "Avowing—the Impossible: 'Returns,' Repentance, and Reconciliation." In E. Weber (ed.), *Living Together: Jacques Derrida's Communities of Violence and Peace*. New York: Fordham University Press, 18–41.

Deutsch, Helen, and Mary Terrall, eds. (2012). *Vital Matters: Eighteenth-Century Views of Conception, Life, and Death*. Toronto: University of Toronto Press.

Di Paolo, Ezequiel A. (2018). "The Enactive Conception of Life." In AlbertNewen, Leon De Bruin, and Shaun Gallagher (eds.), *The Oxford Handbook of 4E Cognition*. Oxford: Oxford University Press, 71–94.

Diagne, Souleymane Bachir (2002). "Keeping Africanity Open." *Public Culture* 14:3, 621–3.

Diagne, Souleymane Bachir (2011). *African Art as Philosophy: Senghor, Bergson and the Idea of Negritude*. Trans. Chike Jeffers. London: Seagull.

Diagne, Souleymane Bachir (2016). *The Ink of the Scholars: Reflections on Philosophy in Africa*. Dakar, Senegal: Council for the Development of Social Science Research in Africa (CODESRIA).

Diagne, Souleymane Bachir (2019). *Postcolonial Bergson*. New York: Fordham University Press.

Drabinski, John E. (2010). "Review Essay." In Donna V. Jones (ed.), *The Racial Discourses of Life Philosophy: Negritude, Vitalism, and Modernity*. New York: Columbia University Press, 217. *Journal of French and Francophone Philosophy—Revue de la philosophie française et de langue française* 19:2 (2011), 180–8.

Driesch, Hans (1914). *The History and Theory of Vitalism*. London: Macmillan.

Etieyibo, Edwin, ed. (2018). *Method, Substance, and the Future of African Philosophy*. London: Palgrave Macmillan.

Eudell, Demetrius (2015). "'Come On Kid, Let's Go Get the Thing': The Sociogenic Principle and the *Being* of Being Black/Human." In Katherine McKittrick (ed.), *Sylvia Wynter: On Being Human as Praxis*. Durham, NC: Duke University Press, 226–48.

Eze, Emmanuel Chukwudi (2008). *On Reason: Rationality in a World of Cultural Conflict and Racism*. Durham, NC: Duke University Press.

Eze, Michael Onyebuchi (2010). *Intellectual History in Contemporary South Africa*. New York: Palgrave Macmillan.

Fabian, Johannes (1969a). "Charisma and Cultural Change: The Case of the Jamaa Movement in Katanga (Congo Republic)." *Comparative Studies in Society and History* 11:2 (April), 155–73.

Fabian, Johannes (1969b). "An African Gnosis—for a Reconsideration of an Authoritarian Definition." *History of Religions* 9:1 (August), 42–58.

Fabian, Johannes (1971). *Jamaa: A Charismatic Movement in Katanga*. Evanston, IL: Northwestern University Press.

Fabian, Johannes (1998). *Movements of Freedom: Anthropology and Popular Culture*. Charlottesville: University Press of Virginia.

Fanon, Frantz (2008). *Black Skin, White Masks*. Trans. Richard Philcox. New York: Grove.

Fell, Joseph (1979). *Heidegger and Sartre: An Essay on Being and Place*. New York: Columbia University Press.

Fricker, Miranda (2007). *Epistemic Injustice: Power and the Ethics of Knowing.* Oxford: Oxford University Press.

Gerrity, Ellen, Terrence Keane, and Farris Tuma, eds. (2001). *The Mental Health Consequences of Torture.* New York: Springer Science + Business Media.

Glissant, Edouard (1997). *Poetics of Relation.* Ann Arbor: University of Michigan Press.

Graessner, Sepp, Norbert Gurris, and Christian Pross, eds. (2001). *At the Side of Torture Survivors: Treating a Terrible Assault on Human Dignity.* Baltimore, MD: Johns Hopkins University Press.

Graiule, Marcel (1965). *Conversations with Ogotemmeli: An Introduction to Dogon Religious Ideas.* Oxford: Oxford University Press.

Gray, Amber Elizabeth Lynn (2001). "The Body Remembers: Dance/Movement Therapy with an Adult Survivor of Torture." *American Journal of Dance Therapy* 23:1, 29–43.

Greco, Monica (2005). "On the Vitality of Vitalism." *Theory, Culture & Society* 22:1, 15–27.

Grünbaum, Liselotte (1997). "Psychotherapy with Children in Refugee Families Who Have Survived Torture: Containment and Understanding of Repetitive Behaviour and Play." *Journal of Child Psychotherapy* 23:3, 437–52.

Harris, David Alan (2007). "Dance/Movement Therapy Approaches to Fostering Resilience and Recovery among African Adolescent Torture Survivors." *Torture* 17:2, 134–55.

Horton, Robin (1967a). "African Traditional Thought and Western Science. Part One. From Tradition to Science." *Africa: Journal of the International Africa Institute* 37:1 (January), 50–71.

Horton, Robin (1967b). "African Traditional Thought and Western Science. Part Two. The 'Closed' and 'Open' Predicaments." *Africa: Journal of the International Africa Institute* 37:2 (April), 155–87.

Hountondji, Paulin (1996). *African Philosophy: Myth & Reality*, 2nd ed. Bloomington: Indiana University Press.

Hutto, Dan (2011). "Consciousness." In James Garvey (ed.), *The Continuum Companion to Philosophy of Mind.* London: Continuum, 35–53.

Hutto, Dan (2017). "REC: Revolution Effected by Clarification." *Topoi* 36, 377–91.

Ingold, Tim (1992). "Editorial." *Mana* 27:4, 693–6.

Ita, J. M. (1973). "Frobenius, Senghor and the Image of Africa." In Robin Horton and Ruth Finnegan (eds.), *Modes of Thought: Essays on Thinking in Western and Non-Western Societies.* London: Faber & Faber, 306–36.

Janz, Bruce (2008). "Reason and Rationality in Eze's *On Reason.*" *South African Journal of Philosophy* 27:4, 296–309.

Janz, Bruce (2009a). *Philosophy in an African Place.* Lanham, MD: Lexington.

Janz, Bruce (2009b). "Thinking Like a Mountain: Ethics and Place as Travelling Concepts." In Martin Drenthen, Jozef Keulartz, and James Proctor (eds.), *New Visions of Nature: Complexity and Authenticity*, International Library of Environmental, Agricultural and Food Ethics. New York: Springer, 181–95.

Janz, Bruce (2015). "Philosophy-in-Place and the Provenance of Dialogue." *South African Journal of Philosophy* 34:4, 480–90.

Janz, Bruce (2016). "Free Space in the Academy." *Journal of Academic Freedom* 7. https://www.aaup.org/JAF7/free-space-academy#.WigTi0qnFhF (accessed December 6, 2017).

Janz, Bruce (2018a). "Dialogue and Listening." *Dialogues in Human Geography* 8:2, 124–7.

Janz, Bruce (2018b). "Hermeneutics, Third-Person Self-Interpretation and Narrative." In Patrizia Pedrini and Julie E. Kirsch (eds.), *Third-Person Self-Knowledge, Self-Interpretation, and Narrative*. Cham, Switzerland: Springer, 159–75.

Janz, Bruce (2018c). "Peripherality and Non-philosophy in African Philosophy: Womanist Philosophy, Environmental Philosophy and Other Provocations." In Jonathan Chimakonam (ed.), *African Philosophy and Environmental Conservation*. London: Routledge, 9–23.

Janz, Bruce (2018d). "The Problem of Method in African Philosophy." *Social Epistemology Review and Reply Collective* 7:8, 1–7. https://wp.me/p1Bfg0-3ZC (accessed June 22, 2019).

Janz, Bruce (2019). "Scholarly Cognition, Place and the Event." In Leonhard Praeg (ed.), *Philosophy on the Border: Decoloniality and the Shudder of the Origin*. Durban: University of KwaZulu-Natal Press, 54–70.

Janz, Bruce (2022). "Ethnophilosophy and the Wellspring of Philosophy in Africa." In Ada Agada (ed.), *Ethnophilosophy and the Search for the Wellspring of African Philosophy*. Cham: Springer.

Janz, Bruce (in press). "Oruka, Odinga, and Recasting Sage Philosophy." In Kai Kresse and Oriare Nwarwath (eds.), *New Work on Sage Philosophy*. Lanham, MD: Lexington.

Jell-Bahlsen, Sabine (1985). "Ethnology and Fascism in Germany." *Dialectical Anthropology* 9, 313–35.

Jones, Donna (2010). *The Racial Discourses of Life Philosophy: Negritude, Vitalism, and Modernity*. New York: Columbia University Press.

Karavanta, Mina (2015). "Human Together: Into the Interior of Auto/OntoPoeisis." *Symplokē* 23:1–2, 153–71.

Karcher, Sylvia (2001). "'In My Fingertips I Don't Have a Soul Anymore': Body Psychotherapy with Survivors of Torture—Insights into Work with Concentrative Movement Therapy." In Sepp Graessner, Norbert Gurris, and Christian Pross (eds.), *At the Side of Torture Survivors: Treating a Terrible Assault on Human Dignity*. Baltimore, MD: Johns Hopkins University Press, 70–94.

Kazeem, Fayemi Ademola (2012). "H. Odera Oruka and the Question of Methodology in African Philosophy: A Critique." *Thought and Practice* 4:2, 185–204.

Kerzin, Barry (2014). Unpublished correspondence, March 6.

Kezilahabi, Euphrase (1985). "African Philosophy and the Problem of Literary Interpretation." Unpublished dissertation, University of Wisconsin-Madison.

Kramer, Fritz (1985). "Empathy—Reflections on the History of Ethnology in Pre-Fascist Germany: Herder, Creuzer, Bastian, Bachofen, and Frobenius." *Dialectical Anthropology* 9, 337–47.

Lambert, Gregg (2017). *Philosophy after Friendship: Deleuze's Conceptual Personae*. Minneapolis: University of Minnesota Press.

Lanfranchi, Benedetta (2012). "Daring to be Destructive Euphrase Kezilahabi's Onto-Criticism." *Swahili Forum* 19, 72–87.

Lash, Scott (2006). "Life (Vitalism)." *Theory, Culture and Society* 23:2–3, 323–9.

Levi-Strauss, Claude (1966). *The Savage Mind*. Chicago: University of Chicago Press.

Levinson, Sanford (2007). "Slavery and the Phenomenology of Torture." *Social Research* 74:1, 149–68.

Lütticken, Sven (2007). "Unnatural History." *New Left Review* 45 (May–June), 115–32.

MacCormack, Patricia (2020). *The Ahuman Manifesto: Activism for the End of the Anthropocene*. London: Bloomsbury.

MacGaffey, Wyatt (1979). "Review of *The Jamaa and the Church: A Bantu Catholic Movement in Zaire*. By Willy de Craemer." *Africa: Journal of the International African Institute* 49:4, 429–30.

Malpas, Jeff (2006). *Heidegger's Topology: Being, Place, World*. Cambridge, MA: MIT Press.

Marks, John (2010). "Thought." In Adrian Parr (ed.), *The Deleuze Dictionary*, rev. ed. Edinburgh: Edinburgh University Press, 284–6.

Masolo, D. A. (1994). *African Philosophy in Search of Identity*. Bloomington: Indiana University Press.

Mataczynski, David (1986). "A Re-examination of the Jamaa: 'Thick Description.'" *Les cahiers du CEDAF* 1, 1–102.

Mbembe, Achille (2000). "At the Edge of the World: Boundaries, Territoriality, and Sovereignty in Africa." *Public Culture* 12:1, 259–84.

Mbembe, Achille (2001). *On the Postcolony*. Berkeley: University of California Press.

Mbembe, Achille (2002a). "African Modes of Self-Writing." *Public Culture* 14:1, 239–73.

Mbembe, Achille (2002b). "On the Power of the False." *Public Culture* 14:3, 629–41.

Mbembe, Achille (2017). *Critique of Black Reason*. Trans. Laurent Dubois. Durham, NC: Duke University Press.

Mbiti, John (1969). *African Religions and Philosophy*. Nairobi: Heinemann.

Metz, Thaddeus (2007a). "Toward an African Moral Theory." *Journal of Political Philosophy* 15:3, 321–41.

Metz, Thaddeus (2007b). "Ubuntu as a Moral Theory: Reply to Four Critics." *South African Journal of Philosophy* 26:4, 369–87.

Metz, Thaddeus (2011). "Ubuntu as a Moral Theory and Human Rights in South Africa." *African Human Rights Law Journal* 11, 532–59.

Michel, Jean-Claude (2000). *The Black Surrealists*. New York: Peter Lang.

Mudimbe, V. Y. (2005). "An African Practice of Philosophy: A Personal Testimony." *Quest: An African Journal of Philosophy/Revue Africaine de Philosophie* 19: 1–2, 21–36.

Narkunas, J. Paul (2018). *Reified Life: Speculative Capital and the Ahuman Condition.* New York: Fordham University Press.

Odera Oruka, H. ed. (1991). *Sage Philosophy: Indigenous Thinkers and Modern Debate in African Philosophy.* Nairobi: African Centre for Technology Studies.

Odera Oruka, H. (1992). *Oginga Odinga: His Philosophy and Beliefs.* Nairobi: Initiatives.

Odinga, Oginga (1967). *Not Yet Uhuru: An Autobiography.* London: Heinemann.

Oguejiofor, J. Obi (2009). "Negritude as Hermeneutics: A Reinterpretation of Léopold Sédar Senghor's Philosophy." *American Catholic Philosophical Quarterly* 83:1, 79–94.

Okolo, Mary S. C. (2007). *African Literature as Political Philosophy.* Dakar: CODESRIA Books.

Olúwọlé, Sophie (1989). "The Africanness of a Philosophy." In S. Oluwole (ed.), *Readings in African Philosophy: An Anthology.* Lagos: Masstech. Also in Herta Nagl-Docetal and Franz Wimmer (eds.), *Postkoloniales Philosophieren: Afrika.* Vienna: R. Oldenbourg Verlag, 1992, 101–22.

Ott, Michaela (2018). *Dividuations: Theories of Participation.* Cham, Switzerland: Palgrave Macmillan.

p'Bitek, Okot (1964). "Fr. Tempels' Bantu Philosophy." *Transition* 13 (March–April), 15–17.

p'Bitek, Okot (1984). *Song of Lawino & Song of Ocol.* No. 266. Oxford: Heinemann.

Peterson, Christopher (2018). *Monkey Trouble: The Scandal of Posthumanism.* New York: Fordham University Press.

Peterson, Derek. "Reading John Mbiti from Uganda." *Africa Is a Country.* https://africasacountry.com/2019/10/reading-john-mbiti-from-uganda (accessed October 18, 2019).

Praeg, Leonhard (2014a). "African Modes of Writing and Being." In *A Report on Ubuntu.* Durban: University of Kwa-Zulu Natal Press, 83–132.

Praeg, Leonhard (2014b). *A Report on Ubuntu.* Durban: University of Kwa-Zulu Press.

Praeg, Leonhard, and Siphokazi Magadla, eds. (2014). *Ubuntu: Curating the Archive.* Durban: University of Kwa-Zulu Press.

Presbey, Gail (n.d.). "African Sage Philosophy." *Internet Encyclopedia of Philosophy.* http://www.iep.utm.edu/afr-sage/ (accessed December 5, 2017).

Rabbitt, Kara (2006). "Suzanne Césaire's Significance for the Forging of a New Caribbean Literature." *French Review* 79:3 (February), 538–48.

Rabbitt, Kara (2008). "The Geography of Identity in Suzanne Césaire's 'Le grand Camouflage.'" *Research in African Literatures* 39:3 (Fall), 121–31.

Rabbitt, Kara (2013). "In Search of the Missing Mother: Suzanne Césaire, Martiniquaise." *Research in African Literatures* 44:1 (Spring), 36–54.

Rabbitt, Kara (2015). "History into Story: Suzanne Césaire, Lafcadio Hearn, and Representations of the 1848 Martinique Slave Revolts." *Anthurium: A Caribbean Studies Journal* 12:2, Article 3. http://scholarlyrepository.miami.edu/anthurium/vol12/iss2/3.

Ramose, Mogobe (1999). *African Philosophy through Ubuntu*. Harare, Zimbabwe: Mond.

Rosemont, Franklin, and Robin D. G. Kelley, eds. (2009). *Black, Brown, & Beige: Surrealist Writings from Africa and the Diaspora*. Austin: University of Texas Press.

Russell, William P. (2003). "'Time Also Moves Backwards': John Mbiti's Traditional Concept of Time and the Future of World Christianity." *Studies in World Christianity* 9:1, 88–102.

Saldanha, Arun (2006). "Reontologising Race: The Machinic Geography of Phenotype." *Environment and Planning D: Society and Space* 24, 9–24.

Saldanha, Arun (2013). "Introduction: Bastard and Mixed-Blood Are the True Names of Race." In Arun Saldanha and Jason Michael Adams (eds.), *Deleuze and Race*. Edinburgh: Edinburgh University Press, 1–34.

Sawyer, Michael E. (2018). *An Africana Philosophy of Temporality: Homo Liminalis*. Cham, Switzerland: Palgrave Macmillan.

Schrempp, Gregory (2002). *Magical Arrows: The Māori, the Greeks, and the Folklore of the Universe*. Madison: University of Wisconsin Press.

Scott, David, and Sylvia Wynter (2000). "The Re-enchantment of Humanism: An Interview with Sylvia Wynter." *Small Axe* 8, 119–207.

Sembène, Ousmane (1971). *Les bouts de bois de Dieu: banty mam yall*, vol. 871. Paris: Pocket.

Senghor, Léopold Sédar (1956). "African-Negro Aesthetics." *Diogenes* 16 (Winter), 23–38.

Senghor, Léopold Sédar (1973). "The Lessons of Leo Frobenius." In Eike Haberland (ed.), *Leo Frobenius: An Anthology*. Wiesbaden: Franz Steiner Verlag Gmbh., vii–xiii.

Sharpley-Whiting, T. Denean (2002). *Negritude Women*. Minneapolis: University of Minnesota Press.

Shutte, Augustine (1993). *Philosophy for Africa*. Cape Town: University of Cape Town Press.

Smedley, Edward (1845). *Encyclopaedia Metropolitana; or, Universal Dictionary of Knowledge, on an Original Plan: Comprising the Twofold Advantage of a Philosophical and an Alphabetical Arrangement, with Appropriate Engravings*. Ed. Edward Smedley, Hugh Jam Rose, and H. John Rose (Text: voll. XXVI. Plates: voll. III. Index: vol. I. XII). London: B. Fellowes, Rivington, Ducan, Malcolm, Suttaby, Hodgson.

Sontag, Susan (1981). "Fascinating Fascism." In *Under the Sign of Saturn*. New York: Vintage, 71–105.

Soyinka, Wole (1976). *Myth, Literature and the African World*. Cambridge: Cambridge University Press.

Strathern, Marilyn (1988). *The Gender of the Gift*. Berkeley: University of California Press.

Sylvain, Renée (1996). "Leo Frobenius: From *Kulturkreis* to *Kulturmorphologie*." *Anthropos* 91, 483–94.

Taylor, Keeanga-Yamahtta, ed. (2017). *How We Get to Be Free: Black Feminism and the Combahee River Collective*. Chicago: Haymarket.

Tempels, Placide (1959). *Bantu Philosophy*. Paris: Presence Africaine.

Tempels, Placide (2001). *La Philosophie Bantu*. Augmentée du huitieme chapitre inédit; Avant-propos et Edition critique de la Traduction française par le Prof. Emer. A.J. SMET C.P. (c). http://www.aequatoria.be/tempels/FTCriticalEditon.htm.

Tempels, Placide ([1948] n.d.). "Catéchèse Bantoue." *Bulletin des Missions* 22. Bruges: Abbaye de Saint-Andre, 258–79.

Thiam, Cheikh (2014). *Return to the Kingdom of Childhood: Re-envisioning the Legacy and Philosophical Relevance of Negritude*. Columbus: Ohio State University Press.

Varela, Francisco, Humberto R. Maturana, and Ricardo Uribe (1974). "Autopoiesis: The Organization of Living Systems, Its Characterization and a Model." *BioSystems* 5, 187–96.

Viveiros de Castro, Eduardo (2014). *Cannibal Metaphysics*. Minneapolis, MN: Univocal.

Wa Thiong'o, Ngugi (2018). *Petals of Blood*. London: Random House.

Weber, Elisabeth (2012). "Living—with—Torture—Together." In E. Weber (ed.), *Living Together: Jacques Derrida's Communities of Violence and Peace*. New York: Fordham University Press, 243–8.

Wilder, Gary (2015). *Freedom Time: Negritude, Decolonization and the Future of the World*. Durham, NC: Duke University Press.

Wiśnewski, J. Jeremy, and R. David Emerick (2009). *The Ethics of Torture*. New York: Bloomsbury.

Wuketits, Franz M. (1989). "Organisms, Vital Forces, and Machines: Classical Controversies and the Contemporary Discussion 'Reductionism vs. Holism.'" In Paul Hoynlngen-Huene and Franz M. Wuketits (eds.), *Reductionism and Systems Theory in the Life Sciences: Some Problems and Perspectives*. Dordrecht: Kluwer Academic, 3–28.

Wynter, Sylvia (1969a). "Bernardo De Balbuena, Epic Poet and Abbot of Jamaica 1562-1627. Part One." *Jamaica Journal: Quarterly of the Institute of Jamaica* 3:3 (September), 3–12.

Wynter, Sylvia (1969b). "Bernardo De Balbuena, Epic Poet and Abbot of Jamaica 1562-1627. Part Two." *Jamaica Journal: Quarterly of the Institute of Jamaica* 3:4 (September), 17–26.

Wynter, Sylvia (1984). "The Ceremony Must Be Found: After Humanism." *boundary 2*, 12–3, On Humanism and the University I: The Discourse of Humanism (Spring–Autumn), 19–70.

Wynter, Sylvia (2001). "Towards the Sociogenic Principle: Fanon, Identity, the Puzzle of Conscious Experience, and What It Is Like to Be Black." In Mercedes Durán-Cogan and Antonio Gómez-Moriana (eds.), *National Identities and Sociopolitical Changes in Latin America*. New York: Routledge, 30–66.

Wynter, Sylvia (2015). "The Ceremony Found: Towards the Autopoetic Turn/Overturn, Its Autonomy of Human Agency and Extraterritoriality of (Self-)Cognition." In Jason Ambroise and Sabine Broeck (eds.), *Black Knowledges/Black Struggles: Essays in Critical Epistemologies*. Liverpool: Liverpool University Press, 184–245.

Zawidzki, Tadeusz (2018). "Mindshaping." In Albert Newen, Leon De Bruin, and Shaun Gallagher (eds.), *The Oxford Handbook of 4E Cognition*. Oxford: Oxford University Press, 735–54.

Further Reading

Adorno, Theodor. *The Jargon of Authenticity*. Evanston, IL: Northwestern University Press, 1973.
American Historical Association (AHA). https://www.historians.org/ (accessed October 30, 2021).
American Philosophical Association (APA). https://www.apaonline.org/ (accessed October 30, 2021).
Appiah, K. Anthony. "Inventing an African Practice in Philosophy: Epistemological Issues." In V. Y. Mudimbe (ed.), *The Surreptitious Speech: Presence Africaine and the Politics of Otherness, 1947–1987*. Chicago: University of Chicago Press, 1992, 227–37.
Araeen, Rasheed. "Modernity, Modernism and Africa's Authentic Voice." *Third Text* 24:2 (March 2010), 277–86.
Araeen, Rasheed. "Preface: Why 'Beyond' Negritude?" *Third Text* 24:2 (March 2010), 167–76.
Babalolak, Sunday Fumilola, and Olusegun Ayodeji. "African Concept of Time: A Socio-cultural Reality in the Process of Change." *Journal of Education and Practice* 4:7 (2013), 143–7.
Badiou, Alain. *Being and Event*. New York: Continuum, 2005.
Balibar, Etienne. "From Bachelard to Althusser: The Concept of 'Epistemological Break.'" *Economy and Society* 7:3 (August 1978), 207–37.
Ballangee, Jennifer. *The Wound and the Witness: The Rhetoric of Torture*. Albany, NY: SUNY, 2009.
Bassett, T., C. Blanc-Pamard, and J. Boutrais. "Constructing Locality: The *Terroir* Approach in West Africa." *Africa* 77:1 (2007), 104–29.
Bergson, Henri. *A Study in Metaphysics: The Creative Mind*. Totowa, NH: Littlefield Adams, 1965.
Berktay, Asli. "Negritude and African Socialism: Rhetorical Devices for Overcoming Social Divides." *Third Text* 24:2 (March 2010), 205–14.
Bernasconi, Robert. "The Assumption of Negritude: Aime Cesaire, Frantz Fanon, and the Vicious Circle of Racial Politics." *Parallax* 8:2 (2002), 69–83.
Bernasconi, Robert "Lévy-Bruhl among the Phenomenologists: Exoticisation and the Logic of 'the Primitive.'" *Social Identities* 11:3 (May 2005), 229–45.
Bogues, Anthony, ed. *Caribbean Reasonings: After Man, towards the Human: Critical Essays on Sylvia Wynter*. Kingston, Jamaica: Ian Randle, 2006.

Bromberger, Sylvain. "Natural Kinds and Questions." In Matti Sintonen (ed.), *Knowledge and Inquiry: Essays on Jaakko Hintikka's Epistemology and Philosophy of Science*. Amsterdam: Rodopi, 1997, 149–63.

Bromberger, Sylvain. *On What We Know We Don't Know: Explanation, Theory, Linguistics, and How Questions Shape Them*. Chicago: University of Chicago Press, 1992.

Buber, Martin. "Dialogue." In Robert Gregor Smith (trans. and introduction), *Between Man and Man*. London: Collins, 1947, 17–59.

Burbules, Nicholas, "The Limits of Dialogue as a Critical Pedagogy." In Peter Trifonas (ed.), *Revolutionary Pedagogies: Cultural Politics Instituting Education and the Discourse of Theory*. New York: Routledge, 2000, 251–73.

Burns, Lorna. *Contemporary Caribbean Writing and Deleuze: Literature between Postcolonial and Post-Continental Philosophy*. New York: Continuum, 2012.

Case, Holly. *The Age of Questions*. Princeton, NJ: Princeton University Press, 2018.

Casey, Edward. *The World on Edge*. Bloomington: Indiana University Press, 2017.

Cash, Mason. "Cognition without Borders: 'Third-Wave' Socially Distributed Cognition and Relational Autonomy." *Cognitive Systems Research* 25–26 (2013), 61–71.

Césaire, Aimé. *Discourse on Colonialism*. Trans. Joan Pinkham. New York: Monthly Review, 2001.

Chemhuru, Munamato. "Pursuing the Agenda of Africanising Philosophy in Africa: Some Possibilities." *South African Journal of Philosophy* 35:4 (2016), 418–28.

Chimakonam, Jonathan. "Addressing Uduma's Africanness of a Philosophy Question and Shifting the Paradigm from Metaphilosophy to Conversational Philosophy." *Filosofia Theoretica: Journal of African Philosophy, Culture and Religions* 4:1 (January–June 2015), 33–50.

Chimisso, Cristina. *Gaston Bachelard: Critic of Science and the Imagination*. London: Routledge, 2001.

Chitumba, William. "University Education for Personhood through Ubuntu Philosophy." *International Journal of Asian Social Science* 3:5 (2013), 1268–76.

Collingwood, R. G. *The Idea of History*. Oxford: Oxford University Press, 1994.

Condé, Maryse. "The Stealers of Fire: The French-Speaking Writers of the Caribbean and Their Strategies of Liberation." *Journal of Black Studies* 35:2 (November 2004), 154–64.

Conroy, John. *Unspeakable Acts, Ordinary People: The Dynamics of Torture*. New York: Alfred A. Knopf, 2000.

Cooren, François. *Action and Agency in Dialogue: Passion, Incarnation and Ventriloquism*. Amsterdam: John Benjamins, 2010.

Dasaolu, Babajide Olugbenga, and Ademola Kazeem Fayemi. "Oral Tradition in African Philosophical Discourse: A Critique of Sophie Olúwọlé's Account." *African Symposium* 15:1 (July 2015), 57–68.

Deleuze, Gilles. *Bergsonism*. Trans. Hugh Tomlinson. New York: Zone, 1988.

Deleuze, Gilles. *The Fold: Leibniz and the Baroque*. Foreword and trans. Tom Conley. Minneapolis: University of Minnesota Press, 1993.

Deleuze, Gilles. *The Logic of Sense*. Trans. Mark Lester with Charles Stivale. New York: Columbia University Press, 1990.

Deleuze, Gilles. *Spinoza: Practical Philosophy*. San Francisco, CA: City Lights, 1988.

Deleuze, Gilles, and Claire Parnet. *Dialogues II*. Columbia University Press, [1987] 2002.

Derrida, Jacques. *Of Spirit: Heidegger and the Question*. Chicago: University of Chicago Press, 1989.

Diagne, Souleymane Bachir. "Bergson in the Colony: Intuition and Duration in the Thought of Senghor and Iqbal." *Qui Parle* 17:1 (Fall/Winter 2008), 125–45.

Diagne, Souleymane Bachir. "In Praise of the Post-Racial: Negritude beyond Negritude." *Third Text* 24:2 (March 2010), 241–8.

Diagne, Souleymane Bachir. "On Prospective: Development and a Political Culture of Time." *Africa Development Senegal* 29.1 (2004), 55–70.

Dirlik, Arif. "Historical Colonialism in Contemporary Perspective." *Public Culture* 14:3 (2002), 611–15.

Drabinski, John E. *Glissant and the Middle Passage: Philosophy, Beginning, Abyss*. Minneapolis: University of Minnesota Press, 2019.

Eboussi-Boulaga, Fabien. "Le Bantou Problématique." *Présence Africaine*, new series, No. 66 (2e Trimestre 1968), 4–40.

Ekpo, Denis. "Introduction: From Negritude to Post-Africanism." *Third Text* 24:2 (March 2010), 177–87.

Ellis, Mary Lynne. "Languages of Trauma; Towards a Phenomenological Response." *Psychodynamic Practice* 20:4 (2014), 314–27.

English, Parker. "Kalumba, Mbiti, and a Traditional African Concept of Time." *Philosophia Africana* 9:1 (March 2006), 53–6.

Eyene, Christine. "Sekoto and Negritude: The Ante-Room of French Culture." *Third Text* 24:2 (March 2010), 423–35.

Eze, Emmanuel Chukwudi. *Achieving Our Humanity: The Idea of a Postracial Future*. London: Routledge, 2001.

Eze, Michael Onyebuchi. *The Politics of History in Contemporary Africa*. New York: Palgrave Macmillan, 2010.

Fabian, Johannes. "Philosophie Bantoue—Placide Tempels et son oeuvre vus dans une perspective historique." *Etudes Africaines du CRISP, Centre de recherche et d'information sociopolitiques* Issue 108–9 (1970), 1–28.

Fabian, Johannes. "Popular Culture in Africa: Findings and Conjectures. To the Memory of Placide Tempels (1906–1977)." *Africa: Journal of the International African Institute* 48:4 (1978), 315–34.

Fassin, Didier. "On Resentment and Ressentiment: The Politics and Ethics of Moral Emotions." *Current Anthropology* 54:3 (2013), 249–67.

Foucault, Michel. "Polemics, Politics and Problematizations: An Interview with Michel Foucault." In Paul Rabinow (ed.), *Ethics: Subjectivity and Truth. Essential Works of Michel Foucault Vol. 1. 1954–1984*. New York: New Press, 1997, 111–19.

Frobenius, Leo. *Paideuma: Umrisse Einer Kultur- und Seelenlehre*. Munich: C. H. Beck'sche Verlagsbuchhandlung Oskar Beck, 1921.

Gadamer, Hans-Georg. *Truth and Method*, 2nd rev. ed. Trans. Joel Weinsheimer and Donald G. Marshall. London: Continuum, [1975] 1989.

Gallagher, Shaun. *Enactivist Interventions: Rethinking the Mind*. Oxford: Oxford University Press, 2017.

Gallagher, Shaun. "Precis: *Enactivist Interventions*." *Philosophical Studies* 176 (2019), 803–6.

Gallagher, Shaun. "The Socially Extended Mind." *Cognitive Systems Research* 25–26 (2013), 4–12.

Gallagher, Shaun, Lauren Reinerman-Jones, Bruce Janz, Patricia Bockelman, and Jörg Trempler. *A Neurophenomenology of Awe and Wonder: Towards a Non-Reductionist Cognitive Science*. London: Palgrave Macmillan, 2015.

Gallagher, Shaun, and Dan Zahavi. *The Phenomenological Mind*. London: Routledge, 2012.

Garraway, Doris. "'What Is Mine': Cesairean Negritude between the Particular and the Universal." *Research in African Literatures* 41:1 (Spring 2010), 71–86.

Gerard, Albert. "Historical Origins and Literary Destiny of Negritude." *Diogenes* 48 (Winter 1964), 14–38.

Giddy, Patrick. "The Ideal of African Scholarship and Its Implications for Introductory Philosophy: The Example of Placide Tempels." *South African Journal of Philosophy* 31:2 (2012), 504–16.

Gill, Alex, ed. "Aimé Césaire and the Broken Record." http://record.elotroalex.com/secondary-sources/ (accessed April 30, 2018).

Gilroy, Paul. "Toward a Critique of Consumer Imperialism." *Public Culture* 14:3 (2002), 589–91.

Guyer, Jane. "Contemplating Uncertainty." *Public Culture* 14:3 (2002), 599–602.

Haberland, Eike, ed. *Leo Frobenius: An Anthology*. Wiesbaden: Franz Steiner Verlag Gmbh., 1973.

Hallen, Barry, and John O. Sodipo. *Knowledge, Belief and Witchcraft: Analytic Experiments in African Philosophy*. Stanford: Stanford University Press, 1997.

Hantel, Max. "Rhizomes and the Space of Translation: On Edouard Glissant's Spiral Retelling." *Small Axe* 42 (November 2013), 100–12.

Harding, Sandra. "The Curious Coincidence of Feminine and African Moralities: Challenges for Feminist Theory." In Eva Feder Kittay and Diana T. Meyers (eds.), *Women and Moral Theory*. Lanham, MD: Rowman & Littlefield, 1987, 296–315.

Harney, Elizabeth. "Rhythm as the Architecture of Being: Reflections on a Black Soul." *Third Text* 24:2 (March 2010), 215–26.

Heidegger, Martin. *Being and Time*. Trans. John Macquarrie and Edward Robinson. Oxford: Blackwell, 1962. Originally *Sein und Zeit*, 1927.

Heidegger, Martin, "The Question Concerning Technology." In William Levitt (trans. and introduction), *The Question Concerning Technology and Other Essays*. New York: Garland, 1977, 3–35.

Henry, Paget. *Caliban's Reason: Introducing Afro-Caribbean Philosophy*. New York: Routledge, 2000.

Henry, Paget. "Wynter and the Transcendental Spaces of Caribbean Thought." In Bogues, Anthony (ed.), *After Man, towards the Human: Critical Essays on Sylvia Wynter*. Kingston, Jamaica: Ian Randle, 2006, 258–89.

Hintikka, Jaakko. *Socratic Epistemology: Explorations of Knowledge-Seeking by Questioning*. Cambridge: Cambridge University Press, 2007.

Hook, Derek, and Ross Truscott. "Fanonian Ambivalence: On Psychoanalysis and Postcolonial Critique." *Journal of Theoretical and Philosophical Psychology* 33:3 (2013), 155–69.

Hörl, Erich, and James Burton, eds. *General Ecology: The New Ecological Paradigm*. London: Bloomsbury Academics, 2017.

Hountondji, Paulin. "Intellectual Responsibility: Implications for Thought and Action Today." *Proceedings and Addresses of the American Philosophical Association* 70:2 (November 1996), 77–92.

Hountondji, Paulin. "The Particular and the Universal." *SAPINA Bulletin* 10:2 (1997), 3–52.

Hountondji, Paulin. *The Struggle for Meaning*. Athens: Ohio University Center for International Studies, 2002.

Hunt, Nancy Rose. "Rewriting the Soul in a Flemish Congo." *Past and Present* 198 (February 2008), 185–215.

Iyer, Arun. *Towards an Epistemology of Ruptures: The Case of Heidegger and Foucault*. London: Bloomsbury Academic, 2014.

Jackson, Jeanne-Marie. *The African Novel of Ideas: Philosophy and Individualism in the Age of Global Writing*. Princeton, NJ: Princeton University Press, 2021.

Jacques, Tomaz Carlos Flores. "Philosophy in Black: African Philosophy as a Negritude." *Sartre Studies International* 17:1 (2011), 1–19.

Janz, Bruce. "The Folds in Paulin Hountondji's *African Philosophy: Myth and Reality*." *Philosophical Papers* 39:1 (March 2010), 117–34.

Janz, Bruce. "Forget Deleuze." In Lorna Burns and Birgit M. Kaiser (eds.), *Postcolonial Literatures and Deleuze: Colonial Pasts, Differential Futures*. Basingstoke, England: Palgrave Macmillan, 2012, 21–36.

Janz, Bruce. "Philosophy As If Place Mattered: The Situation of African Philosophy." In Havi Carel and David Gomez (eds.), *What Philosophy Is*. London: Continuum, 2004, 103–15.

Janz, Bruce (2019). "Ramose, the Limits of Cosmopolitanism and the Being to Come." In Helen Lauer and Helen Yitah (eds.), *The Tenacity of Truthfulness: Mogobe Ramose*. Dar-es-Salaam, Tanzania: Mkuki Na Nyota, 251–70.

Janz, Bruce. "The Terror of the Place: Anxieties of Place and the Cultural Narrative of Terrorism." *Ethics, Place and Environment* 11:2 (2008), 189–201.

Janz, Bruce. "Virtual Place and Virtualized Place." In Erik Champion (ed.), *The Phenomenology of Real and Virtual Places*. London: Routledge, 2019, 60–75.

Jauss, Hans Robert. *Question and Answer: Forms of Dialogic Understanding*. Minneapolis: University of Minnesota Press, 1989.

Jeffers, Chike. "Recent Work on Negritude." *Journal of French and Francophone Philosophy* 24:2 (2016), 304–18.

Jewsiewicki, Bogumil. "The Subject in Africa: In Foucault's Footsteps." *Public Culture* 14:3 (2002), 593–8.

Johnson, Clarence Shole. "An Analysis of John Mbiti's Treatment of the Concept of Event in African Ontologies." *Quest* 9:2, 10:1 (1995–6), 139–57.

Jules-Rosette, Benetta. "Afro-Pessimism's Many Guises." *Public Culture* 14:3 (2002), 603–5.

Kalumba, Kibujjo M. "A New Analysis of Mbiti's 'The Concept of Time.'" *Philosophia Africana* 8:1 (March 2005), 11–19.

Kavoulakos, Konstantinos. *George Lukács's Philosophy of Praxis: From Neo-Kantianism to Marxism*. London: Bloomsbury Academic, 2018.

Khandker, Wahida, "Life as Method: The Invention of Problems in Deleuze's Bergsonism." In Paul Ardoin, S. E. Gontarski, and Laci Mattison (eds.), *Understanding Deleuze, Understanding Modernism*. London: Bloomsbury, 2014, 21–32.

Knappett, Carl, and Lambros Malafouris. *Material Agency: Towards a Non-anthropocentric Approach*. New York: Springer, 2008.

Koralus, Philipp. "The Erotetic Theory of Attention: Questions, Focus, and Distraction." *Mind and Language* 29:1 (February 2014), 26–50.

Lapoujade, David. *Aberrant Movements: The Philosophy of Gilles Deleuze*. South Pasadena, CA: Semiotext(e), 2014.

Lauer, Helen. "African and Non-African Time: To Contrast or Not To Contrast? The Geopolitical Convenience of Conceptual Dichotomization." *Thought and Practice: A Journal of the Philosophical Association of Kenya, New Series* 5:1 (June 2013), 1–24.

Leitner, Isabella. *Fragments of Isabella*. New York: Thomas Y. Crowell, 1978.

Leitner, Isabella, and Irving A. Leitner. *Isabella: From Auschwitz to Freedom*. New York: Anchor, [1978] 1994.

Levinas, Emmanuel. *Of God Who Comes to Mind*. Stanford: Stanford University Press, 1998.

MacCormack, Patricia, ed. *The Animal Catalyst: Towards Ahuman Theory*. London: Bloomsbury, 2014.

Malpas, Jeff. *Place and Experience: A Philosophical Topography*, 2nd ed. London: Routledge, 2018.

Maniglier, Patrice. "What Is a Problematic? Bachelard and the Concept of the Problematic." *Radical Philosophy* 173 (May/June 2012), 21–3.

Maranhão, Tulio, ed. *The Interpretation of Dialogue*. Chicago: University of Chicago Press, 1990.

Marcel, Gabriel. *Mystery of Being Vol 1: Reflection and Mystery*. South Bend, IN: Gateway Editions, 1950.

Marshall, Donald. "On Dialogue: To Its Cultured Despisers." In Bruce Krajewski (ed.), *Gadamer's Repercussions: Reconsidering Philosophical Hermeneutics*. Berkeley: University of California Press, 2004, 123–44.

Mascarenhas, Salvador, and Philipp E. Koralus. "Illusory Inferences: Disjunctions, Indefinites, and the Erotetic Theory of Reasoning." CogSci (2015). https://pdfs.semanticscholar.org/218e/a080b2770d9cef6bb3e31be4d3d214cd17fe.pdf (accessed March 20, 2018).

Matolino, Bernard. "Tempels' Philosophical Realism." *South African Journal of Philosophy* 30:3 (2011), 330–42.

McKittrick, Katherine, ed. *Sylvia Wynter: On Being Human as Praxis*. Durham, NC: Duke University Press, 2015.

Meyer, Michel. *Of Problematology: Philosophy, Science, and Language*. Chicago: University of Chicago Press, 1995.

Meyer, Michel. "The Revival of Questioning in the Twentieth Century." *Synthese* 74:1 (January 1988), 5–18.

Meyers, Diana Tietjens. "Decentralizing Autonomy: Five Faces of Selfhood." In John Christman and Joel Anderson (eds.), *Autonomy and the Challenges to Liberalism: New Essays*. Cambridge: Cambridge University Press, 2005, 27–55.

Mignolo, Walter. "Sylvia Wynter: What Does It Mean to Be Human?" In Katherine McKittrick (ed.), *Sylvia Wynter: On Being Human as Praxis*. Durham, NC: Duke University Press, 2015, 106–23.

Monga, Celestin. *Nihilism and Negritude: Ways of Living in Africa*. Cambridge, MA: Harvard University Press, 2016.

Moreau, A. Scott. "A Critique of John Mbiti's Understanding of the African Concept of Time." *East African Journal of Evangelical Theology* 5:2 (1986), 36–48.

Mudimbe, V. Y. *The Idea of Africa*. Bloomington: Indiana University Press, 1994.

Mudimbe, V. Y. *The Invention of Africa*. Bloomington: Indiana University Press, 1988.

Mudimbe, V. Y. "Placide Tempels and African Philosophy." *Bulletin des seances de l'Academie royale des sciences d'Outre-mer* 32:3 (1986), 349–58.

Mugerauer, Bob. "Maturana and Varela: From Autopoiesis to Systems Applications." In Darrell P. Arnold (ed.), *Traditions of Systems Theory: Major Figures and Contemporary Developments*. London: Routledge: 2014, 158–78.

Mweshi, John. "On Africanising the Philosophy Curricula: Challenges and Prospects." *South African Journal of Philosophy* 35:4 (2016), 460–70.

Nardal, Paulette. *Beyond Negritude: Essays from* Women in the City. Albany, NY: State University of New York Press, 2009.

Newen, Albert, Leon De Bruin, and Shaun Gallagher, eds. *The Oxford Handbook of 4E Cognition*. Oxford: Oxford University Press, 2018.

Ngcoya, Mvuselelo. "Ubuntu: Toward an Emancipatory Cosmopolitanism?" *International Political Sociology* 9 (2015), 248–62.

Òkè, Moses. "From an African Ontology to an African Epistemology: A Critique of J. S. Mbiti on the Time Conception of Africans." *Quest* 18 (2005), 25–36.

Olúwọlé, Sophie. *Socrates and Orunmila: Two Patron Saints of Classical Philosophy*, 3rd ed. Lagos, Nigeria: Ark, 2017.

Ong, W. *Orality and Literacy: The Technologizing of the Word*. New York: Routledge, 1982.

Osha, Sanya. "Legacies of a Critique of Ethnophilosophy: Hountondji's *African Philosophy: Myth & Reality* Revisited." *Quest: An African Journal of Philosophy/Revue Africaine de Philosophie* XVII (2005), 13–34.

Paphitis, Sharli Anne, and Martin H. Villet. *The Demographic Diversity of Philosophy and the Possibilities for Transforming Philosophy in South Africa*. Rhodes University, January 2017.

Presbey, Gail. "Who Counts as a Sage? Problems in the Further Implementation of Sage Philosophy." *Paideia Project Online*, 1998. http://www.bu.edu/wcp/Papers/Afri/AfriPres.htm (accessed December 5, 2017).

Prigogene, Ilya, and Isabelle Stengers. *Order Out of Chaos: Man's New Dialogue with Nature*. New York: Bantam, 1984.

Prior, Mary, and Arthur Prior. "Erotetic Logic." *Philosophical Review* 64:1 (January 1955), 43–59.

Protevi, John. "Adding Deleuze to the Mix." *Phenomenology and the Cognitive Sciences* 9 (2010), 417–36.

Protevi, John. "Deleuze, Guattari and Emergence." *Paragraph* 29:2 (2006), 19–39.

Quayson, Ato. "Obverse Denominations: Africa?" *Public Culture* 14:3 (2002), 585–88.

Rabasa, José. "Dialogue as Conquest: Mapping Spaces for Counter-Discourse." *Cultural Critique*, No. 6, The Nature and Context of Minority Discourse (Spring 1987), 131–59.

Ram-Prasad, Chakravarthi. *Human Being, Bodily Being: Phenomenology from Classical India*. Oxford: Oxford University Press, 2018.

Ramose, Mogobe. "But Hans Kelsen Was Not Born in Africa: A Reply to Thaddeus Metz." *South African Journal of Philosophy* 26:4 (2007), 347–55.

Ramose, Mogobe. "On the Contested Meaning of 'Philosophy.'" *South African Journal of Philosophy* 34:4 (2015), 551–8.

Ramose, Mogobe. "Transcending Cosmopolitanism." *Diogenes* 59:3–4 (2014), 30–5.

Ramose, Mogobe. "Ubuntu: Affirming a Right and Seeking Remedies in South Africa." In Leonhard Praeg and Siphokazi Magadla (eds.), *Ubuntu: Curating the Archive*. Durban: University of Kwa-Zulu Press, 2014, 121–36.

Ratcliffe, Matthew, Mark Ruddell, and Benedict Smith. "What Is a 'Sense of Foreshortened Future?' A Phenomenological Study of Trauma, Trust, and Time." *Frontiers in Psychology* 5 (2014), 1–11.

Relph, Edward. *Place and Placelessness*. London: Pion, 1976.

Rettova, Alena. "Afrophone Philosophies: Possibilities and Practice. The Reflexion of Philosophical Influences in Euphrase Kezilahabi's *Nagona* and *Mzingile*." *Swahili Forum* 11 (2004), 45–68.

Ricoeur, Paul. *Interpretation Theory: Discourse and the Surplus of Meaning*. Fort Worth: University of Texas Press, 1976.

Roitman, Janet. *Anti-crisis*. Durham, NC: Duke University Press, 2014.

Romano, Claude. *Event and Time*. New York: Fordham University Press, 2014.

Romano, Claude. *Event and World*. New York: Fordham University Press, 2009.

Romano, Claude. *There Is: The Event and the Finitude of Appearing*. New York: Fordham University Press, 2016.

Rorty, Richard. *Philosophy and the Mirror of Nature*. Princeton, NJ: Princeton University Press, 1979.

Saldanha, Arun, and Jason Michael Adams, eds. *Deleuze and Race*. Edinburgh: Edinburgh University Press, 2013.

Schuhmann, Karl, and Barry Smith. "Questions: An Essay in Daubertian Phenomenology." *Philosophy and Phenomenological Research* 47:3 (March 1987), 353–84.

Segall, Kimberly Wedeven. "Postcolonial Performatives of Victimization." *Public Culture* 14:3 (2002), 617–19.

Senghor, Léopold Sédar. *On African Socialism*. Trans. and introduction by Mercer Cook. New York: Frederick A Praeger, 1964.

Stamenov, Maxim I. "The Rheomode of Language of David Bohm as a Way to Re-construct the Access to Physical Reality." In Gordon G. Globus, Karl H. Pribram, and Guiseppe Vitiello (eds.), *Brain and Being: At the Boundary between Science, Philosophy, Language and Arts*. Amsterdam: John Benjamins, 2004, 149–66.

Strawser, Michael. "The Ethics of Love in Spinoza and Kierkegaard and the Teleological Suspension of the Theological." *Philosophy Today* 51:4 (Winter 2007), 438–46.

Tabensky, Pedro, and Sally Matthews. *Being at Home: Race, Institutional Culture and Transformation at South African Higher Education Institutions*. Durban: University of KwaZulu-Natal Press, 2015.

Tempels, Placide. http://www.aequatoria.be/tempels/index.htm (accessed December 2, 2017).

Tichy, Pavel. "Questions, Answers and Logic." *American Philosophical Quarterly* 15:4 (October 1978), 275–84.

Tomasik, Timothy. "Certeau à la Carte: Translating Discursive *Terroir* in *The Practice of Everyday Life: Living and Cooking*." *South Atlantic Quarterly* 100:2 (Spring 2001), 519–42.

Tyler, Stephen. "Ode to Dialog on the Occasion of the Un-for-seen." In T. Maranhão (ed.), *The Interpretation of Dialogue*. Chicago: University of Chicago Press, 1990, 292–300.

Uduma, Uduma Oji. "The Question of the 'African' in African Philosophy: In Search of a Criterion for the Africanness of a Philosophy." *Filosofia Theoretica: Journal of African Philosophy, Culture and Religions* 3:1 (January–June 2014), 127–46.

Varela, Francisco. "Neurophenomenology: A Methodological Remedy for the Hard Problem." *Journal of Consciousness Studies* 3 (1996), 330–49.

Varela, Francisco, and Jonathan Shear. "First-Person Methodologies: What, Why, How." *Journal of Consciousness Studies* 6:2–3 (1999), 1–14.

Vergès, Françoise. "The Power of Words." *Public Culture* 14:3 (2002), 607–10.

Vogler, Candace. "Social Imaginary, Ethics, and Methodological Individualism." *Public Culture* 14:3 (2002), 625–7.

Wahman, Jessica, Jose M. Medina, and John J. Stuhr. *Cosmopolitanism and Place*. Bloomington: Indiana University Press, 2017.

Walsh, Harold T. "Whewell and Mill on Induction." *Philosophy of Science* 29:3 (July 1962), 279–84.

West-Pavlov, Russell. *Space in Theory: Kristeva, Foucault, Deleuze*. Amsterdam: Rodopi, 2009.

Whately, Richard. "Logic." In the *Encyclopaedia Metropolitana*, 2nd rev. ed. London: John Joseph Griffin, 1849.

Wiedorn, Michael. *Think Like an Archipelago: Paradox in the Work of Édouard Glissant*. Albany: SUNY, 2018.

Wilks, Jennifer M. *Race, Gender, and Comparative Black Modernism: Suzanne Lacascade, Marita Bonner, Suzanne Césaire, Dorothy West*. Baton Rouge: Louisiana State University Press, 2008.

Williams, James. *Gilles Deleuze's Logic of Sense: A Critical Introduction and Guide*. Edinburgh: Edinburgh University Press, 2008.

Wiredu, Kwasi. *Cultural Universals and Particulars: An African Perspective*. Bloomington: Indiana University Press, 1997.

Wiśniewski, Andrzej, and Dorota Leszczyńska-Jasion. "Inferential Erotetic Logic Meets Inquisitive Semantics." *Synthese* 192 (2015), 1585–608.

Wynter, Sylvia. "Bernardo De Balbuena: Epic Poet and Abbot of Jamaica 1562–1627. Part Three." *Jamaica Journal: Quarterly of the Institute of Jamaica* 4:1 (March 1970), 11–19.

Wynter, Sylvia. "Bernardo De Balbuena: Epic Poet and Abbot of Jamaica 1562–1627. Part Four." *Jamaica Journal: Quarterly of the Institute of Jamaica* 4:3 (September 1970), 6–15.

Wynter, Sylvia. "Jonkonnu in Jamaica." *Jamaica Journal: Quarterly of the Institute of Jamaica* 4:2 (June 1970), 34–48.

Wynter, Sylvia. "Unsettling the Coloniality of Being/Power/Truth/Freedom: Towards the Human, After Man, Its Overrepresentation—an Argument." *CR: The New Centennial Review* 3:3 (2003), 257–337.

Wynter, Sylvia, and Katherine McKittrick. "Unparalleled Catastrophe for Our Species? Or, to Give Humanness a Different Future: Conversations." In Katherine McKittrick (ed.), *Sylvia Wynter: On Being Human as Praxis*. Durham, NC: Duke University Press, 2015, 9–89.

Index

Afro-pessimism 162, 175–7
Afro-politanism 162, 175–7
Agamben, Giorgio 166, 171, 173–5, 183
agency 13, 32, 55, 89, 185, 201–2
   and colonialism 49–50
   and freedom 30
   and narrative 161
ahumanism 12–13, 19–21, 24–5, 40–3, 129, 146, 148, 216
Améry, Jean 167, 170–3, 190–1
apartheid 3, 17, 21, 80, 160, 162–5, 175–9, 183, 191–3, 199, 219, 228
archive 9, 136, 139–40, 142, 149, 158
Asouzu, Innocent 118
autopoiesis 12, 25, 129, 204, 220,
   and African philosophy 16–18, 197
   and creativity 9, 131, 133
   and emergence 20
   and Wynter 31–5, 37, 39–40, 223

be-ing 119–21
Bergson, Henri 46, 49, 51, 58–9, 61, 63, 180, 200
Braidotti, Rosi 162, 177, 182–5

Césaire, Aime 197, 202, 204, 206, 208
Césaire, Suzanne 9, 15, 17, 19–20, 134, 195–214, 216, 219
cognition 6–7, 15, 25, 77, 122–4, 127–30, 133, 221–3
   cognitive processes and practice 75, 79, 121, 157, 197, 199, 206, 226
   cognitive science 28–9, 119, 219
   cognitive systems 86, 88, 117
   and narrative 138
   and place 176
   scholarly cognition 10, 224–5, 229
   shared cognition 10–11, 17, 119, 129, 131, 217
   social cognition 8
   traditional cognition 87

colonialism 3, 9, 17, 20–1, 24, 26, 48–9, 57, 87, 90–1, 108, 110, 112, 116, 123, 129–31, 141–2, 150–1, 196, 204–6, 209–10, 228–9
   anti-colonialism 37, 184
   colonial violence 55, 127, 132
   ideology 213–14
   neocolonial 59
   postcolonial 89, 136
   slavery, colonialism, apartheid 160, 163, 175–9, 185, 191, 193, 199, 219
   systems of 14, 18
conceptual personae 106, 181–2
consciousness 64, 126, 128, 150, 156, 177, 193
   Black consciousness 91, 164, 213
   class consciousness 152
   and culture 87
   intentional consciousness 61
   and memory 83
   self-consciousness 90, 118
   sentiment conscious 146
   and Sociogeny 28–32
   and time 71
   unconscious 120, 130, 205, 212
cosmopolitanism 175–80, 182–5, 191

Deleuze, Gilles 7, 34, 82, 107, 125, 140, 167, 180–5, 200–1
Derrida, Jacques 90, 139, 140, 166, 175
De Craemer, Willy 51, 53–4, 57
Diagne, Souleymane Bachir 58–62, 101–2, 162, 180–1, 197–9, 202
dialogue 2–3, 8–9, 59–62, 134, 198, 217
   and literature 139–42
   and sage philosophy 94–8, 101–2, 106–7
Du Bois, W. E. B. 90–1, 205

embeddedness 12–13, 40, 86, 89, 172, 195, 197, 220

and culture 16–17, 55, 57, 71, 80–1, 133, 216
and institutions 76, 178
and networks 64, 184
embodiment 17, 29, 34, 117, 133, 188, 219
and place 21, 165, 176–7
and practice 121
and torture 169, 189
empathy 11, 146,
enactivism 52, 56, 67, 81, 94, 156, 195, 215, 218–25
and cognition 6–21, 30–2
and Négritude 202, 204, 208–9
and place 136
and race 159
and time 85–6, 91
and Ubuntu 118, 121, 129, 133
and vitalism 56
ethics 4, 11–12, 101, 104, 184–5
and cognition 30
and concepts 228
and environment 37
and torture 165–6, 169–71
and Ubuntu 17, 115–18, 122, 128, 130, 133
ethnophilosophy 79, 148, 216
and Hountondji 2, 45, 51–2, 132, 141
and Jamaa 48, 54, 56, 63, 65–7
and sage philosophy 93, 95, 97
and time 88, 91
event 3–4, 18–20, 207
and becoming 15, 106, 209–10, 226–9
and colonialism 162–4, 168
and narrative 134, 138–42, 145–6, 160
and problematics 9–10, 63, 191–2
and sage philosophy 102, 109–10
and time 73, 75–80
and Wynter 35, 41
Evola, Julius 213
extendedness 8, 16, 29, 81, 227
Eze, Emmanuel 196–9, 202, 214
Eze, Michael Onyebuchi 117–19

Fabian, Johannes 51–7, 65
Fanon, Frantz 24–31, 34, 72, 90–1, 172, 178
first- second-third-person 8, 28, 218
focal length 8–9, 12, 220, 227
Foucault, Michel 90, 139, 167, 200

Frobenius, Leo 205–8, 211, 212
Functionalism 94

genocide 166, 183, 222
Glissant, Edouard 161, 178
Goddard, Neville 212
Graiule, Marcel 51

Holocaust 166–7, 170, 172–3, 190, 192, 222
Hountondji, Paulin 2, 15, 45, 51, 63–4, 93, 95, 97, 105, 132, 140–1, 143–6, 148, 217–18
humanism 90–1, 145–8, 178, 183–4, 216
and ahumanism 12–13
and Jamaa 57
and Ubuntu 119, 127–9
and Wynter 15, 19–21, 23–5, 31–8, 40–2

intentionality 8–9, 29, 32, 119

Jamaa movement 16, 51–7, 63–7, 216, 224
Jones, Donna 199–202
Julian of Norwich 168

Kagame, Alexis 45–6, 51, 59, 141, 143
Kezilahabi, Euphrase 21, 72–3, 148–60, 162, 218

Lebensphilosophie 207
Lefebvre, Henri 167
Levy, Primo 170
literature 17, 46–7, 109, 200, 218–19
and Kezilahabi 149–51, 153–4, 156–60
and Olúwọlé 135–43, 147–8, 162
and philosophy 8–10
and surrealism 209, 211
and torture 186
and Ubuntu 117, 133,
and Wynter 21, 23, 25, 38–40, 42–3

Mbembe, Achille 17, 21, 133, 161–4, 174–85, 191–3, 218–19, 222
Mbiti, John 2, 16, 20, 51, 69–91, 157, 217–18, 224
Ménil, René 208
metaphilosophy 2

Metz, Thaddeus 117
mindshaping 11, 38
minor literature 82, 140–1, 203
mode of thought 7, 10, 20, 23–4, 85, 101, 131, 139–40, 145, 148, 215, 220
Musselman 173–4, 183

Narkunas, J. Paul 19, 41–2, 127
narrative 58, 180, 196, 202, 217, 219, 229
    and African philosophy 2–3, 11, 14, 15–16, 19
    and literature 136–40, 151, 154, 157
    and Mbembe 163–4, 176–7
    and time 73–4, 80, 82
    and Wynter 33–8, 39
necropolitics 183
Négritude 66, 143, 147, 219
    and Bergson 51
    and Césaire, Suzanne 15, 17, 19, 21, 134, 195–214
    and Kezilahabi 153, 156
    and Mbiti 79–82
    and vitalism 59, 60
Nyerere, Julius 56, 72

Olúwọlé, Sophie 21, 133, 135, 141–9, 158–60, 162, 218
Oruka, H. Odera 2, 16, 20, 93–114, 137, 217

Paideuma 19, 205–8, 212–13, 219
pain 21, 30, 154, 168–9, 172, 175–6, 186, 188, 191
P'Bitek, Okot 51, 152
personhood 2, 4, 13, 223
phenomenological cognitive science 6, 121
phenomenology 5, 14, 19, 136, 197
    and cognitive science 6
    and sage philosophy 94, 104
    and time 71, 75, 87, 157
    and torture 21, 167, 169–70, 172–3, 186, 189, 193
    and Ubuntu 116, 117, 121
place 1, 122, 151, 195–6, 202, 215–25, 226–9
    African 48, 119
    and cognition 15–21, 122, 129, 199
    and concepts 101

and culture 53
and Jamaa 64–6
and Mbembe 161–79, 182–5, 188–93
and Olúwọlé 135–40, 148
philosophy-in-place 5, 6, 8–12, 151
and time 76
and vitalism 55–6
Praeg, Leonhart 117, 162, 181–2
pragmatic sage 111, 217
pragmatism 1, 10
praxis 25, 42, 108,
Presbey, Gail 93, 96
problematic 6, 18, 159–60, 163, 195, 227, 229
    and ahuman 20
    and Bachelard 38
    and Mbiti 71, 86, 88–91
    and Mbembe 179, 181–2, 191, 193
    and Oruka 93, 104, 109–11
    and questions 9–11
    and Ramose 115, 117, 119, 133–4
    and Tempels 47–50, 58, 60–3, 67
    and Wynter 23

Quassia 133, 152–7
questions 179, 195
    and African philosophy 13, 181–2, 221–9
    and literature 135–42, 145,
    and philosophical method 1–7, 20–1, 35, 115–17, 215–16, 218–19
    and place 12
    and power 65–7
    and problematics 11, 63, 191–2
    and propositions 9–10
    and rheology 121–5
    and sage philosophy 94–9, 102, 104–10, 112–13
    and sociogenesis 27–30
    and Tempels 47–9, 57
    and time 69–75, 86, 89–91
    and torture 165–8
    and Ubuntu 17, 118
    and vitalism 201–2

race 4, 179, 184, 192–3, 211
    discourse 26
    as productive event 14, 158–9
    and rationality 196–9

and temporality 89–90
  and Wynter 30–1, 34, 38
racism 18, 90–1, 158–9, 213
  racialization 14, 183–4
  and Wynter 30
Ramose, Mogobe 17, 20, 115–34, 197, 218
representationalism 3–4, 227
  Africa 11, 151, 206, 215–17, 221
  and creation 19
  cultural representation 10, 63–4, 101–2
  and discourse 140, 154, 181
  mental representation 9, 16
  nonrepresentation 8, 20, 29, 32, 195, 201, 219
  and race 13–14
  and sage philosophy 105, 110
  and time 75
  and torture 165–6
  and Ubuntu 130, 132–3
rheomode, rheology 118, 121–6, 130, 218
Riefenstahl, Leni 206

Sawyer, Michael 89–91
scaffolding 8, 10, 122, 127, 136–7, 220, 224, 227–8
Scarry, Elaine 169
Senghor, Leopold Sedar 51, 59, 143, 147, 197–9, 202, 206–7
sociogenesis 25–33, 35–6, 38, 41
solitary confinement 162, 165, 168–9, 175, 177, 179
space of thought 15, 19–21, 65, 209, 223–4
  and literature 139–40, 144, 160
  vs. mode of thought 85, 145, 148
  and Négritude 195–7, 213
  and new concepts 103
  nonlinear 9
  philosophical method 1, 3–4, 6, 11–13, 136, 215–18
  and problematics 115
  and questioning 181, 221
  and Ubuntu 118, 131, 133–4
  and vitalism 58
  and Wynter 23, 27, 42–3
spatial philosophy 5, 17

Tempels, Placide 2, 20, 45–50, 71, 83, 118, 141, 143, 216
  Bantu Philosophy 16, 51–67
temporality 216–7, 219 (*see also* time)
  and Cesaire, Suzanne 21, 195, 210
  and Kezilahabi 149, 152, 157–8
  and Mbiti 71–6, 78, 86–91, 129
  and Oruka 16, 108–9, 111, 114
  and Ubuntu 133
  and Wynter 35, 42
textuality 136–7, 142–3, 162, 225
  and space of thought 20–1
  and temporality 109–10, 114
time 12 (*see also* temporality)
  and Mbembe 163, 175, 180
  and Mbiti 2, 16, 69–91, 217–18, 224
  and Oruka 16
  and Tempels 51
  and text 20–1
  and Wynter 35, 42
torture 17, 21, 162, 165–177, 179, 183, 185–93, 199, 219, 222

Ubuntu 2
  as cognition 17, 224
  and language 49
  metaphysics 11, 51
  and Praeg 181–2
  and Ramose 20, 117–23, 126–34, 197, 218

vitalism 12, 133, 183
  as emergence 35
  and Négritude 199–202, 207
  Tempels 20–1, 45–6, 51, 53, 55–63, 65–7, 216–17

Whewell, William 215
Whitman, Walt 158
Wiredu, Kwasi 143, 145–6
Wynter, Sylvia 9, 13, 15, 19–21, 23–43, 89–91, 134, 138, 146, 148, 195–6, 211, 216, 223

www.ingramcontent.com/pod-product-compliance
Lightning Source LLC
Chambersburg PA
CBHW062130300426
44115CB00012BA/1873